Emily Lau
and the PLUM BLOSSOM SWORD

Emily Lau and the PLUM BLOSSOM SWORD

TIMOTHY STONE

WRITTEN IN STONE PUBLISHING, LLC
SANTA ANA

First paperback edition 2021

Cover & Interior Design by Damonza.com

ISBN 978-1-7377212-0-8 (paperback)

ISBN 978-1-7377212-1-5 (ebook)

Printed in the United States of America

10 9 8 7 6 5 4 3 2 1

Published by Written in Stone Publishing, LLC

www.timmstone.com

For my friends and family, without whom
this wouldn't have been possible.

CHAPTER 1

THE GIRL THAT
DESTINY CHOSE

SOMETHING STIRRED IN the air. It started off small, like the moment when a performance ends and the applause begins. Then it built up until it was something Emily could taste and feel. It reminded her of the scent of rain before it fell. It was the moment of anticipation after lightning and right before thunder crashed.

Someone coughed, clearing their throat, and the silence crumbled around her. Emily raised her head from her book. Her teacher sat behind his desk with his feet perched on the corner. He had a packet in his left hand and a red pen in his right.

A classmate to her right started gathering her things and Emily glanced up at the clock. Only a few minutes left in class. Other classmates started clearing their desks, spurred to do the same thing by the sound of Emily's neighbor. Emily just turned a page in her book.

"Ahem." Her English teacher peered around the room, his eyes just barely above his glasses. "I've still got you for a few more minutes. Keep working on the assignment. And if you've finished, just sit at your desk quietly. No packing up."

Emily shifted her attention back to the story unfolding in front of her. A unicorn was being herded toward the ocean by a red bull and time was running out to save her. A prince asked a wizard what use was magic if it couldn't save a unicorn. *That's what heroes are for*, she read. The weight of the words sent a shiver down her body. She rested the book against the edge of her desk and leaned back into her chair just to appreciate the story.

Movement in the corner of her eye drew her attention to her left. Her desk neighbor was resting his head on his arm. His right hand was propped up holding a pen to paper but his eyes were shut. Shallow, quiet breaths escaped his lips and Emily couldn't help but admire his bravery at sleeping in class. She was always afraid she'd snore or get caught.

A thin, slip of a smile formed at the corners of her mouth and she started reading again. She had read this book five times so she knew what was going to happen next, but she couldn't help rereading it. It was her favorite. It had almost everything she wanted. Magic, heroes, adventure. The only thing it needed more of, for her tastes, were fights. Daring sword fights, magic duels. Just a little more action.

"All right, that's enough." Her teacher suddenly stood up and walked toward the front of the class. "Everyone pass your papers forward."

Emily took the paper from the student behind her and passed it forward with her own. The person behind her sleeping neighbor tried to nudge him awake with their own paper, but there was no way he could feel it. Emily reached and poked him hard in the ribs. He jolted awake and looked around the room aimlessly before turning toward Emily.

He hit her with a grimace, but she gestured behind him before whispering, "Almost time to go. We're turning in the assignment."

His head swiveled around the room again before he took the paper from behind him to pass forward with his own. "Thanks."

She smiled and put her bookmark in her book before closing it.

"I have one last nugget of wisdom for you all before you leave," said their English teacher. He turned toward the white-board, picked up a marker, and started writing across it in big green letters. "'The only person you are destined to become is the person you decide to be.' Ralph Waldo Emerson."

He tapped the whiteboard with the marker and let his gaze sweep across the room.

"You're all freshmen," he said. "Life is just getting started for you. The things you decide to do now matter, though. Think about it. What kind of person do you want to be?"

The bell in the class rang, ending the poignant speech. Everyone started packing up their stuff again knowing he couldn't stop them this time. Everyone but Emily. She let her eyes rest on the quote and read it again to herself. Her eyes were drawn a little to the right to her smiling English teacher.

He nodded and then put the marker down. "Have a good weekend, everyone."

Emily grabbed her binder and slid it into her backpack

along with her copy of *The Last Unicorn*. She followed her classmates out and smiled when the warm California sun greeted her.

"See you on Monday, Emily," said someone as they walked by.

The classmate she had woken up was waving at her as he walked toward the parking lot.

"See you," she said with a wave.

Emily started walking farther into the school. Entire throngs of students were busy either leaving or loitering near lockers and classrooms. They moved in packs like animals and those people walking solo attempted to avoid the larger groups of people. Emily followed the wall on her right, passing lockers and classrooms until she came to the corner. There was a giant building in front of her with an enormous knight painted on its side, showing off the mascot for Foothill High School.

She set her backpack down at her feet and spun the dial until it unlocked. There wasn't much in her locker: a mostly empty bag that she carried her lunch in, a few books, and binders for her first classes of the day. She pulled her planner out of her backpack and pored over her notes from the day to check what homework she had for the weekend. Someone bumped into her just as she pulled out her math book.

Emily spun on her heels and smacked her elbow into her locker door. Pain shot up her arm like it only can when it's been hit in the exact right spot.

"OW!" She clutched at her elbow, hissed through her teeth, and glared at the girl who had bumped into her. "Allison!"

"Sorry!" said Allison through her laughter. "I didn't mean for that to happen. How was English?"

Emily checked her elbow. She peeled some torn skin away and brushed at it with her right hand. "Good. I got a lot of reading done. How was math?"

"Oh, you know," replied Allison, "I added. I subtracted. I zoned out. The usual."

Emily shook her head. Allison was taller than Emily with curly, raven hair and dark eyes.

"Are you ready for your audition?" Emily dropped her math book inside her backpack.

When Allison didn't reply, she turned. Allison had a worried look on her face. "I guess so," she said finally. "I don't think I'm going to get it though."

"What? Why not? You're the best singer I know."

"But I'm a freshman," said Allison. "There are upperclassmen auditioning for Belle too. One of them is bound to get it."

"You never know," said Emily. "It's a new teacher, isn't it?"

"Yeah, but the juniors and seniors are *so* good."

"Allison," said Emily with weight in her voice. "You're great. It's actually crazy. You're so shy around everyone else. I don't get how you can sing in front of all those people."

Allison shrugged. "It's like I can show off who I am for the first time. Like people can hear me, actually hear me. It's a rush."

"I could never," replied Emily. She lifted her backpack and rested it against her knee while she grabbed the last book she was going to need. The book brushed the bottom of a picture that Emily had put on the back wall of her locker and sent it falling. She caught it with her left hand against her body but dropped her backpack to do it. The books dropped on her toe and she kicked her leg back. "Ouch."

"You've got no luck today," said Allison, chuckling.

"Yeah, I know." Emily clutched at the photo with her hand and pulled it back up. There were four people standing near a wooden railing. Past them was an endless expanse of sea and sky. Emily was standing with two women at her sides. On the far right was her dad, tall and proud. He was typically more fit than her classmates' dads. He worked out a lot and took Emily with him when he did. He was proud of how healthy he was. His hair was a true black while Emily's was almost as brown as her mom's.

Between Emily and her dad was her mom. She had none of the features Emily's father had. She had brown hair and hazel eyes. She was a full head taller than Emily too. Emily had inherited a mix of both their appearances, but she was clearly half Asian.

To the far left of the picture on Emily's other side was a woman who was a lot like the man on the far right. She was taller than Emily's mom, and had dark hair like pools of black ink. Her skin was tanner than Emily's father's, and she had a rough edge to her. She wasn't burly or masculine, but she was toned like an athlete. She had a wry smile that said she was the only person in on the inside joke.

Emily stuck the photo back onto the adhesive she had put on the wall of her locker. The four of them were standing in a typical pose: everyone lined up with their arms together. Emily remembered that day trip and something inside her felt lighter because of the picture. She zipped her backpack shut and then slung it over her shoulder. The weight of it rocked her back and she teetered a little bit. "Want me to wait with you at the audition?"

Allison shut her own locker. "No, it's okay. I don't know how many people are auditioning, or who's going first."

"All right. Well, I'll talk to you later? Text me when you're done," said Emily.

"Of course."

Emily turned to start walking toward the junior parking lot and found another student standing a few feet away. He eyed Emily warily and it made Emily stop in her tracks. His eyes trailed to his left toward Allison and back to Emily before they went wide. His nose twitched, he took a step back, and then he spun on his heels and started walking the other way. Allison snorted and Emily spun back to her.

"What was that about?" she asked Allison.

"That's Jeff," Allison said like it should explain everything, but Emily shrugged.

"You don't remember?" Allison swung her backpack over her shoulder and said, "You punched him."

"What! When?"

"Back in elementary school," replied Allison. "It was the first day we met. He was teasing me, and you punched him in the face. I'm pretty sure you broke his nose."

Emily searched her memories and remembered a boy with a shaved head antagonizing Allison.

"Oh yeah!" she exclaimed. "Jeff! He was such a little prick. How is he now?"

It was Allison's turn to shrug. "Still scared of you, apparently. He never bullied me again. I'm pretty sure he hasn't spoken to me since then. I remember a really awkward group project, now that I think about it."

Emily bit back the smile that was threatening to form.

"Okay, well, I'll talk to you later." Emily turned and joined the stream of fellow students making their way to the exit. Two groups of people converged around her and squished her personal space. An image of a school of fish trying to make its way upstream flashed in her mind. She stopped walking and lurched forward when someone behind her walked right into her.

"Sorry!" said the person behind her.

Emily spun on her heels. A large boy stood there with his arm roped around a girl in a cheerleader's uniform.

"No, it's my fault," said Emily. "I shouldn't have stopped like that. I just wanted to get out of this crowd of people."

"Hey Emily!" called a girl's voice.

Emily shifted her attention to the girl. She recognized her from her math class. "Oh, hey!"

"Are you going to the game tonight?"

"No, I've got something after school."

"Aw, well, have a good weekend!"

"You, too!" Emily turned back toward the junior parking lot and started walking again. She hoped her dad hadn't found out there was a football game. If he did, there was a chance that he would make her go. She went to Foothill High School and she didn't care about their sports teams as much as her dad did.

She reached the end of the walkway and stood on the precipice of the sidewalk. Cars full of parents were lined up and the sound of horns honking filled the air like they were surrounded by geese.

"Emily!" screamed a familiar voice.

Emily stood up on her tiptoes so she could see above everyone. Her breath caught in her throat when her eyes rested on a woman leaning against a blue sedan. She was dressed casually in sweatpants and a tank top but she managed to pull off the outfit like it wasn't something other women wore to bed. She had the same black hair as she had in the photo. She pulled her sunglasses off her face and there was a subtle shift in the woman's muscles. Emily couldn't help but notice that she was darker now than she was in the picture.

"Aunt Elaine?" yelled Emily.

"Hey!"

Aunt Elaine stood tall and with the confidence of an adult who's really seen the world. She wasn't like the adults who looked down on you because you were younger. Rather, Aunt Elaine had experienced what life really had to offer and it had polished her until she shone like a diamond. She radiated with life.

Emily crossed the street, and her aunt threw her arms out.

The tank top left her arms bare to the autumn sun. She had some small scars on her arms and other places on her body that made Emily wonder. Growing up she had always asked her aunt where they came from, and her aunt always had an answer. One was from a troll that didn't like it when she refused to pay the bridge toll. Another she got in a duel to protect a healing spring. She always had the best stories for where they came from. Emily probably got her love of fantasy books from her aunt's stories. Her parents never liked them, but she did.

Her aunt stopped telling the stories now that Emily was

older. She wasn't quite sure why, but it probably had to do with the fact that the last time her aunt tried to tell Emily a story her dad and aunt got into a huge argument that Emily could hear three rooms away.

Emily didn't have siblings, so she never got to experience a sibling argument herself, but her dad and his sister gave her a pretty good idea of what they were like. Her aunt was a few years younger than her dad, but she appeared even younger than that. The blessing of Asian genes, you always come off younger and then one day you turn ancient. Emily had to stand on her toes to get her chin above her aunt's shoulder. Her aunt pulled Emily in for a hug and squeezed her tight. Her hair smelled like spices, cinnamon maybe.

"How's my favorite niece?" she asked after they let go of each other.

"I'm your only niece."

"Yeah, but I could have said you were my least favorite," replied her aunt. Emily managed to stop herself from snickering. "Let me get a look at you."

Her aunt stepped back and held Emily at arm's length. Emily's toes squirmed in her shoes and she pulled her left arm closer to herself. She clutched it with her right hand and her body shrunk in on itself.

"Now, now, chin up," said Aunt Elaine. She lifted Emily's chin with her hand until Emily stood up straight and unfurled her arms. "Sheesh, are you finished growing yet? You're so tall now."

"I haven't gotten taller," said Emily with a frown. It was a sore subject.

"Well, I didn't get shorter," replied her aunt. "Maybe

you're just finally standing up straight." Emily rolled her eyes. "What? You slouch. Bad posture isn't good for anyone."

"Okay, can you not be my mom right now?" asked Emily.

"Fine. Need a ride?"

"Do my parents know you're here?" asked Emily.

"Of course, they do," replied Aunt Elaine. "Why do you think I'm here picking you up?"

CHAPTER 2

THE LESSON

"So, do you like your karate instructor?" Aunt Elaine asked as they pulled into the parking lot. Her aunt slowed down and let a group of dancers dressed in tights and carrying their ballet slippers in their hands cross in front of them. Emily watched them climb the stairs in front of her karate dojo that led to the dance studio upstairs.

"Ben? He's really nice," replied Emily. "I've learned a lot from him."

"Is he strict?" asked Aunt Elaine while she parked.

"Yeah, when he has to be." Emily grabbed the bag that had her gear and *gi* inside it. She rifled through the bag quickly to make sure she hadn't forgotten anything when she had packed that morning. "Did you grab this from my mom? Or did you get to the house early?"

"I got there a little after your dad left to take you to school," replied Aunt Elaine. "I asked your mom if I could pick you up today and she said yes."

"You know karate too, right?" asked Emily.

"Yeah, a little bit," said her aunt with an odd inflection to her voice, part-sarcastic and part-mysterious, like she was holding back some big secret that she couldn't wait to get out.

They walked into the studio together and a bell chimed when the door opened. Emily turned to the front of the dojo and bowed when she entered. The karate studio was pretty plain. The walls were painted white and there were three rooms to her immediate right. The first and closest was a closet that stored cleaning supplies, next to that was the changing room, and last was the bathroom. Just past that was an office, but the entry was around the corner where all the chairs were set up next to a display case. The back of the studio where she had entered had pads and a few punching bags piled up. A chain hung from the ceiling to hang the bag from.

Her instructor came out from his office and waved at Emily and her aunt. He was just around Aunt Elaine's height, so he was kind of short for a guy but he was stocky. He was full blooded Asian and had black hair buzzed short to go with his dark eyes.

"Hey, Emily."

"Hey, Sensei! Remember my Aunt Elaine?"

"Hello." Aunt Elaine stepped forward and brought her hands up. Her right hand formed a fist and her left blanketed it. She bowed slightly to him. "Thank you for teaching my niece. I was hoping I could watch her lesson."

"That's totally fine," replied Ben. He walked up and held out his hand to her.

Aunt Elaine slapped his hand away, and then went in for a hug. They both laughed and embraced briefly. Emily was dumbfounded.

They slapped each other's back as friends do then separated after a second. Aunt Elaine turned and noticed Emily staring. "What?"

"I mean, I know you and Dad are friends with him. I just didn't think you guys would hug one another."

"Why not? We're old family friends," said Ben. "That's why your dad sent you to me for training."

"Yeah, still weird," replied Emily.

"Go get dressed for your lesson," said Ben.

Emily bowed to her teacher and made her way to the changing room.

Emily was kneeling with her eyes closed. She breathed in through her nose and then out through her mouth. Ben and Aunt Elaine's voices were just barely audible through the walls. They were muffled but whatever they were talking about must have been serious; the volume wasn't what she had expected from two friends catching up. Their voices were quieter, muted, like they were sharing secrets. She tried to focus on what they were saying, then realized she was supposed to be meditating. She refocused on her breath like she had been taught. It was normal to have distractions and for her focus to slip away, but she still had to work on centering herself even after all her years of karate.

So, she took a deep breath in through her nose, and then she felt the moment of inaction before she breathed out. She did it again and focused on the cool air as it passed through her nostrils, and then the warm brush of air against the top of her lip. She counted in her head repeatedly. One on the inhale, two on the exhale. She didn't count how long her breaths were; she just noticed when they happened.

Her nose started to itch and she resisted the urge to scratch at it. The tickle persisted and she clenched her fists in her lap. She forced herself to focus on anything but that incessant itch that just wouldn't go away.

The voices in the office grew a little louder, but they were still garbled noises since the door was closed. And then the sound of voices stopped suddenly. She leaned a little to the right and then the door burst open. Her body jolted back to a straight position and she almost opened her eyes. She managed to keep them shut, but her eyes were doing the closed variation of squinting. She relaxed her eyes and her body followed suit.

"Okay, let's get started," said Ben.

Emily opened her eyes. Her teacher stood in front of her while Aunt Elaine was sitting on one of the chairs at the front. "We're going to be doing something of a comprehensive lesson for your aunt. You're going to show off a little bit. We'll start out simple and then we'll get to the harder stuff, all right?"

Emily's brow furrowed. Why did her teacher want Emily to show off for her aunt? Her aunt knew martial arts but showing off was something she had been taught to never do—by Ben no less. Her eyes darted to her aunt in a furtive glance. She was going to bring her attention back to her teacher quickly, but she locked eyes with her aunt. They held each other's gaze for a solid second before her aunt smiled and nodded.

"Yes, Sensei," said Emily, though she was still confused.

"Okay, stand up."

Emily stood and held both hands out in front of her in the same hand motion she had made when she came in. Her right hand was a fist and her left hand covered it with her elbows winged out.

"Bow," said Ben. Emily bowed to her sensei who bowed slightly to her. "All right, show me defense maneuver six."

Emily immediately shifted to her stance. Her feet were shoulder width apart, her knees bent slightly, and her hands were in front of her in a defensive position. She took a breath, then deliberately raised her right knee in front of her, and finally kicked forward.

"*Kiai*!" she cried out when she kicked. She brought her leg back so her knee was up at waist level like before and then she let it fall to her left so her legs were crossed. Finally she took another step back diagonally with her left leg, so she was farther away from her invisible assailant.

"Good," said Ben. "Now show me seven."

The lesson continued in that fashion for a good deal of time. Ben told her which maneuver to do, Emily did it, and then he said a different one. They moved from defense maneuvers to all the punches and kicks she knew and then finally to the forms she had been taught. Emily didn't have any time to catch her breath, but she did them all silently and correctly. At least she assumed she did, Ben didn't stop to give her any comments. He just stood at the head of the dojo with his arms crossed.

Emily caught glimpses of her aunt occasionally in the corner of the room. Aunt Elaine sat quietly, her legs crossed, and leaning on the chair's armrest with her elbow. Her chin rested on her closed fist, but she never took her eyes off Emily. She was pretty sure her aunt never blinked or looked away. Not to check her phone, to check the time, to watch someone walking by. Nothing. Emily had checked the time at least twice, it had been forty-seven minutes, longer than a normal private lesson. Some people walked by multiple times. Dancers had gone upstairs and then back downstairs. Pedestrians walked by and a few people stopped at the windows to watch. Emily remained silent throughout the entire ordeal and then finally she ended her last form. Her instructor didn't say anything.

Ben studied Emily for a moment after she had bowed. Then he turned to face Aunt Elaine. "So, what do you think?"

Emily turned her head in her aunt's direction. Aunt Elaine stood up and walked closer, so she stood next to Ben.

"She's good," said Aunt Elaine. "You've done a good job."

A swell of pride rose inside Emily and her lips curled up into a smile.

"How's her sparring?" asked Aunt Elaine.

"Why don't we find out?" said Ben. He turned to face Emily. "Go get your gear on."

Emily turned and started to walk toward the changing room where her bag was, but had only made it a couple steps before Aunt Elaine interrupted.

"Wait."

Emily turned back to her instructor as her aunt said, "She won't need any. We'll just go barehanded."

Emily almost tripped over her own feet. Ben cleared his throat. "We don't really do that here."

"Trust me," said Aunt Elaine. "I'm not going to hurt her."

Emily studied her teacher for a moment and there was an uncomfortable expression on his face, but Aunt Elaine just kept staring at him.

"Fine," said Ben, but his voice said it was anything but.

"Can we get a little privacy?" asked Aunt Elaine.

"Sure. Emily, can you shut the blinds and then lock the door in the back? I'll get these ones in the front."

Emily ran to the back and shut the blinds while Ben closed the rest in the front and then they both locked the doors. Emily returned to the front of the class and stood at attention, her hands back in front of her with her left over her right. Aunt Elaine had removed her jewelry and was standing in front of Emily. She stood loosely, almost aloof, whereas Emily felt stiff standing up straight and in her *gi*. Ben stood at the corner of the room.

"Do you want me to referee?" he asked.

"No, that won't be necessary," Aunt Elaine said. "Do you spar much?"

"Every so often," replied Emily. "Always with gear."

"Yes, well, I don't think there's any chance you'll hurt me," said Aunt Elaine. "And I'll go easy on you."

"What?"

"You heard me," said Aunt Elaine. "This is just a test to see what you can do. Attack me however you want."

"I'm not going to attack you," said Emily. "Not bare-handed. I'm a black belt, Aunt Elaine. I could hurt you."

"You could try," snorted Aunt Elaine. "Tell you what. I'll give you two minutes."

"What?" said Emily again.

Aunt Elaine turned to Ben. "Ben, if Emily can't hit me in two minutes then she's not allowed to study martial arts here ever again. Okay?"

Ben considered the words for a moment. His face said he

wasn't sure but then his eyes settled on Aunt Elaine. It steeled him for some reason. "Understood."

"*What?*" repeated Emily a little louder.

"You heard him," said Aunt Elaine. She pulled her phone out and showed it to Emily. A timer was set to two minutes. "You've got two minutes. Don't worry, I won't hit you."

She pressed start.

Emily wasn't sure how to react. She turned to Ben, but her teacher was checking his watch. He looked up finally and said, "Don't look at me; the clock's ticking."

Emily turned back to Aunt Elaine who stood with her arms crossed like she was waiting for a late bus. "One minute and fifty seconds left."

Emily exploded into action. She lunged forward with a front kick at her aunt. Aunt Elaine turned slightly, caught Emily's foot, and pulled her forward. Emily lurched as her back leg stumbled and dragged across the floor. Aunt Elaine dropped Emily's foot and she fell into a half split and then on her side. Emily grimaced up at her aunt who was checking her phone again.

"One minute and forty-seven seconds left."

Emily spun on the ground and rolled onto her feet. She attacked again, throwing a punch with her right hand. Aunt Elaine slapped Emily's hand away. "What was that?"

Emily spun on her heel and swung her left hand in a sweeping motion and aimed for her aunt's head. Aunt Elaine stepped back and watched Emily's hand swing past, then stepped forward again and shoved her body into Emily's back. Emily stumbled forward and then turned to face her aunt again with her hands up.

"You can throw more than one attack at a time," said Aunt Elaine.

Emily jumped forward and threw a punch at her aunt, but she just stepped out of the way again. Emily landed and then turned and attempted a roundhouse kick. Aunt Elaine stepped in toward Emily and pinned Emily's leg between her arm and shoulder then shoved her down. Emily toppled onto the ground again and Aunt Elaine stepped back. She sighed, pulled out her phone, and started tapping at it again.

"What are you doing?" asked Emily.

"Well, if you're not going to take this seriously, then I'm just going to answer some emails," said Aunt Elaine.

"We aren't finished yet," said Emily. "I've got more time."

"Yes, you do," agreed Aunt Elaine while still working on her phone. "Are you just going to sit there? Or are you going to show me what you've got?"

Emily lunged forward again and attacked. She threw a series of hand strikes at her aunt aiming for her head and body. Aunt Elaine turned to the side and started deflecting Emily's attacks with only her right hand. Emily's frustration was mounting. She aimed a kick low at her aunt's legs, something she was taught never to do, but her aunt lifted her leg and stopped Emily's kick with her own foot. She just stepped on Emily's foot and all the momentum from her kick disappeared. Aunt Elaine put her foot down and Emily's came down with it. Her aunt shifted so her foot and leg slid behind Emily's leg and then swept her leg back. Emily lurched forward again and lost her balance.

She tried to pull her leg back just like her aunt had, but the foundation of her stance was gone, and she couldn't get the same strength behind it. Her aunt didn't even falter. She was tapping away on her phone with her left hand and wasn't even glancing at Emily. Emily shrieked and threw a punch at Aunt Elaine's stomach that had no technique in it whatsoever. It was just pure, unbridled rage. Aunt Elaine thrust her hand out and stabbed Emily's upper arm with her pointer and index finger. Sharp pain exploded in her arm and she pulled it back. Aunt Elaine lunged forward and shoved Emily back with her shoulder. Emily's leg was still behind her aunt's and she tripped backward and landed on her butt.

The phone started beeping loudly. Aunt Elaine tapped at the screen, put her phone away, and then directed her gaze at Emily. "Time's up. You didn't hit me."

Emily turned desperately toward her teacher and he just shrugged. "Sorry. You're no longer my student."

All the energy inside her disappeared. She felt like she just got hit in her chest and the air was sucked out of her. She loved karate. It was something she had grown up doing. It was the first thing she bonded with her father over, and now it was gone. Shame and fury were threatening to expose themselves as tears. Aunt Elaine stepped forward, extended her hand out to Emily, and said, "How would you like to be mine?"

CHAPTER 3

A GIFT

"WHERE DID YOU learn that?" asked Emily in disbelief. Her lesson was over and they were picking up dinner for the family. "I mean I know you learned karate but that was... unreal."

The restaurant was so crowded and noisy she could barely hear her aunt laugh in response. Emily and Aunt Elaine were both seated on a pair of stools with seats shaped like bottle caps. The walls of the restaurant were painted in segments of red and yellow and occasionally some black. A menu hung behind them on a black chalkboard with handwritten items on there. There were signs and sayings and decorations across the whole restaurant. A side room to her right had a flat screen TV hanging from the corner with a basketball game on.

The sound of noisy eating and conversations filled the air and Emily was jostled by someone walking by. He called an apology and Emily just waved him by without even turning his way. She was too focused on her aunt. Her aunt was watching the cars searching for spaces in the parking lot that was too small for the number of people in the burger joint. The door next to Emily was held ajar by people standing in a line that stretched out into said parking lot.

"Here and there," replied Aunt Elaine without a care in the world. She adjusted a bracelet on her wrist and then turned to face Emily. "I learned when I was your age."

"Yeah, but I can't do any of the stuff you can do," said Emily. "What belt are you?"

Her aunt shrugged. "I'm older than you. I've had a lot more time to train and learn new things. And I don't think I was ever given a belt."

"No belt?" asked Emily.

"Our teachers weren't really big on belts for us," said Aunt Elaine. "They just taught us what they knew when they thought we were ready."

"Who were your teachers?" asked Emily.

"Family members mostly. Some monks," said Aunt Elaine.

"You said we, who's we?"

"Me and your dad," said Aunt Elaine.

Emily's jaw almost dropped when Aunt Elaine said "your dad." Her dad had never mentioned learning karate. Ever. She opened her mouth to speak and found words failing her. Could her dad do what Aunt Elaine could do?

She started to ask that very question when Aunt Elaine spun toward the menu. "Are you sure we shouldn't have ordered gooey fries?"

"My dad?" she said, ignoring the question about gooey fries. "My dad can do that too?"

"I don't know if he can anymore," replied Aunt Elaine.

"He stopped learning years ago, just when he was a little older than you."

"You're serious though? About teaching me?" asked Emily. Her aunt nodded. "Does this mean you'll be staying a while?"

"As long as I can," said Aunt Elaine. "Now really, what about the gooey fries?"

Emily's eyes narrowed. There was something she almost missed on her aunt's face. It was only there for a moment, and then it was gone. A flash of sadness. Then her aunt was smiling again. Emily wasn't sure what to do or say; she wasn't even sure her aunt was actually sad. "My mom doesn't like them. Too sweet. She just likes sweet potato fries on their own. They're also too much."

"Got it," replied Aunt Elaine. She sipped her soda and studied the room. "So, this place is super busy."

Emily turned around and saw that the line hadn't shrunk at all. "It's the best burger place in Tustin in my opinion."

"Looks like people agree with you," said Aunt Elaine.

"So, where did you come from this time?"

"Northern California," said Aunt Elaine. "Was there for a little bit of work."

"What kind of work?" asked Emily, her interest piqued. They never talked about what her aunt did for work. "Do you teach martial arts?"

"Sometimes," said Aunt Elaine. "I was visiting family."

"My mysterious cousins?" Emily picked up a fry and tried to pretend that it was interesting. "What are they like?" She tried to ask as nonchalantly as she could.

Aunt Elaine shrugged. "You know, they're family."

"I really don't," said Emily under her breath.

She had never met any of her cousins. Neither of her parents had really kept in touch with their family, but Emily knew she had cousins on her dad's side. He just never talked about them. They never visited, they never called. She wished she knew them. Her *yeye* used to tell her stories about their family before he passed. Fantastical stories that never happened but Emily still wished she had cousins she could go on adventures with. Aunt Elaine was her only connection with her mysterious family, and she had taken on her grandpa's role of telling her family's stories.

"Hey, don't worry about it," said Aunt Elaine. "Our family likes to keep to themselves. I only saw them this last time because I had to."

Emily sipped her own soda. "Why's that?"

"Oh, just had to pass along some news. Looks like our food's ready."

Emily's phone dinged as soon as she sat down inside her aunt's car. She pulled her phone out and a photo of herself with Allison grinned back at her. Emblazoned over that photo was a notification for a new text message from Allison. She punched down on her phone on the message and opened it.

"Hey! What are you up to?"

Emily tapped at the virtual keys on her phone while her aunt started the car and backed out of the parking spot.

"With my aunt picking up dinner. She surprised me at school after you went to tryouts. How did it go?"

"Good! Jeremy tried out for *Beast*."

"Wait. THE Jeremy?"

"YES. We had to try out in front of everyone and he told me after that he really hoped I got the part."

"WHAT? WHAT DID YOU SAY?"

"I barely said anything. I just kind of smiled and I'm positive I blushed. I just said he was really good."

"Wow, that's a big step. I mean you actually talked to him. Don't you normally just stare from far away? And then look away when he actually looks at you."

"Shut up!"

"This is good though! You guys will both get the parts, then you'll fall in love during rehearsal. It's like a movie."

"Are you going to be on that thing the whole ride home?" her aunt asked suddenly.

Emily slipped the phone back inside her pocket ignoring the chime from it that meant Allison had replied. "Sorry. That was Allison."

"Oh, how is she?" asked Aunt Elaine.

"Good, she auditioned for a part in the school musical today."

"What musical?"

"*Beauty and the Beast*," said Emily. She picked a fry out of the bag and started eating it. Then she pulled another one out and held it up for her aunt who took it after a second glance. "She tried out for Belle."

Aunt Elaine snorted. "I figured. She used to sing that song all the time."

"The one at the beginning, in the town, right?" said Emily.

"That's the one," replied her aunt. She was silent for a moment as she made a left turn onto a small street. "Hey, are your parents going to be home when we get there?"

Emily checked the clock on the dashboard. "Doubt it. Dad usually works late and Mom's showing a house tonight. Why? What's up?"

"I've got something for you. I think you'll like it a lot."

"What is it?" asked Emily.

"Wait till we get home," said her aunt. "Hand me another fry though."

Emily dropped the bags of food on the kitchen counter and then slipped her backpack and karate bag off her shoulder. She ran outside and grabbed the duffle bag her aunt offered her and led her aunt to the guest room. She crossed through some double doors and put the bag down on the floor at the foot of the unmade bed.

"Are the blankets in the same spot?" asked Aunt Elaine.

"Yeah," said Emily.

Her aunt opened the closet and was pulling down some sheets. Emily grabbed one end of the sheet and helped her aunt make the bed. Once they were finished, her aunt sat down at the foot of the bed and then patted the bed next to her. Emily sat down while her aunt started rummaging through her duffle bag. She pulled something out of the bag and cupped it in her hands in her lap. She unfolded her hands and revealed a lacquered wooden box. It was painted red and had a brass latch to keep it shut.

Aunt Elaine held the box reverently while Emily attempted to bore holes into it with her eyes. Her aunt brushed her hand against it. She did it lovingly, but there was something sad about the way she did it too.

"Aunt Elaine?" said Emily.

"Hmm?"

"Is everything okay?"

"Yeah," said Aunt Elaine. She knocked on the box twice and then she opened it.

Emily's breath caught in her throat. The box was filled with a shiny, gray-blue cloth, and resting in it was a ring. The ring was a silver band that had small tree branches forking along the edges of it with flowers on it. There was one flower that was larger than the rest that must have marked the intended center of the ring. It had five petals and stalks exploding out of the center like a firework.

Aunt Elaine picked up the ring and lifted it out of the box for Emily. Emily reached out to take the ring between her forefinger and thumb.

The ring touched her fingertips and shocked her with a quiet pop. Emily's hand recoiled on instinct. "Ow!"

"You okay?"

"Yeah," said Emily. "Just shocked me."

She held her hand out and her aunt placed the ring in Emily's palm. She turned the ring over in her hand to admire it. Leaves and flowers on the branches intertwined around the ring, but the flowers were smaller versions of the large flower that was facing up when her aunt opened the box.

Her aunt let out a breath like she had been holding it and then smiled at Emily.

"Do you like it?"

"I love it," said Emily. "What kind of flower is it?"

"It's a plum blossom."

"It's beautiful," said Emily. "Does a plum blossom mean anything?"

"Perseverance. And hope."

Emily studied the flower for a moment longer, then slid the ring on her ring finger on her right hand. She thought it was going to be too big when she was holding it in her palm, but it fit her finger perfectly. It was like it was made for her. She threw her arms around her aunt. "Thank you."

"You're welcome." Her aunt returned the hug and squeezed her tight. The sound of tires rolling along the driveway pulled Emily away from her aunt. A muffled thud came from the front yard. It sounded a lot like a car door being shut, and then there was the beep of a car being locked. Both Emily and her aunt peered out the window in the living room.

"I better put my bags in my room," said Emily. "Mom gets mad when I leave them lying around."

Emily slipped her backpack over her shoulder, grabbed her karate bag, and ran upstairs. She stepped inside her room, shut the door behind her, and set her bags down by her desk. She crossed the room to her bed and set the box down on top of it. Emily sat down at the foot of her bed, held the ring up to the light, and admired the silver band wrapped around her finger.

"Emily!" called a voice.

"Yeah, Mom?" she called back.

"Dad's home too! Come on down for dinner!"

Emily slipped down the stairs just as her dad was walking in through the garage.

"Hey Emily," he said. "How was your day?"

"Hey Dad!" said Emily. "It was good! Glad it's Friday. How about yours?"

"Long," replied her dad. "Hey, Elaine."

"Hey Chris," said Aunt Elaine from behind Emily.

Her dad dropped his briefcase and hugged Emily. She let him go after a few seconds, and moved out of the way for her aunt. Her dad and aunt shared what passed for a hug for the two of them. It was short, the hug lasting barely the length of a breath, and it was stiff. It was almost formal, like they were from a different planet and were taught what a hug was with pictures. Emily frowned at the two of them but bit back a comment that was building up.

"Good to see you, Elaine," said Emily's dad.

"You too," said Aunt Elaine. "I bet you're glad to be home."

"You have no idea," he replied.

"Tell us about it," said Aunt Elaine.

He picked up his briefcase again and the three of them made their way into the kitchen where the smell of burgers and fries was wafting in the air.

Her dad set his briefcase down on a table that was set up next to the kitchen table. It was a kind of catch-all for Emily's parents to put all their work stuff so it was out of the way. They had an office, but everyone always gravitated around the dinner table to do their work.

"Just clients late with their information," said Dad. "It's always the same. They say we never sent it to them, but we always do. Then it's late and they're blaming us."

"That sounds awful," said Aunt Elaine.

"Yeah, well, there's nothing we can do about it really. Thanks for picking up dinner for us."

"You're welcome," said Aunt Elaine. "It was a cute place. A lot of people there."

"It's super good," chimed in Emily. "You'll see."

Aunt Elaine sat down next to Emily and Emily's parents sat down across from them. Emily picked up her turkey burger, pulled the paper down a bit, and found a side with avocado before taking a bite.

"Oh my God this *is* good," said Aunt Elaine. She had taken the wrapper off completely and chopped lettuce was spilling out the back of it.

"Best burger in Tustin," said Emily's dad. "Maybe Orange County."

"Their gyros are good too," said Emily's mom with one hand up to cover her mouth. "Everything's good there."

"I believe it. I wanted to get gooey fries, but someone told me no," said Aunt Elaine. She gave Emily a healthy dose of side eye.

"It would have been too much," said Emily.

"She's right," said Mom. "They're good but we'd never finish them."

Aunt Elaine picked up a sweet potato fry and pointed it at Emily's mom. "That sounds like a challenge, Jessica."

"It's not," said her dad. "Just a fact."

"All right, fine," said Aunt Elaine while holding her hands up in a placating motion. "You win."

"So, how was your karate lesson?" Dad asked Emily before he stuffed three ranch-dipped fries in his mouth.

Emily glanced over at Aunt Elaine, who didn't react at all. She just kept on eating. "It was interesting."

"Learn anything new?" asked her mom. She was using a fork to spread tzatziki sauce on her gyro.

"Nope," replied Emily. Her voice cracked and she started talking again just to hide it. "He just kind of ran me through everything. Like, *everything*."

"Maybe he's getting ready to test you," said her mom. "That would be good, right?

"Yeah," said Emily. "That would mean another rank up."

"Did you watch her, Elaine?" Her dad's face was stern.

Aunt Elaine was in the middle of taking a bite of her burger. She leaned forward and covered her mouth with her hand and coughed a little bit. "Sorry. Middle of eating. Yeah, I watched."

"What'd you think?" he asked.

"Pretty good," said Aunt Elaine. Emily's dad appeared content with that answer because he picked up his food again. "That said, I think Emily needs a better teacher."

Emily's eyes shifted from her aunt to her dad who had paused mid-bite. He put his turkey burger down, wiped his mouth with a napkin, and tilted his head at Aunt Elaine. He looked annoyed. "What makes you say that?"

Aunt Elaine pushed her plate toward the center of the table and leaned on her elbows. "Ben is a good teacher, and he's a good person, but Emily needs to be great."

There was a silence after Aunt Elaine spoke as everyone in the room absorbed what she had said. What did Aunt Elaine mean when she said Emily had to be great? Emily's dad was frozen like a statue as he stared hard across the table. Emily turned to her aunt. Aunt Elaine had a softer expression, but she returned her brother's steely gaze.

"What did you do?" whispered Emily's father.

Emily's eyes shot toward her dad. His voice only got that low and quiet when he was angry. But what could he be angry about?

Aunt Elaine closed her eyes, took a deep breath, and then opened her eyes again. "Emily, could you hold up your hand?"

A weird feeling formed in the pit of Emily's stomach as confusion and worry stormed her thoughts. She slowly lifted her right hand, the only one that her aunt could have been talking about, and showed the ring to her family.

"Now hold your hand out with your palm down. Like you're reaching for the next rung of a ladder or like you're grabbing a bubble out of the sky."

Emily twisted her hand and closed it on the empty air. Then her hand was full. A weight pulled her arm down and Emily couldn't believe her eyes. There, in her hand, was a sword.

"I've chosen Emily as my successor," said Aunt Elaine.

CHAPTER 4

SUCCESSOR

TWO QUESTIONS POPPED into Emily's head. The first was where did this sword come from? The second was, what was going on?

She hadn't dropped the sword, which had surprised her. She brought it closer so she could inspect it. It was long and sheathed, and it wasn't very wide, so she could tell the sword was thin. The sheath was made of black wood with brass ornaments at the tip and near the mouth. The black wood was glossy and there was something painted along it. Emily turned the sword slightly and saw that there were branches with white flowers on them.

The same flower was on the hilt embossed on the metalwork. She recognized the shape and raised her hand to compare the ring with the flower on the sword. Her ring was gone. She opened her mouth to speak but stopped herself when she noticed that her aunt was still staring across the table.

Emily turned to her father. He was glaring at her with a cold fury in his eyes that burrowed into her bones.

"What is my daughter doing with that?" Her dad enunciated each word with such venom that Emily was surprised he didn't actually spit the words out. And then Emily realized he wasn't shooting hateful glares at her, but at the sword. She studied his face for a moment longer. He wasn't surprised.

He definitely had surprise written on his face, but not the kind of surprise that Emily was expecting or that her mother was showing. There was recognition in his face. Emily was sure he had seen the sword before.

"I told you," said Aunt Elaine. "Emily is my successor."

"Wait, can someone tell me what's going on?" broke in Emily.

Aunt Elaine and Emily's dad both turned to Emily. The anger on his face dissipated for a moment, then his gaze fell to the sword in her hands. Anger flashed across his face again.

"Emily, go to your room," he said suddenly.

"What? Why?" asked Emily.

"Your aunt and I need to have a conversation."

"But what's going on?" cried out Emily. "Where did this sword come from? What happened to my ring?"

Emily's dad jumped up from his seat and Emily reeled back from the table. "YOU DIDN'T TELL HER?"

"Come on, Emily let's go upstairs," whispered her mother. Emily didn't even realize her mom had crossed the room. Her mother lifted Emily gently, helping her to stand up while Emily kept clutching the sword.

"What about—"

"Just take it with you," said her mom.

Emily allowed herself to be dragged from the room, but she spared one last glance over her shoulder. Her father was seething, and Emily swore there was literal steam coming off him. Aunt Elaine was still sitting calmly, her hands folded on the table in plain view.

"Chris, you need to calm down," said Aunt Elaine just as Emily was pulled from the room.

"DON'T!" yelled her dad, but he stopped. Emily was making her way up the stairs, but her dad's voice carried to the stairwell. "Don't tell me to calm down."

He sounded strained, like he was holding everything back. Emily was just outside her room now and her mom was ushering her in.

"Does she even know—"

Emily didn't get to hear the rest. Her mother shut the door and leaned against it. She closed her eyes and let out a deep breath. She had an embarrassed expression on her face. It was something that Emily was used to seeing in movies or on TV when someone was apologizing with their eyes for their loved one.

"Not exactly the best family meal," Mom said.

"Mom, what's going on?" asked Emily.

"Why don't we sit down?"

"What?" Emily wanted to do anything but sit. In fact, she had started pacing back and forth in her room. Her mom sat on Emily's bed and just waited. "Mom, how can you just sit down? What's going on?" She held the sword up in front of her. "Where did this come from?"

"Emily." Her mother patted the bed beside her. "Sit down."

Emily sat on the bed next to her mom and lay the sword down across her lap. Now that the sword's weight was resting on her, she realized she hadn't had a chance to look at the actual sword. Curiosity burned inside her and suddenly she was like a kid on Christmas morning. She lifted the sword and ran her eyes along the entirety of the sheath.

It was beautiful. The painted tree branch forking across it like lightning had intricate details. The white flowers along the branch were round and had five petals and tiny stems coming from the center. Emily traced her hand along the sheath until she came to the guard on the hilt.

"A plum blossom," murmured Emily. She let her fingers slide across the guard and onto the handle and then to the brass pommel at the end. Emily wrapped her fingers around the handle and was about to pull when her mother's hand covered hers and stopped her.

"Let's not," she said.

Emily attempted to hide her disappointment at being stopped and then relinquished her grip on the sword.

"Mom," said Emily. "What's going on?"

"I don't know really," said her mother. "I have an idea, but I don't want to give you a wrong answer. I think the best thing to do right now is wait for your dad and aunt to figure it out."

"Dad recognized this sword," said Emily. "He did, right?"

Her mom pursed her lips. "Yes. I think I do too."

"You recognize it?" repeated Emily. "How? Mom please."

Her mother gestured to the sword and said, "Can I see it?"

Emily passed the sword to her mother, who took it. She held it carefully, like it was a fragile vase, or like she expected something to pop out of it. She rested it on her lap just as Emily had and ran her hands along it like she was smoothing out a blanket.

"It's beautiful." She lifted it just below the guard with her left hand, grabbed the handle with her right, and pulled.

Emily resisted the urge to scream "no." That sword was hers. Aunt Elaine gave it to her. It appeared in *her* hand. She should be the first one to unsheathe it! To catch the glint of light off its blade. But if she were to have any chance of keeping the sword she had to let everything run its course.

So, she closed her eyes. She was determined to let the first time she saw it be when she was holding it. She waited for a gasp, a word or two from her mother, or even the grind of the blade against the scabbard but there was nothing. Only a click and a strained grunt from her mom.

Emily chanced a peek. Her mother was still pulling, but the sword didn't budge. It was stuck in the sheath.

"Huh," said her mom. "Well, that's okay."

She passed the sword back to Emily and stood up. "I'm going to make sure those two don't do anything stupid. Don't play with the sword."

"Mom—"

"Promise me, Emily," said her mom, cutting her off.

Emily was trying to come up with something to say, for an answer, but her mom just gave her that parent face that said the conversation was over. No answer was coming to her now. "Okay."

Her mother shut the door behind her and left Emily alone in her room. Emily closed her eyes and listened to the footfalls of her mom as she walked down the stairs. She opened her eyes and ran her hands along the sword and the sheath again. She found herself wondering where it came from, but then a new question formed in her mind.

What good is a sword that can't be drawn? Her dad had recognized the sword, so he should know Emily couldn't draw it. Why would he get so mad about a sword that couldn't be unsheathed? Unless…

Emily turned the sword over slowly and ran a finger along the space where the guard met the sheath. There was nothing there. No lock or any glue seeping out.

She stood up and held the sword out in front of her. She pulled and the sound of metal rang out. Emily had to stop herself from letting out an excited squeak. She didn't draw it completely, but enough that her reflection shone off the thin sword.

"Wow," whispered Emily. She tilted the sword a little and light glared across it. The light shifted and Emily froze.

There was a face there, but it wasn't hers. She blinked in surprise, but the face was her own again. Emily was sure of what she saw. This woman's face was older, but still young. She had hair black as night where Emily had brown hair, and her skin was paler than Emily's.

She tilted the sword and the reflection shifted leaving her own. She was sure she had seen it, or had she?

"Emily!" cried her mom from downstairs and Emily jumped. The sound of her mother's footsteps up the stairs were like a drum beat. The footsteps grew closer and Emily's heart matched pace with the steps. She frantically sheathed the sword and sat down on her bed again just before her mother opened the door. "Come on downstairs. They want to talk to you."

CHAPTER 5

FAMILY SECRETS

EMILY HELD THE sword close to her chest; clutching at it as if someone might appear from the shadows and take it from her. She followed her mother to the living room instead of the kitchen. Her father stood by a window with his back turned to everyone while Aunt Elaine sat in one of the lounge chairs. Emily's mom sat down on the couch and Emily joined her.

"Your mom thought that you should be here for this," said her dad. He turned around and Emily expected the guise of fury to be plastered on his face still. Instead, he appeared tired and worn, like he had been up all night working. "Why don't you put the sword down?"

Emily set the sword on the coffee table. Her mom handed her a steaming cup of tea and Emily took a sip before setting it down on the table in front of the sword.

"Dad, what's going on? You're all kind of scaring me."

"I'm sorry for yelling earlier," he said. "We're going to explain it to you. It's just a hard story to tell."

He sat down in the empty lounge chair and buried his face in his hands.

"You have to understand, Emily," he said suddenly. "You have a choice in this. You always have a choice. You should have been told."

"I'm sorry, Chris," said Aunt Elaine. "You all came home before I could tell her."

"Why hide it from us?" Dad replied. "We're her parents."

"I'm sorry. I just—I wasn't sure how you'd take it."

"Maybe you guys should just tell her," said Mom.

Dad and Aunt Elaine shared a look, then he gestured at Aunt Elaine. She stood up and picked up the sword.

"Emily. You're not going to believe what I'm about to tell you. That doesn't mean it isn't true. I need you to understand that, okay?"

"Okay," replied Emily.

Aunt Elaine held the sword out in front of her. "This is Meihua."

"May-Hwa?" repeated Emily, sounding the word out.

Her aunt nodded. "She's a magic sword that's been passed down in our family for generations. Since our family was in China. You see, a long time ago there was a war. One of your ancestors was drafted into the army and took this sword with him. The sword helped him survive the war, and he passed the sword down to his child, and so forth until it came to your *yeye*." She gestured to Emily's dad. "Our dad."

Aunt Elaine paused and Emily took the moment to sneak a peek at her father. He had a pained, sickly expression on his face.

"Do you want me to?" asked Aunt Elaine.

"I can do it," he said. Aunt Elaine offered him the sword, but he put his hands up and practically jumped away from it. He looked a little queasy. "No, thank you."

Aunt Elaine sat down in her chair and let the sword rest on her lap.

"It has been the destiny of those born in our family to become warriors," said her dad. "Every person who inherited the sword trained their children so they could take over."

"Take over what?" asked Emily.

"The family business," said Aunt Elaine, "and protecting the sword."

Emily waited for more of an explanation but neither her parents nor her aunt expanded, so Emily asked, "Which is?"

Her parents both turned to Aunt Elaine. "I'm a bodyguard. I'll explain it later. Let your dad finish."

Emily turned back to her father. She realized she was sitting at the edge of her seat and she was holding her breath. Anxious energy toyed with her head and insides, so she grabbed the mug of tea, took a sip, and held it in her hands.

"The guardian of the sword trained all their kids," said her dad. "But they usually had someone picked out in their head. *Yeye* did, too."

"He picked Aunt Elaine?" asked Emily. "Is that why you're so mad?"

Her father wouldn't meet Emily's gaze. "No. He picked me."

"What?" said Emily.

"I was the eldest, and he trained me to take over, but then something happened."

Her dad fell silent, and there was a weight to that silence.

It pressed down on her chest and built something up in her until she couldn't hold the question back anymore.

"What?" she whispered.

Her dad placed his hand over his eyes and managed a single cough before he spoke, and when he did Emily could hear the tears in his voice.

"He came back from a job really hurt," he said. "The family physicians saved him, but he couldn't fight anymore. So, he had to retire, and he had to name his successor. I was ready. God, I was ready. But then he picked Elaine."

Emily didn't say anything. There were so many questions in her mind, but she couldn't ask them. She wasn't sure where to start, or if she should.

"I was just as shocked as your dad was," said Aunt Elaine. "He got angry and stormed off when Meihua was given to me."

"Why?" asked Emily.

"Because Meihua isn't just a sword," said Aunt Elaine. "You'll see, but she can think, talk, she can choose. She usually agrees with whoever her holder chooses, but not always. She doesn't have to. She chose me. I tried to change her mind and give her to your dad, but she won't let anyone but who she chooses wield her."

"And after that I left the family business," said Dad. "I met your mom, fell in love, and we had you."

"What happened to *yeye*?" asked Emily.

Aunt Elaine's eyes darted to Emily's dad, and then back to Emily. "Remember what I said earlier? About not believing in something and it being true anyway?"

"Yeah."

"Well, all those stories you read? All the stories he told

43

you about? About monsters and magic? They're all real in some way. The family business. We're all bodyguards really. We protect people from monsters. And well, your *yeye* got hurt protecting someone."

Her gaze shifted to the shelf with all their family photos. Her eyes found one picture in particular with her grandpa holding a younger Emily in his lap. He was smiling happily, and his eyes were nearly closed, but now Emily was drawn to the little scars on him that she had never paid attention to before. She imagined where they all came from, and all the stories he used to tell her, and what he had made up when he told her about them. She wondered how many of those stories were true.

And she remembered all her aunt's scars. The stories she had told about the troll, the healing spring, and all those monsters. Were they true too?

Emily's voice disappeared and so did her ability to think. She tried to say something, anything, but nothing was coming out.

"Which brings us to today," said Aunt Elaine. "I'm retiring while I can. I need a successor and we chose you."

"And that's why I was so mad," broke in her father. "She didn't tell me or ask me. She just did it."

"I had no choice," said Aunt Elaine. "Meihua chose her."

"You had a choice," said Emily's dad coldly. "And so does Emily." He turned to Emily just as she raised her head. "The sword chose you. Only you can wield it."

"*Her*, not it," corrected Aunt Elaine.

Dad waved Aunt Elaine off and kept his focus on Emily. "You are the one who decides to use the sword or not."

"He's right," said Aunt Elaine. "And I'll stay around no matter what you choose. I'll still teach you."

Both her dad and aunt were giving her expectant faces. The only one who didn't have an eager gleam in their eyes was her mom.

"Mom, what do you think?"

Everyone turned to Emily's mom. She smiled weakly, took Emily's hand in her own, and gave it a gentle squeeze.

"I think it's your decision and you have to make it," she said. "I don't want you to fight monsters, but they both said you don't have to. Your father will tell you he doesn't regret what happened and leaving it all behind. He better not at least. That choice gave him you and me. But he would be lying if he said he didn't miss it."

Emily leaned forward and reached for the sword. Her aunt handed it to her, and Emily let it rest gently on her lap like she had earlier. She slid her left hand across the sheath and the flowers painted on it. She traced her fingers over the guard and then took hold of it by the handle. Holding it just felt right.

"I don't have to make a decision now, do I?" asked Emily.

"No, of course not," said her mother.

"But you'll still teach me, right Aunt Elaine?"

"Of course, I will," said her aunt.

Emily turned to her parents. "Is that okay with you guys?"

Her mom squeezed her hand again. "Of course." There was a supportive tone to her voice when she said it, which was quickly dropped for a more serious tone. "As long as it doesn't affect your schoolwork."

"Wait, I'm not sure I'm okay with it," said her dad.

Her mom threw her arms up in frustration, rolled her eyes, and slapped her hands down on her knees before she turned to face her husband. "Well, honey, you're the one that went on and on about how she has a choice. You can't take it from her now."

"Yeah, I can. I'm her dad," he replied.

"Yup, and what kind of parent gives their child a choice and then says no because he didn't like it?" asked Mom.

Dad pursed his lips. "Fine."

Emily's mom patted her husband's leg. "Just think of this as a parenting lesson."

"Hey guys," said Emily. "Do you think we can finish dinner now? I'm still hungry."

Her mom laughed. "Of course."

"Well I think I'm going to go to bed early," announced Aunt Elaine. They were all sitting in the TV room pretending to watch whatever was on. Her dad had put on the Laker game and they always watched it together. Tonight, it was more like background noise while they all ignored one another. "Could I talk to Emily before I do though?"

"Sure," said Emily.

Her dad just kind of shrugged and Emily got up from the couch. She followed Aunt Elaine to the guest room and leaned the sword against the desk by the entrance. Her aunt shut the doors and Emily sat down on the office chair. She pulled her knees up to her chest, so her feet were clutching at the edge of the seat and hugged her legs.

"What's up?" asked Emily when her aunt sat at the edge of her bed.

"I just thought I should talk to you before you went to sleep. Answer any questions you have about Meihua."

"Oh. Probably a good idea."

"I'm sure you've got plenty," said Aunt Elaine. "Shoot."

"Okay, well you said it's a magic sword, right?"

"She," said Aunt Elaine.

"What?"

"She," repeated her aunt. "Meihua is a *she*."

"How do you know?"

"It's pretty obvious once you talk to her," said Aunt Elaine, like talking to a sword was completely normal.

"How do you talk to her?" asked Emily.

"She's pretty intuitive." Aunt Elaine stretched her arms behind her head and fell back onto the bed. "Meihua is a thinking, talking being. She's more of a spirit than a sword. A sword is just the shape she's in."

Emily sat there for a moment to let that information sink in. She wasn't sure why but she was okay with that. "What else can she do? Why is she so magical?"

Her aunt smiled. "Aside from being a thinking sword with her own will?"

"Yeah, aside from that."

"I already told you that she only allows people she chooses to use her. Have you drawn her out of the sheath yet?"

"Yeah, a little," admitted Emily. "I wasn't supposed to, but I couldn't resist."

"That's good," said Aunt Elaine. "At least she still likes you. Let's see, what else... Ah, have you noticed how you're not freaking out about how you just got told magic and monsters are real? And how you have a magic sword?"

Emily thought back to an hour ago, to just a minute ago. "I have, actually. Like just now, you told me she was a spirit in a sword's body, right? I just kind of accepted that."

"Yeah, I saw that too," said Aunt Elaine. "Well, that's Meihua. It's hard to explain. She takes an edge off, I guess. She helps you get used to situations, to stay calm and analyze."

"That's cool," said Emily. "What else?"

"Does there need to be more?" asked Aunt Elaine with a raised eyebrow.

"Is there more?"

Her aunt shrugged. "I think that's enough for now. You can figure the rest out on your own."

Emily frowned but her aunt had already started rummaging through her duffle bag. She was pulling out clothes and a toiletry bag and wasn't even paying attention to Emily anymore.

"But—"

"Don't run before you can walk, Emily," said Aunt Elaine. "Everything in time."

Emily took a deep breath and wondered what that meant. "All right, good night."

"Oh, one more thing, Emily," said Aunt Elaine. Emily turned to face her aunt who was now standing. "You can't tell anyone about Meihua. She's a family secret."

"What about Allison?"

"No," said Aunt Elaine. "Not even Allison. You can't tell her about any of it."

"Nothing?" said Emily.

"Think about it. We told you that magic is real and there's this whole secret world out there. Do you believe it? Like, *really* believe it."

Emily thought for a moment. "No, not really. It's like I know the sword is magic, and you told me about everything but I haven't seen it yet. So, it's hard for me to believe it."

Aunt Elaine nodded sagely. "What would anyone else say?"

Emily frowned. "I guess they wouldn't believe it."

"Also, it's dangerous."

"How?"

"Believing, really believing, makes things real," said Aunt Elaine.

Emily shifted her weight onto her right foot and crossed her arms. "What is that supposed to mean?"

Her aunt crossed the room and put both her hands on Emily's shoulders. She held Emily in place and locked eyes with her. "It means that when you really believe in something, you can see it. Most of the time monsters don't want to be seen. And Allison doesn't deserve to see what monsters are capable of."

Emily let out a nervous laugh. "What? And I do?"

"No," said Aunt Elaine. "But we don't always get what we deserve. If you can keep it from Allison, wouldn't you want to?"

"Yes," said Emily immediately.

"Good girl," replied Aunt Elaine. She relinquished Emily's shoulders and reached past her to push the door open. "Good night, Emily. Sweet dreams."

CHAPTER 6

SWEET DREAMS

KNOCK, KNOCK.

"Come in," said Emily. She was sitting up in her bed, holding Meihua in her hands. The sword was unsheathed a couple inches and she was about to touch one of the edges when both of her parents walked in.

"Emily!" cried her mother.

She drew her hand back and slid the sword fully into its sheath. "I just wanted to see how sharp it was."

"Let's just assume the sword is pretty sharp," said her dad. He came in and sat at the edge of Emily's bed near her feet. "We wanted to see how you were doing. Tonight was crazy."

"I'm okay," said Emily. "Apparently the sword helps keep me calm."

"Right," said Dad.

"How are you guys okay with this?" asked Emily.

Her parents looked at one another and then her mom shrugged. Emily's dad turned to face Emily, but he couldn't quite meet her eye. His face was either embarrassed or unsure,

Emily couldn't tell. But he wasn't the confident person she had grown up with and seeing him like this made her uncomfortable.

"I don't know that we are," he said. "But like your mom said, I gave you a choice. Plus, you're still fourteen. You're still our kid. You're not going to be doing anything but training."

"It's just like an after-school activity," added her mom. "Nothing's really changed. Just now you have a sword. You've still got to go to school. You're still going to college."

"Yeah, but—" Emily held the sword up in front of her. "Magic is real. How are you not freaking out, Mom?"

Her mother stepped around her husband and sat down between him and Emily. "I knew already."

"What?" said Emily.

"Your dad told me before we got married."

Emily shifted her attention to her dad. "How come you guys never told me?"

"I left that life behind, Emily." He glanced down at the sword in Emily's hands and his face shifted like he was in pain. But he had something else in his eyes too. Hunger. Emily put the sword down next to her against her nightstand. Her dad broke his stare and turned away. "I had no intention of coming back to it. I still don't."

"Yeah, but *magic*, Dad," said Emily. "All I do is read books, play games, and watch shows about magic and heroes. How could you not tell me?"

"Maybe I was afraid," he whispered.

Emily didn't know what to say. What could her dad have been afraid of? She opened her mouth to speak but her dad slapped his knee with his right hand and stood up. "Well, I'm going to sleep."

The memories still hurt her dad. She could tell. She had so many questions she wanted to ask but she knew they would have to come later.

He stepped toward Emily and kissed her forehead. "Good night, honey."

Emily's mom leaned in and kissed her forehead too. "Good night, I love you."

"Love you too, Mom." Emily's eyes followed her dad's slumped shoulders as he made his way out of her room. "Hey, Dad?"

He turned. "Hmm?"

"I love you."

He smiled, and this time there was no pain or shame. There was only the truth. "I love you too, Emily. Sweet dreams."

There was no way Emily was going to sleep. How could she? She was going to learn martial arts from her aunt, who also gave her a magic sword, and she just learned that magic was real. There was that thing her family had said about monsters, but Emily wasn't sure how to react to that just yet. All her books and movies and games had taught her everything about monsters, and that included that monsters weren't always monsters. Plus, Aunt Elaine loved Emily and wouldn't do anything to hurt her. She wouldn't have let Emily take the sword if it were dangerous.

Resigned to the safety of her decision, Emily picked up the sword and rested it on her bed instead of the floor. She was probably going to knock it off the bed, but she wanted it next to her. She couldn't just admire it all night, but she doubted she could sleep right now. Excitement and curiosity had taken root in her mind. She grabbed her book from her nightstand and opened it up toward the end. The hero was about to sacrifice himself to save the unicorn. Emily loved the part when the unicorn finally fought back despite the fear that was pressing into her chest.

The words were difficult this time though. She tried to read a page and found she had skipped a line or two. She went back to read the paragraph over, but her eyes became heavy. She leaned forward and drifted in and out of sleep. She had tried to read the same paragraph three times now and each time she had managed to read less than she had before. Emily willed herself to stay awake one last time to at least get through the chapter, but the battle was lost. She rested her head on her pillow and drifted into the soft embrace of her dreams.

And then she woke up right after she shut her eyes.

The first thing she thought was how monumentally unfair it was for her to wake up that quickly. The first sleep on a weekend was something to be cherished. It didn't matter how late she went to bed because it was followed by freedom. There would be no alarm waiting for her in the morning. There would only be the warm, sweet promise of more sleep.

Emily turned over and opened her eyes in an attempt to find the clock on her nightstand. She lifted her arm, and noted that it took enormous effort to do so, and dropped it as gently as she could on the clock. Blue digital numbers appeared on the face of the clock to inform her that it was 12:47 a.m. Roughly forty-seven minutes since she went to sleep.

She groaned and rolled over in her bed. She hid her arm under her blankets again and curled herself into a ball.

More sleep was the only thing she wanted. Except, she wasn't tired. It was like she had gotten the exact amount of sleep she needed. Emily rolled over so she was on her back and watched the blades of her ceiling fan spin clockwise.

Emily Lau.

Emily poked her head up. Fear and panic struck chords in Emily's body as she searched the corners of her room for the source of the voice. The only thing amiss was the outline of her door. A bright, yellow light was shining behind it, leaving a dim glow to light up the room.

"Hello?" whispered Emily.

Emily Lau, came the voice again. Emily was on high alert now. The voice didn't exactly frighten her. It was a woman's voice, light and gentle as gossamer. It was soft, curious, and a tiny bit wary. It was like the beginning of a song, or a promise spoken to a friend on a moonlit night. Simply, it was beautiful.

And it had come from the other side of the door.

Emily pulled the covers off and slipped out the right side of her bed. She tested the floor with the tips of her toes expecting cold to lance up her feet, but instead the floor was warm and comforting. Like it had been kissed by the afternoon sun.

She crossed the room to her door and put her hand on the doorknob. It was warm too, but not quite as warm as the floor. She turned the knob and the lock clicked as it came undone. She pulled the door open, and light flooded her eyes.

She covered her face with her arm and waited for her eyes to adjust to the bright light and stepped closer to the doorway.

Her feet hit something soft and she looked down. The toes of her left foot were resting in green grass. She inhaled sharply and the scent of the grass came to her along with something gentle and sweet.

The sound of birds chirping and the rush of wind through grass and trees swept through the air like music while the cool caress of a breeze gently slid across her arms and face.

Emily lowered her arm and a green valley stretched out in front of her. The sun shone brightly in a blue sky littered with clouds so large they were like crashing waves.

"What is this?"

She stepped out into the field and basked in the warmth of the sun. A trio of birds flew past her and Emily spun to the direction they had come from.

A lone doorframe stood attached to no walls. The door was pushed in and Emily's bedroom was on the other side with a night sky through her windows. Around and behind her door though was more grass and hills that eventually led to mountains.

Emily stepped toward her room and pulled the door shut. She held onto the doorknob and pushed the door open again. Still her room. She shut the door, let go of the doorknob, and opened it again. Still her room.

Emily Lau, said the voice a third time. Emily spun around. The voice was so close, it almost brushed against her ear.

No one was behind her. Or at least no one was *right* behind her.

Some ways away the grass sloped up a hill, and on top of that hill was a massive tree bathed in so much white that Emily thought it was covered in snow, even in all this sun.

Standing at the top of the hill and at the base of the tree was a person dressed in white. They stood perfectly still, but the wind that made the branches sway also blew the person's long hair in the wind. Emily was sure the person was a woman; the voice had been a woman's, after all, and they were the only two people present. The way she stood was telling too. She stood tall and proud, but she exuded a gentleness that Emily thought no man could pull off.

Emily started walking toward the tree and the familiar tickle of grass between her toes disappeared. In its place was something soft but sturdy.

Her clothes had changed. She was wearing her favorite sneakers, her most comfortable pair of black jeans, a t-shirt, and a jacket. It was pretty much her favorite outfit.

"Not the worst dream," said Emily.

The lone figure stood atop the hill staring down at Emily. It wasn't a tall hill so Emily could actually make out some features on the person. Definitely a woman.

"Hello," called Emily. "Who are you? Where am I?"

The woman tilted her head and walked away from Emily.

"Hey!" she cried. She ran up the hill and found the woman standing beneath the tree. Emily stopped, stricken in awe by the tree towering over her. "Whoa."

The tree was massive. The trunk erupted from the ground sending forking branches in each direction until it reached its pinnacle. It was like the ground was a storm cloud and the tree was a bolt of lightning.

The branches were littered with countless white flowers. A wind rushed through the branches sending blossoms and petals tumbling down around Emily. She turned in a circle and let the flowers fall around her like snow. She couldn't even begin to describe the scent. It was beautiful and wonderful. Joy sprang up inside her and she felt an irresistible urge to laugh.

"Do you like it?" asked the woman.

Emily stopped spinning and came face to face with the only other person there.

She was taller than Emily and stood without the barest hint of a slouch. She had a heart-shaped face that was paler than Emily's. Her skin was flawless, and her lips had just a hint of color to them that made them stand out next to her skin. Her hair was long and waved gently in the wind. It was dark and glossy and poured from her head like black ink. She was dressed all in white, wearing a robe that Emily recognized as a *hanfu*. The *hanfu* folded against itself and drew a stark contrast to her hair. Her robe swayed in the wind like seafoam leftover after the crash of waves.

She exuded nobility. Emily almost bowed but managed to stop herself. The voice that had called to Emily in her room belonged to this woman. It was the same face that was in the reflection of the sword.

"Meihua?" asked Emily.

The woman smiled and nodded.

"What do you think?" asked Meihua with a sweeping gesture to the tree.

"It's beautiful," said Emily.

Meihua caught some of the petals falling all around them in her hand. *"I think so too."*

There was something to Meihua's face that Emily had seen a lot of in the past few hours. It was a sad expression, like remembering better days. Her aunt had it and now Meihua. Her dad had a similar face, but it was different. Aunt Elaine's and Meihua's had been about memories, and her dad's was more about what might have been.

"Are you okay?" asked Emily.

Meihua turned to Emily and there was pride on her face, like she was happy for herself. *"See? That's why I chose you. Here you are, your life turned upside down, and you're asking if I'm okay."*

"You chose me?" asked Emily.

"We both chose you," replied Meihua. *"But my choice matters a little more."*

"Why me?" asked Emily. "I mean, how does it even work? We've never met."

"No, not officially," admitted Meihua. *"But I was always with your aunt. I watched you grow up."*

Meihua sat down effortlessly and gestured next to her. *"Join me."*

Emily moved and sat next to Meihua. The woman sat perfectly still, and Emily was actively trying to keep herself from fidgeting. Her eyes kept darting sideways at Meihua and eventually she started to pluck at the grass beneath her.

"What is this place?" she asked finally.

"It's your dream," said Meihua. *"You know that."*

"No, I mean, what is this?" asked Emily, gesturing all around her. "I've never seen it."

"Ah, I just kind of made it up so we could talk," replied Meihua.

"About what?" asked Emily.

"About me. And you," said Meihua. *"What I can do. What you can expect. Any questions you have."*

"Aunt Elaine told me what you can do," said Emily.

"She told you some, not all."

Emily focused all her attention on Meihua and gloated. "So, there was more."

"A little."

Emily was about to ask what else there was when something landed on her head. She tilted her head up and a flower fell down, brushing her face. Emily caught it in her hand and held it in her palm. It felt delicate, like it would fall apart if Emily pressed it too hard.

"First off, I wanted to meet you," said Meihua. *"Actually meet you. Face to face. The only time we can really do this is in reflection. Right now, it's only during dreams. Eventually we can meet while you're meditating. I don't like to do this when you're awake because it takes a lot of concentration to see something that isn't there.*

"I always take the time to introduce myself to my new guardians. So they can get to know me before they make a decision."

Meihua glanced sideways at Emily. *"Is that okay?"*

The confidence and nobility that had been practically dripping off Meihua had lessened now. She was like a new student introducing herself to her new class on her first day.

"Of course," said Emily.

"Thank you," replied Meihua. *"Like your aunt said, I am a spirit. I have been handed down in your family for generations. I remember when your name wasn't Lau."*

"Wow," whispered Emily.

"Indeed," said Meihua. *"Lie down with me."*

They laid down on their backs and studied the canopy stretching out above them. Meihua reached up with her right hand and spread out her fingers. *"Imagine every single one of those falling flowers and petals are past guardians."*

Emily stared in wonder at the countless flowers. How long had Meihua lived?

"Some lived a long time, and some only had me for a short time," said Meihua. *"But I remember them all. Every moment, every choice, everything."*

Emily stayed silent. She was locked in thought, trying to imagine what it must be like to remember all of that. To remember everything. Her family had troves of pictures and videos saved of just moments in their lives, but Meihua had every second.

She watched the petals dance in the wind as they fell. Some were whole flowers; others were just a single petal. They were all different. Some were torn and some were intact. There was one that had just started to wilt and part of its flower was browning. She found herself wondering if the lone petals were those who had Meihua for the shortest time, and the full flowers were guardians who had held her for a long time. Or maybe the full flowers were the ones she liked more. Most of the flowers were so vibrant and alive. Which one of those represented her aunt? A flash of color caught her eye, or more a lack of color. There was one flower still attached to the tree, at the very edge of its thin branch, and there were no other flowers near it. And unlike all of the white flowers dancing in the air around them, this flower was jet black and wrinkled, like it had been burned.

"When you're my guardian, we have a direct connection," said Meihua. Emily tore her eyes away from the odd flower and back to Meihua. *"I can speak to you and you can speak to me."*

"How does that work?" asked Emily.

"*Well, no one else can hear me,*" said Meihua. "*I speak directly in your head. I can show you when you wake up.*"

"And how do I talk to you?"

"*You can speak aloud, but I'm not sure I'd recommend doing that all the time,*" said Meihua. "*Or you can just think to me. I experience everything you do. I see what you see, hear what you hear. All of it. I'll remember it all.*" She was quiet for a moment. "*It takes some getting used to.*"

"I bet," replied Emily.

"*There's more,*" said Meihua. "*I've always been connected to my guardians. And I remember everything. Do you understand?*"

"Yeah, you told me that already," said Emily.

"*Like your aunt said, I have been handed down by the members of your family. It started with surviving a war. Then it was defending the family, then others. Most of my guardians were warriors. You have that option in the future too.*"

"Right," said Emily. "Aunt Elaine is going to teach me."

"*Yes, and I remember everything from every warrior before you,*" said Meihua. "*Every fight, every lesson, every victory, every defeat.*"

Meihua snapped her fingers and the scene around them changed. Windows that looked like TV screens without the TVs had just appeared all around them, circling in the air like fish in a giant aquarium. There were people she didn't recognize moving in all of them. It was like watching hundreds of martial arts films all at once. Then Meihua swiped her hand in front of her and they all disappeared.

"*Everything you just saw you are capable of.*"

"What? How?"

"*The connection,*" replied Meihua. "*I am able to move your body for you."* Emily was horrified at the prospect of that, and it must have shown on her face because Meihua held up her hands with splayed fingers. *"I would never do it. I could never do it without your permission. You would have to let me."*

"Oh, okay," said Emily as calmly as she could, but her body recoiled just a little bit. The reaction wasn't lost to Meihua.

"I'm sorry," said Meihua. *"I didn't mean to scare you. I just have to tell you what I am capable of. This is a partnership. I want to do what makes you happy. I don't want to scare you. I just don't want you to—"*

Meihua stopped and dropped her gaze down to her hands. Now she was the one trying not to fidget.

"You don't want me to what?" asked Emily in a low voice.

Emily watched Meihua look sideways at her. *"I don't want you to leave me behind. To lock me away for days... years. I'm awake for all of it. Or aware at least."*

There was a silence between them as the words Meihua said burrowed into Emily like roots. She tried to imagine what that would have been like. To sit in silence and emptiness for countless seconds and minutes and moments. Do you even keep track of time like that? Are you aware of how much time has passed?

"Meeting you," started Emily. Her voice was weak and cracked. She cleared her throat and sat up so her voice would be stronger. "Talking to you. Seeing you. I don't think I could do that to you. Or anyone."

Meihua visibly relaxed and there was relief in her eyes.

"I don't think I can carry a sword around with me all the time though," said Emily.

"That won't be a problem," said Meihua. She waved her

hand in the air and new shapes orbited in the air in front of Emily. There was a brooch, a comb, a hair pin, a pendant, a watch, an anklet, and more. All of them had some sort of plum blossom design to them. *"I can change my shape into pretty much anything you like. These are some samples of what previous guardians chose."*

Emily studied each and then her eyes fell on a familiar shape. "How about the ring? The way Aunt Elaine gave you to me."

Meihua bowed her head slightly and Emily caught the barest slip of delight on Meihua's face. *"Of course."*

CHAPTER 7

WHAT YOU DON'T KNOW

EMILY WOKE, THANKS to her alarm screaming at her repeatedly. She peeked one eye open, angry that her dream was over, and then slapped the button on her clock to make it stop. Sunlight crept through the blinds on her windows. Emily rubbed at her eyes with her right hand and pushed herself up with her left. She yawned, stretched both arms up above her, and flared them out. The sweet stretch of her muscles brought a smile to her face. Her arms dropped next to her on her bed and her hand hit something cold and metallic.

Meihua lay beside her on the comforter. Emily traced her fingers along the flower feeling the familiar grooves of the engraving.

"Meihua?" whispered Emily. "Are you there?"

The sword began to glow and then it shrunk until it was the size of a firefly. It flew toward her finger and the light disappeared to reveal a plum blossom ring fitting perfectly around her right ring finger.

Always, replied Meihua's voice in Emily's head. Emily shuddered in surprise from the sound of the voice and how it came to her and then giggled. She raised her hand up and admired the ring.

"So that's how it works," she said. "I just kind of talk and you reply to me in my head."

Correct, said Meihua.

"And you're a ring now, how do I turn you back into a—" There was another flash of light and the ring was gone, and the sword was back in Emily's hand. "And back to—"

Another flash, and Emily had a ring on again.

"So, I just think it and it kind of happens?" asked Emily.

Yes, said Meihua. *I can read your intention when you're thinking about it.*

"You can read my mind?" asked Emily.

No, not really, said Meihua. *I told you that you can think your answers to me. I pay attention. You think what you're going to say before you say it. Thought is always faster than speaking.*

"That makes sense," replied Emily.

It might seem like I'm reading your mind, but I'm not, said Meihua.

Emily brought the image of the sword to her mind and Meihua appeared in her hand as a sword again. She thought back to the ring and Meihua was a ring again a second later. "Cool."

Knock, knock.

"Come in," said Emily while bringing the sword back.

The door opened and Aunt Elaine stood in the doorway just as the sword reappeared. She leaned against the doorframe and watched Emily turn the sword over in her hand. There was an extra gleam in her eyes that Emily wasn't quite sure how to place. Maybe Aunt Elaine was proud.

"Getting the hang of things, I see," said Aunt Elaine.

The sword turned back into a ring on Emily's finger.

"Yup," said Emily.

"Well, Meihua isn't a toy," said Aunt Elaine.

"I know."

"Then stop playing with her," retorted Aunt Elaine. "Now come downstairs. There's something I want to talk to you about."

Emily kicked the covers off herself and rolled out of bed. She slipped her feet into her slippers, grabbed a hooded jacket, and snaked her arms through the sleeves while following her aunt downstairs.

Aunt Elaine led Emily back to the guest room and shut the doors behind them. The bed was unruffled and made with clean corners. There was a bamboo stick, a couple of paper cups, a stone, and some plastic knives resting on it.

"Sit down," said Aunt Elaine. They both sat on the floor facing one another in silence with their legs crossed. Emily did her best to stifle a yawn and her aunt just smiled at her. Finally, she gestured to Emily's hand and spoke, "So I assume you two have met."

"Yeah," said Emily excitedly.

"What did you think of her?" asked Aunt Elaine with an eager edge to her voice. Emily imagined her aunt would have been on her toes if she were standing.

"She's beautiful," admitted Emily. "And scary."

Aunt Elaine frowned. "Scary how?" Emily recounted what Meihua had said about taking over her body and Aunt Elaine sat there silently, taking it all in before answering. "I've let it happen before."

Emily's head shot up. "What? You have?"

"A few times," said Aunt Elaine. She was peering off into the distance now, remembering something. "It's not as bad as it sounds. You always know what's happening. And you can always stop it whenever you want. It saved my life a couple times."

Emily must have had a skeptical grimace on her face because her aunt continued, "It's not like Meihua wants your body. She just wants to help you. Anyway, that's not what I really wanted to talk to you about. I wanted to talk to you about your future."

"My future?" repeated Emily.

"Yes," said Aunt Elaine. "From this day going forward I am your teacher. You listen to what I have to say, and you do it. No lip, got it?"

Emily sat up a little straighter.

"I won't make you call me *shifu*, but you have to treat me with respect. Now, you're a black belt, right?"

"Yup," said Emily. Aunt Elaine narrowed her eyes at her and Emily rephrased it. "Yes."

"So, you know a lot about martial arts, right?"

Emily nodded.

"Wrong. I'm going to teach you how little you know. What can you tell me about *qi*?"

"*Chi*?" repeated Emily, sounding the word out.

"Yes."

"Isn't that just made-up stuff?" asked Emily. "Like in movies and anime?"

Her aunt laughed at Emily like she was a newborn child.

"You've got a magic sword that talks to you and that's really what you think? Like I said, everything you don't know.

"Qi is like your life essence, your vital force. Every living thing has it. Martial artists use qi to strengthen their techniques. You've been taught some martial arts. My job is to continue your education. The next natural step to that is qi."

Emily opened her mouth to speak but her aunt started, "You look like you don't believe me."

"It's not that," said Emily. "But yeah, it's hard to believe. I mean, Meihua is a sword. I know she's magic. I saw it. I can feel it."

"Which brings us to the visual portion of my presentation. I'm going to show you what someone is capable of with qi."

Her aunt reached up and grabbed two paper cups from the top of her bed. They were stacked inside one another and she handed them to Emily. "Take a look."

Emily took the cups and turned them over in her hand. She pulled them out of one another and studied each one individually. She set one down on the ground and then traced her finger along the bottom of one of them. They were just paper cups. She stacked them together again and held them out to her aunt. "Okay?"

"Normal paper cups, right?"

"Yeah."

Her aunt pulled the cups out again and laid them both out on the floor in front of her, so the bottoms were facing up. Then she gestured at them again. "Pick one."

Emily pointed at the cup on her left. Aunt Elaine put her right hand over it and then pressed down. The paper cup crumpled under the weight of her hand.

"Pretty normal still," her aunt said. "But with qi we can do some amazing things. One of those is a method of making your body light. Remember all those *wuxia* movies we used to watch? With Jet Li, Chow Yun-Fat, Michelle Yeoh, and Ziyi Zhang? You know all the acrobatic stuff they do? That's what I'm talking about. It's real. With qi we can do stuff like that too. Though you have to be pretty good to do all the stuff they can do. But something like this..."

Aunt Elaine stood up and took a step back. She bent over at her waist, set her left hand on the ground, and then put the pointer finger of her right hand on the top of the remaining cup. She kicked her legs up, so she was doing a handstand. Then she lifted her left hand and placed it behind her back. She pushed herself up until her right arm was extended straight.

Emily's eyes widened and she leaned forward. Her aunt's finger was balanced on the surface of the cup, but it wasn't pressing through.

"How?" whispered Emily.

"Qi," said Aunt Elaine. She began switching fingers one at a time from pointer to index to ring then back to her pointer finger again. "With training you can do this too. I won't lie though. It will be difficult and not everyone is good at it."

Aunt Elaine deftly landed on her feet like it was the easiest thing in the world.

"You'll teach me how to do that?"

Aunt Elaine's eyes lit up like she was watching fireworks for the first time, and when she spoke there was excitement there. "I can teach you techniques that will make you quicker, lighter, and make you feel like you're in one of those martial arts movies. There's more than that though."

She reached over to the bed, picked something up, and tossed it to Emily. Emily caught it with both hands. It was an oblong stone that was just a little bigger than the palm of her hand. It was smooth to the touch, had the color of a dark storm cloud, and was shaped like a slightly flattened egg. Emily knocked on the stone, but she couldn't find anything out of the ordinary.

"Okay, I don't get it."

"Toss it back," said Aunt Elaine with her hands up. Emily tossed it gingerly to her aunt.

Aunt Elaine held her hand out with her palm up and the stone at the center. She closed her fingers around the stone and squeezed. At first there was nothing, but then there was a sound like the frozen surface of a lake cracking. Emily leaned forward to try and focus her eyes on the spaces between her aunt's fingers. Lines forked across the stone like lightning and then the stone shattered in her aunt's hand. Dust and shards of stone fell through her fingertips to the floor below.

"That's all qi?" asked Emily through breathless lips.

"Yes," said Aunt Elaine while grabbing the bamboo pole from the bed. "But wait, there's more."

She held the bamboo stick up right between the two of them. It was about three feet high and three inches thick. She produced a plastic knife with her right hand and slashed at the bamboo. The plastic knife snapped with a crack and the blade flew across the room. She pulled out another knife and started sawing the bamboo. She had managed a few motions before that knife snapped too. She then pulled out a third plastic knife and showed it to Emily. "Now with qi."

She slashed at a downward angle at the top of the bamboo

stick. The knife passed through like a hot knife through butter. The bamboo dropped where the knife had cut, leaving a smooth, sharp edge. Aunt Elaine shifted her left hand down the bamboo shaft then swept the knife from left to right in a horizontal cut. The top half of the remaining bamboo toppled. She raised her hand over her head and brought the knife down in a vertical slash. Aunt Elaine stopped the slash an inch from where her left hand was. She let go of the knife and left it in place in the bamboo.

"Power and control," said Aunt Elaine. She handed the bamboo and knife to Emily. "That is only a little of what I can teach you."

Emily took the bamboo in her hands and tried to cut through the last few inches, but the knife wouldn't budge. She twisted it and the knife snapped in half.

"You can teach me how to do that?" asked Emily.

"Yes," said Aunt Elaine. "It's going to be difficult. You're going to struggle. You might fail. But if you succeed, I can teach you to fly. Do you want to learn?"

"Yes," said Emily hungrily.

"Do you promise to listen to what I tell you? To do as I say? To train and work even when your body is screaming in pain? No matter what I tell you?"

"Yes," said Emily again.

"Good," said Aunt Elaine. "Now go do some homework."

"What?" said a confused Emily.

"I have to prepare," said Aunt Elaine. "And you need to get your homework done now."

"Why now? Can't I just do it later?"

"No," said Aunt Elaine matter-of-factly.

"Why not?"

"Because," said her aunt like she had been waiting all morning to say this, "after we're done training, you won't be able to move."

CHAPTER 8

TRAINING

EMILY'S LEG BOUNCED impatiently as her dad checked her planner. All her homework assignments were written in it for each class, and each class had its own color so she could differentiate between them. Of course, that meant she had to carry a lot of pens, but it made it easier for her. Plus, she liked all the colors.

All the lines in her planner were crossed out now. She always crossed them out when she finished them. Now, all her homework was stacked in a neat pile next to her father, textbooks and all. He licked his finger, turned a page, and started tracing his finger along an entry in the planner.

Her parents always checked to make sure Emily had done her homework, but her dad was being deliberately slow this time. Emily tried to roll her eyes and show her aunt how exasperating this was, but Aunt Elaine was lounging against the kitchen island. She was thumbing through a magazine like she didn't have a care in the world.

"Huh," said her aunt. She lifted the magazine and held it up for Emily. "Did you know they were dating?"

The article had a photo of two celebrities that would have shown them walking down the street holding hands, if not for the illustrated rip dividing them.

"They're not anymore," said Emily.

"I can see that," replied Aunt Elaine. She set the magazine down on the counter and then mumbled, "I didn't even know they were dating."

Emily turned her attention back to her dad who was studying her math book. His eyes darted from her planner to her textbook and then to her homework. He shut the textbook suddenly and the impact rattled the table.

"Looks good to me," he said.

"Great! Can Aunt Elaine and I train now?"

"It's okay with me," he replied. "Good job getting all your homework done. Where do you plan on training anyway? We don't really have a big enough backyard or anything."

"Actually," said Aunt Elaine. "I was hoping we could use the closet."

A few moments later, the three of them were standing outside the closet in the hallway near the kitchen. Her dad stood directly in front of it, scratching his chin with his right hand and cradling his right arm with his left. Emily and Aunt Elaine each stood behind him while he studied the closed door.

"The closet," said Dad.

"Yup," replied Aunt Elaine.

Emily's dad reached forward and opened the closet. He flipped a switch inside on the right and the light bulb hanging inside illuminated the chaos.

"This closet," said her dad. Jackets hung from hangers and boxes were strewn along the floor. A shelf above the jackets revealed even more boxes covered in a thin layer of dust. Three padded folding chairs were leaning against the wall on the left. A broomstick was tilted into the right corner. "Not a lot of room in there."

"You don't use it very often, right?" asked Aunt Elaine.

"Nope," said Dad, then he muttered to himself, "So that's where that broom is."

"It's perfect then," said Aunt Elaine.

"Umm... How?" asked Emily.

Aunt Elaine pulled something out of her pocket and held it up. It was a large, ornate brass key with a purple marble inlaid in the handle. The marble looked like amethyst and it swirled like it held a vortex inside of it.

"Do you remember what a demesne is, Chris?" asked Aunt Elaine. Emily's dad took a sharp breath and Emily stepped forward to try and figure out what they were talking about. Her dad's eyes were wide with excitement and he reminded Emily of a kid in a toy store.

"You have one?" he asked.

"I do," said Aunt Elaine proudly.

"Okay, who's going to tell me what a demesne is?" asked Emily.

Her dad turned to face her and held up his hands like he was holding an invisible ball. "A demesne is—"

Aunt Elaine put a hand on his shoulder and he stopped. He turned his head and she was smiling. She wagged the key at him. "Let's show her first. Then you can explain."

"Okay!" He sounded like a kid who was just told he could

do that one thing he really wanted to do more than anything. He closed the closet door and backed away from it. He gave his sister a little bow and gestured toward the door.

Aunt Elaine stepped forward and held the key in line with the doorknob. Confusion flooded Emily because there was no way that huge key was going to fit in the doorknob's keyhole. In fact, that door had never been locked as far as she knew, and she wasn't even sure that it had a lock.

That didn't stop Aunt Elaine. There was the sound of metal scraping on metal, and then a lock that shouldn't have been there clicked loudly. Aunt Elaine pulled open the door.

The jackets, boxes, chairs, broom, and light were gone and in their place was cavernous darkness. Aunt Elaine stepped through and reached her hand out to the wall on her right. She flipped a switch and the sound of lights turning on erupted like heavy claps as one-by-one different sections of an enormous room were revealed.

Her aunt stepped farther into the room, then Emily's dad stepped past Emily and through the doorway into what used to be a closet. "Come on."

She took three steps and passed through. She didn't feel anything course through her body when she did, but her jaw dropped once she was inside. Their closet had been replaced by an enormous room. It was like an industrial warehouse, but comfortable.

There were hard concrete floors, but they were obviously designed for living rather than labor. The corner to her immediate right was furnished like a living room. There was a couch, a TV, a small shelf filled with books, a couple of lounge chairs, and a coffee table. Beneath all that were carpets laid out to keep your toes warm, probably. Past the makeshift living room was the cleanest kitchen Emily had ever seen. It was all a monotone gray with hard edges and lines. The island was a perfect, concrete rectangle. And then past the kitchen was a room. Walls jutted out and a barn door hid whatever was inside from view.

The left side of the room was a gym. The wall was lined with mirrors and there was a rack of weights and various other exercise machines that Emily couldn't begin to name. And past all that in the back corner was another room with a closed door. That door had a sign that indicated it was a bathroom. Along the wall next to it was a futon with a night-stand beside it.

"What is this?" breathed Emily.

"This is my demesne," replied Aunt Elaine.

"Demesne is an old word," said Emily's dad. "It refers to all the land retained by a lord for his use. Demesnes like this are like pocket dimensions. They're created by magic and have set sizes and rules. It takes a lot of magic and skill to make one of these. They're exceedingly rare."

"I was gifted this by a grateful client," said Aunt Elaine. "A very grateful client. It's got a room for me to sleep if I want. And as you can see, everything I need to train. Everything I need to train you. So, what do you think?"

"It's unbelievable," said Emily. "Do you live here?"

"I could, if I wanted," replied Aunt Elaine. "The demesne isn't tied to a single place. It's tied to that key I showed you earlier. As long as I have the key, and a door to stick it in, I have a place to stay. The problem is if it's a door that's regularly used, someone could come in."

"Couldn't you just lock it?" asked Emily.

"Yes," said Aunt Elaine. "And that would work. But let's say I close that door, lock it, and then sleep. Then your mom or your dad or you come by with a key and unlock the door. Your key still works. It would open that door. And instead of your closet you find this."

Aunt Elaine gestured all around to the furniture and the vaulted ceilings.

"Not exactly what you'd expect," said Aunt Elaine. "It'd be worse on the street. Plus, it's no home."

"Hello!" called a new voice. The three of them turned to the door. "Who left the closet door open?" yelled Emily's mom.

She stepped into view with a bag in her arms and froze in front of the doorway before she dropped the bag.

Fifteen minutes later Emily and Aunt Elaine were alone in the demesne. They had assured Mom that she still had a closet and nothing permanent was done to the house. Aunt Elaine had laid out one of the stacked mats on the concrete floor. Emily had changed into workout clothes and was standing on one leg with her right leg kicked back and held against her with her right hand.

"So, what are we going to do first?" asked Emily. "Sword techniques? Are you going to teach me how to float and all that?"

"No weapons," said Aunt Elaine. "And no lightness techniques either."

"What? Why not?"

"Because you're not ready. Ben taught you a lot, but we

need to go further. He didn't teach you how to cultivate your qi. Switch legs."

Emily dropped her right foot and then kicked her left foot up. "Okay, what then?"

"Your training is going to consist of three parts. Well, more than that, but I've put them into three broad categories."

Her aunt let her foot drop and Emily did the same. "Kneel." They both knelt down on their knees and Emily let her hands rest on her thighs.

"First," said Aunt Elaine with one finger pointing up, "calisthenics. You're not in good shape."

"What?" said Emily, offended.

"You're not," said Aunt Elaine. "Not by my standards. So we're going to work out. A lot. Lots of cardio to get you up to snuff."

"But—"

"Don't interrupt me, Emily," said Aunt Elaine. "Here, I am your *shifu*. Do you interrupt your teachers at school?"

"No."

"Then don't do it here. Understand?"

"Yes."

"Good," said Aunt Elaine. "Up to this point, you've had no qi training or cultivation. So, we're going to do that."

Emily's hand shot up like she was in her classroom.

"What is it?"

"How do we do that?"

"Meditation, breathing, exercises, forms," replied Aunt Elaine. "Qi cultivation is a long, slow process. We'll have to do it a little bit at a time. Like writing a book."

Emily nodded to show she understood, but excitement

had built up in her when her aunt had started talking about qi. Qi was like magic to her. It was something she read about, something she wished desperately to have, and something she was sure didn't exist. Until it did.

"Lastly," said Aunt Elaine interrupting Emily's thoughts, "I'm going to teach you martial arts. The family's martial arts."

"Our martial arts?" asked Emily.

"There are hundreds of kinds of martial arts. People used to create variations and have schools and teach their techniques to students. Now, a lot of martial arts are taught by instructors. Before modern martial arts, a lot of secrets were passed down through manuals."

"Manuals? Like books?" broke in Emily. Aunt Elaine gave Emily a withering stare. "Sorry."

"Yes, like books," said Aunt Elaine. "But we're not going to use that. We have something better. Meihua."

Emily glanced down at the ring on her finger. She had taken it off when she came back into the demesne for training because jewelry wasn't worn in her karate classes, but Aunt Elaine had said they would need Meihua.

"How did you learn karate?" asked Aunt Elaine.

"From Ben," said Emily. "He would show us how to do a move, and then we'd practice it until we got it right."

"That's how we're going to do it too," said Aunt Elaine. "But I have to warn you—you're not going to like this."

"Why?" asked Emily.

"Meihua is an encyclopedia of martial arts," said Aunt Elaine. "She remembers every move, right?" Emily nodded. "And remember, she can move your body for you."

"Oh no," said Emily.

Aunt Elaine held up both her hands to placate Emily. "I know you don't like the idea of it. But what I'm proposing is that you let her show you how to do the move once and that's it. You practice it on your own until you have it. You don't have to do it, but I'm just asking you to consider it, okay?"

Emily pursed her lips and played with the ring on her finger.

I would never hurt you or do anything to betray your trust, came Meihua's voice. The voice was a surprise and Emily was just able to keep herself from jumping.

"I'll think about it," said Emily to both Aunt Elaine and Meihua.

"That's all I ask," said Aunt Elaine. "Now, should we get started?"

Emily had no chance to think about letting Meihua move her body for her. Her aunt had Emily moving from the get-go. First, Emily alternated between running and jogging on a treadmill just to see what her stamina was like. Next she had to hold a plank position for thirty seconds. She did pushups, squats, lunges, leg raises, and then she had to do it all over again. Twice. Finally her aunt led Emily to another apparatus.

"Can you do a pull-up?" asked Aunt Elaine.

"No," said Emily. She had never tried, but she knew she didn't want to try right now. Her breaths were coming out ragged. Her T-shirt clung to her skin like it was glued onto her, thanks to the sweat. She eyed the pull-up bar and felt leaden weight all over her body. There was no way she could do a pull up.

"Why don't you try?" asked Aunt Elaine.

Emily loved her aunt. Her aunt was one of her favorite

people in the entire world, but she hated her aunt right then. She glared at her aunt and her breathing turned to seething.

Aunt Elaine gestured to the bar with her head. Emily let out one more heavy breath and stepped up to the machine. She grabbed the bar where her aunt indicated and then tried to pull herself up.

To her surprise, Emily actually went up, until she didn't. Her body dropped, but her grip remained. Her shoulders and arms burned as she dangled there. She tried to pull herself up again. A deep, primal noise erupted from somewhere inside her, but she didn't go any higher.

"Okay, that's enough," her aunt said.

Emily let go of the bar and fell to the ground. She landed on her feet, but then her knees wavered, and she stumbled back onto her butt.

Her aunt crouched down and patted Emily's shoulder. "That was a good effort. You're a little ahead of where I thought you'd be, but you've still got a long way to go."

Emily would have given her aunt another glare, but all she wanted to do was lie down. So she did. She lay back on the ground and just let gravity press her muscles down. Her chest rose and fell with every breath like it was being pumped by a bellows.

"Come on," said her aunt after a second. She stood up and nudged Emily with her foot. "Time for qi training."

Emily groaned and turned her head from her aunt. Her aunt nudged her again and Emily sat up.

Aunt Elaine led Emily to the center of the room and sat down. Emily sat across from her again and watched as she let out a deep breath.

"You know how to meditate," her aunt stated. "I saw you do it. You've been doing it for years. The problem is you're doing it wrong."

"I thought there was no wrong way to meditate?" said Emily.

Her aunt frowned. "There is and there isn't. For the purpose of qi cultivation, there is."

"I don't understand," admitted Emily.

"When you meditate you focus on your breath, and that's good," said Aunt Elaine. "But how often do you empty your mind? Do you ever just let your thoughts run wild?"

"Yeah," said Emily. "It's hard though. There's so many things to think about besides... nothing."

"In this day and age, no one ever really stops thinking," said Aunt Elaine. "It's always go, go, go. But emptiness is what you need to build up your qi. There's no room for your qi to grow if all you do is fill yourself up with everything else. I'm going to help you to meditate. I need you to try really hard at this. It's going to be difficult at first, but like everything it just takes practice."

"Okay," said Emily.

Aunt Elaine had Emily close her eyes and breathe in and out. She focused on her breath, but tried not to think about it. Aunt Elaine told Emily to empty her mind, to not think, but Emily couldn't help it. Her aunt must have been a mind reader because every time Emily started thinking about anything her aunt would tell her to refocus on her breath and keep it smooth and even. Like a rhythm or a dance.

"Don't hold it too long, and don't let it go too quickly," her aunt said. "Just let it be. Be still."

A comforting warmth spread in her abdomen and she almost clutched at it with her hands but had just managed to stop herself.

"Okay, open your eyes," said Aunt Elaine. Her aunt was smiling at her when she did. "How do you feel?"

"Good," said Emily. She was surprised at how light she felt. Her body still ached but she wasn't as tired as she had been before.

"We'll try meditating again later. Tomorrow we'll start adding in some forms to help out." Her aunt jumped up to her feet and stretched her arms back. "Now, have you thought about what I said earlier? With Meihua?"

Emily hadn't. Thinking about it now didn't really sit well with her though. "I don't think I'm ready to let that happen."

"Okay. Old fashioned way it is. I'll show you a move, you duplicate. I'll tell you what you did wrong and then repeat."

And that was what happened. Aunt Elaine lined up with Emily and performed a technique for her. It was basic but Emily still couldn't get them right on the first try. Her aunt's guidance was a little lacking too.

"Wrong, too much weight on your back foot."

"No, your fist is weak."

"Do it like you're attacking a real person."

There was one time Emily thought she had done a move perfectly and held the pose at the end like a basketball player leaving their hand up after a made shot. Her aunt walked up to her and pushed her with one finger. Emily fell back to the ground like her aunt had shoved her with both hands.

"I swear," started Aunt Elaine, "you've got all the bravery and form of a chicken nugget. We've got a lot of work to do.

Let's break for today. Keep working on your breathing. You want a smooth and even breath. Try to be calm, to be still. That's how you'll build your qi."

Emily left her aunt in the demesne and emerged back inside her house. Both of her parents were sitting on the couch. Her dad glanced over while he had the remote control pointed at the TV.

"How'd it go?" he asked.

Emily groaned and turned away so she could go upstairs to shower.

"That good, huh?" he said as she started up the stairs.

Her legs wavered and she gripped the handrail going up.

That was a good first day, said Meihua. Emily almost fell mid-step but managed to catch herself. *You'll feel better tomorrow.*

"You scared me," snapped Emily.

I'm sorry, said Meihua.

"Just… don't surprise me like that," replied Emily.

I'll try not to, said Meihua. *I really could help. I can tell you how to correct your mistakes better than your aunt can. She's not the best teacher.*

"No," said Emily a little too quickly. "I'll get it. It was just my first day."

As you wish, said Meihua. There was an edge to the voice in her head that time, but Emily ignored it.

"I'm going to take a shower," said Emily once she got inside her room. "What happens if I take you off?"

I'll be where you leave me, said Meihua. *I'll have an idea of my general surroundings. I can come to you if called, but otherwise I will simply be.*

"Be what?" asked Emily.

Be there, replied Meihua.

"Oh, okay," said Emily, a little relieved and confused. "Well, I'll talk to you later."

She slipped the ring off her finger before Meihua could answer.

Emily sat at the edge of her bed dressed in a new set of sweats and a hoodie that was probably one size too large on her. She had just slid her feet into her house slippers and was toying with her still-damp hair that was tied up. She was making a concentrated effort to not pay any attention to Meihua.

The flower was pointed at her like it was watching her, but still she ignored it. New questions had risen for Emily in the shower. Not even questions really; just concerns that she wanted cleared up. So, she stood up and left her room with Meihua still in it.

She made her way downstairs and walked right up to her aunt's room and knocked. There was a shuffling sound inside and then the door opened.

"Emily," said Aunt Elaine with surprise on her face. "What are you doing here?"

"Should I not be here?" asked Emily with a surprised look of her own.

"No, I mean yes, it's fine, it's just… I didn't think you'd want to see me anytime soon."

"Oh, well there was something I wanted to talk to you about," said Emily.

"Sure, come in." She stepped back to let Emily in. Emily stepped inside while her aunt grabbed a book from her nightstand and dropped it in the drawer. Emily only got a short glimpse of the book, but she was pretty sure it was *Teaching for Dummies*. "What's up?"

Emily sat down in the office chair and rested her hands in her lap, left hand over her right. "It's about Meihua." She stopped suddenly, uncertain that by saying the name the ring might appear. Then when Meihua didn't, Emily wondered if she should even say anything. She had already come this far though.

"How long did you have Meihua?" Emily asked.

"Oh, a little over twenty years," said Aunt Elaine.

"How many times did you let her... take over?"

Aunt Elaine tilted her head up at the ceiling. "I can't really remember to be honest. Plenty of times though."

Emily wrung her hands together. "What was it like?"

Her aunt sat down at the foot of the bed so she was just across from Emily and crossed her arms. "It was unnerving at first," said Aunt Elaine. "Giving up control of your body. Have you driven yet?" Emily shook her head. "Well, that analogy is no good then."

She scratched her head and directed her gaze down at the ground. Then she suddenly snapped her fingers and pointed up. "Have you ever gone somewhere and realized you didn't know how you got there? Like you don't remember the steps or what you did to get there? Just that you're there?"

"Yeah," admitted Emily.

"It's like that," said Aunt Elaine. "Like you're on autopilot. You know what your body is doing, but you really only figure out how you did it after the fact. It's like that with Meihua, except you can always take control again."

"Oh," said Emily. She averted her eyes from her aunt and studied a very uninteresting patch of carpet.

"Is something else bothering you, Emily?" asked her aunt.

"No," said Emily looking down. "Well, yes." She raised her head. "How did you get used to it?"

"It?" asked Aunt Elaine.

"Always having something there. *Someone* there," said Emily. She tapped the side of her head with a finger. "In here."

"Ah," said Aunt Elaine as if she had just realized something very important. "That does take some getting used to. I take it that Meihua isn't with us at the moment."

Emily held up her right hand to show a bare ring finger.

"It's just so weird," said Emily. "She doesn't say anything all day, and then suddenly she starts talking to me. I almost fell down the stairs because it scared me so bad."

"That's to be expected," said Aunt Elaine. "She's trying to get to know you. Think about how long it takes for anyone to make friends."

"Umm… it's pretty quick actually," said Emily.

"Is it though?" asked Aunt Elaine. "You may be friendly to each other, but it typically takes a while to build a real friendship. And that's with someone you can see, feel, and actually hear. It's a real person. Think about Meihua. She's bound to the shape she's in. She only experiences things through the person holding her—or wearing her in your case. She can only build on what you allow. If she says or does the wrong thing, you could put her in a box and then just lock her away. Give her a chance. She just wants to be your partner, to be useful. She wants you to like her."

Emily touched her right ring finger and a rush of emotions welled up inside her. She was sick with shame and misunderstanding. Emily had talked to Meihua about that exact subject. And here she was, not twenty-four hours later, having to be reminded that Meihua was just as scared of Emily as Emily was of her. She turned her hand over and brushed her left thumb over the inside of her ring finger. It tickled and she closed her fist.

"Thanks, Aunt Elaine," said Emily suddenly.

She stood up, raised her hands so her left hand covered her right fist, and bowed. Her aunt bowed her head and Emily left the room. She silently made her way up the stairs to the second floor, crossed the hall to her room, stepped inside, and shut the door behind her. She stood there in the silence of her room with star, moon, and streetlight all brushing through her windows. She bore the weight of her aunt's words lingering heavy on her heart, and then she focused on the ring sitting on her desk all alone. She reached her hand out, took the ring, and slid it into place on her hand.

"I'm sorry, Meihua."

Chapter 9

Two Roads

EMILY DROPPED HER backpack at her feet and spun the dial on her locker as quickly as she could. She pulled the latch up, the door out, and was met with an angry grimace coming from inside her locker. The mirror showcased the face Emily was wearing and her mood. Based on how her fellow students had averted their eyes from her, she guessed that she must have looked like that the entire walk toward her locker.

Emily let out a frustrated breath and opened her backpack so she could arrange it for her first two classes. Her legs wavered as she leaned down to pick up the first book and her arms ached when she lifted it. In fact, pretty much every part of her body was sore except for her face. It had been almost a week since she started training. Every day her aunt had some new workout for her to do, then there was qi cultivation training which at times was just like yoga, and then finally her aunt drilled her on techniques that were becoming more and more complex. Additionally, her aunt had not become a better teacher despite the best efforts of the book Emily saw her reading. All of that combined to form a very grumpy Emily.

Allison stepped up next to Emily and started turning the dial on her own locker. "Hey, Emily."

Emily let out a noise somewhere between a groan and a grunt in response.

"What's got you all pissed off?" asked Allison.

"Nothing," said Emily. "I'm just tired and sore. These workouts are killing me."

"Why are you working out so much?" asked Allison.

Emily dropped the last book in her bag and slammed the locker door a little harder than she had meant to. She spun the dial on it to make sure it was locked and then leaned her right side against the wall. She had gone through the first few days without saying anything to Allison so far, but that wasn't without temptation. She had almost told her on accident a few times already. It was only thanks to some timely interventions by Meihua that she was able to stop herself.

And if she was honest with herself, she knew they weren't really accidents. She wanted to tell Allison. To keep this from her went against everything their friendship stood for, but the orders from her family had been absolute.

"Well, you know I take karate, right?" said Emily.

"Yeah," said Allison. "At that place under the dance studio, right?"

"I used to take karate there," said Emily. "Now, my aunt is teaching me."

Allison spun on Emily. "What? Is she still visiting?"

"Yup," replied Emily. "She's going to be staying with us

for a while. She's looking for a place to stay. I think she's waiting for a house on our street to go up for sale."

"Wow," said Allison. "Why didn't you tell me any of this stuff?"

"Sorry, it was just a really crazy week," said Emily. "She showed up last Friday, remember?"

Allison nodded.

"Well, she took me to my karate lesson and decided that I should learn from her now."

"How'd your parents take that?" asked Allison when Emily stopped talking to take a breath. "I mean having someone visit for a little bit is one thing, but a long time? Where does she even teach you? Do you guys have room for that?"

Emily bit her lip when she thought of everything she wanted to tell Allison but couldn't. A wave of panic hit her. She didn't want to lie to Allison, but she didn't know what to say. The silence threatened to become awkward, so she forced herself to say something. "It's a challenge. There's not a lot of room, but we make do with what we have."

Allison's head tilted and Emily knew her friend had noticed what she didn't say. More anxiety roiled inside her, but Allison didn't press Emily.

"So, can we hang out this weekend?" asked Allison. "We didn't talk that much this week. I kind of felt like you were avoiding me."

"What? No, I wasn't," said Emily quickly in an attempt to compensate for the pause, and to hopefully get Allison to believe her.

The first victim of Emily's training, besides Emily herself, had been Allison. Emily was painfully aware of how little they had talked. Allison was such a huge part of her life, but they didn't talk as much now that she was training. And the time she didn't spend training was spent doing schoolwork. "There was just a lot going on. I promise. Let's definitely hang out this weekend. What do you have in mind?"

"Well, you seem pretty tired. Are you up to going out?" asked Allison.

"Yeah, that sounds great."

"How about a movie?" Allison closed her locker and slung her backpack over her shoulder. "Maybe on Sunday?"

"That new hero one?" asked Emily excitedly.

"I knew you were going to want to see that one," said Allison with resignation.

"Hey, you chose last time," remarked Emily.

"Fine," said Allison. "I'll text you later with some times."

"Sound's good," said Emily. Genuine happiness flooded her now that she had something else to look forward to. She bounced happily and then realized what she was doing and stopped. Allison laughed and turned to leave but then spun back like she was on a swivel.

"Oh, one more thing."

"What's up?" asked Emily.

Allison had the barest slip of excitement on her face, and she went up on her toes. Finally, she gestured toward the gym. "It gets announced today."

And suddenly Emily was aware that Allison was not gesturing at the gym. She meant the building behind it.

Emily stepped in so she was closer to Allison than she had to be. "When?"

"After school," she said. "I was hoping you could check with me."

"OF COURSE," said Emily. She slung her backpack over her shoulder. "Meet here after sixth period?"

Emily's body jolted and she jumped in her seat. Laughter sounded in waves around her as her heart jumped into her throat. She clenched her fists tightly and slowly raised her head. The entire room full of teenagers were laughing at her and Emily's fears about falling asleep in class had come true. A tall figure loomed over her. It was her English teacher, Mr. Coulter. She got caught.

Right, English class.

"Finally with us?" asked Mr. Coulter. "Robert Frost too boring for you?"

"Sorry, Mr. Coulter," said Emily. "Haven't been sleeping well lately."

Mr. Coulter's eyes did not have a single shred of sympathy. "Fall asleep in my class again and I'll have to call your parents. Got it?"

"Yes, Mr. Coulter."

"Good." He stepped back to the front of the class and held up a leather-bound book. It was a sort of off-color teal with white trees on the cover. "Robert Frost. One of the greatest poets ever. We're going to be studying his work. I know poetry isn't your favorite, but let's give it a try."

He flipped the book open, cleared his throat, and then held his right hand up for effect and silence. His gaze swept across the room.

"'Two roads diverged in a yellow wood, / And sorry I

could not travel both.'" It was just one line, but he had pulled them all in.

The class listened as Mr. Coulter's performance continued. It was as if they were the tide, and his voice was the moon drawing them in toward the shore.

"'Two roads diverged in a wood, and I— / I took the one less traveled by, / And that has made all the difference.'"

He shut the book as softly as the words he had spoken and nodded to the silent classroom.

"'The Road Not Taken,'" he said. "What do we think that's about?"

"Taking the harder road," blurted someone.

"Yes," said Mr. Coulter, "and no. Not necessarily the harder road. But not a safe one."

"Is there a difference?" another student asked.

"Yes," said Mr. Coulter. "Poetry has different meanings for everyone. What I think Mr. Frost was trying to tell us was to take chances. Take risks. Don't follow a path that's just been given to you. Do you want to be the one following the path? Or do you want to be the one making it? Doing something no one else has done before?"

A bell chimed, stopping Mr. Coulter just as he was about to say something else. "Your assignment tonight is to read this poem and write what it means to you."

"How long does it have to be?" asked a boy.

Mr. Coulter smiled. "As long as you think it should be."

The class started packing their things and Emily was about to leave when Mr. Coulter called her name.

She turned and saw her teacher looking at her from the front of the class. He gestured for her to come over. Emily deflated. She was hoping that her accidental nap wouldn't escalate into a meeting, but those hopes were dashed. Dejected and embarrassed again, Emily made her way toward her teacher.

Mr. Coulter leaned against his desk saying goodbye to the students. Then, when the last student had left, he turned to Emily.

"Is everything okay?"

"Yes," said Emily, a little taken aback.

"It's just… you've been a little off this week," he said. "Don't get me wrong. I catch you reading all the time or doodling, but you've always been a good student. This week you've been inattentive at best. I'm pretty sure I caught you sleeping twice yesterday."

"I'm sorry," said Emily. "I really just haven't been sleeping well."

His face said he expected her to say more, but when she didn't say anything else he showed Emily the book he was holding. *A Collection of Poems by Robert Frost*, read Emily.

"'The Road Not Taken,'" said Mr. Coulter. "I've seen a lot of students in my career, Emily. A lot of them coast through their classes and think they can just coast through life. Life is hard. You have to show up and do the work. Don't become like those other students who gave up on themselves. Take the road less traveled. Okay?"

With nothing else to say, Emily nodded.

Mr. Coulter set the book down on his desk. "Have a good weekend, Emily."

Emily opened her mouth to say something, but her teacher had already turned his back on her and was erasing his notes off the board. She left the classroom.

Sunlight hit her like a warm blanket and blinded her a little, but she started power walking to her locker. Allison was standing there in the distance next to their lockers.

"Hey!" yelled Emily while waving her hand. Allison waved back. Emily stopped at her locker, set her backpack down, and started furiously spinning the dial. "Sorry."

"What happened?" asked Allison.

"I fell asleep in class and Mr. Coulter caught me." She pulled the locker door open and started rummaging through her planner.

"You fell asleep in class?" repeated Allison. "You never fall asleep in class. Are you okay?"

"Why does everyone keep asking me that?"

"Well, you've been a little weird lately," admitted Allison.

Emily slipped one last book into her backpack and then shut her locker. "How?"

Allison shrugged. "You've just been weird. Like a little standoffish? It's like you've got this big sign on your face that says, 'stay away.' Even I've given you some space."

"Sorry," said Emily. "I've just been tired lately. Extra martial arts training."

"Why though?" asked Allison. "Are you going to be like a professional fighter or something?"

"No," said Emily with a snort.

"Then why?"

Emily pursed her lips and threw the backpack over her shoulder. "I don't know." Then to change the subject. "Do you think the results are posted yet?"

Allison's expression changed to something Emily couldn't exactly describe. It was worried with a little bit of hurt and a hint of anger. Emily turned away from her best friend's face. There was a dull ache deep in her chest. She hated not being able to tell her friend the truth. The biggest, best thing in her life and she had to hide it. But there was no changing that. She could only try to be the best friend she could be while lying to Allison.

"Yeah," said Allison quietly. "Let's go see."

They walked past the side of the gym until it curled around the corner. There was a pathway leading up to another building. A large patch of grass on the other side of the gym was bathed in the afternoon sunlight. A small crowd of people stood around the entrance to a glass door. Allison shuddered next to her.

"Are you ready?" asked Emily.

"Yeah," Allison replied.

They walked up and joined the group of people, gently inching closer and closer to a piece of paper posted to the window. A minute later and they were there. Emily stood off to the side while Allison and other students searched for their names.

"Oh my God!" screamed Allison. She spun to Emily.

"Yeah?" asked Emily, excitement building in her.

"Yeah!" she cried.

"Congratulations!" screamed Emily.

The two friends hugged, and other people patted Allison on the back to congratulate her as well. They parted and Emily watched other girls hug Allison and tell her how much she deserved it.

Emily moved back toward the paper showing who got what part and remembered their conversation from the week before. "Who got Beast?"

"Me," came a clear voice.

Emily turned around and saw a boy walking toward them. He wore black skinny jeans and a heather red T-shirt with the name of a band on it. He had tousled dark hair that curled in gentle waves. Emily had to wake up an hour early to get her hair like that. She imagined this boy had achieved that effortlessly.

He stopped in front of Allison. He was half a head taller than her. They shared a moment of silent eye contact that lasted just long enough that Emily wondered if she should look away. They exchanged quiet congratulations, saving Emily from having to awkwardly find someone else to talk to. Emily stepped forward and stood next to her best friend.

"Hi," she said. "I'm Emily."

"Hey," replied the boy. His voice was like silver and slid through the air like a gentle breeze. "I'm Jeremy."

He held out his hand and Emily took it in hers. His hand was as gentle as his voice and he held Emily's eyes in his for the entire handshake. He exuded confidence and Emily instantly understood why Allison had crushed on him so hard. He was just plain attractive.

Jeremy turned his attention back to Allison and his smile appeared again. It was warm and there was a glint in his eyes when he looked at Allison. It was like she was the only thing he saw, and everything else around them was just background noise.

"So, we should probably get together and rehearse sometime," he said to Allison.

"Yeah sure!" she said eagerly.

"Could I get your number then?" he asked coolly. "We can meet up whenever you're free."

Allison recited her number to him, and her cheeks started to flush with each digit. Emily felt the corners of her face stretch and perk up as Jeremy punched Allison's number into his phone. Happiness spread through her body like it was her lifeblood and she knew she was only feeling a fraction of what Allison was feeling. He slid the phone back into his pocket after he was done.

"I'll see you around then."

"Yeah," said Allison again.

He turned to Emily. "It was nice to meet you."

"You too," replied Emily. Jeremy turned and walked away slowly. As soon as his back was to them Allison's hand shot down and clawed at Emily's forearm. Sharp nails dug into her skin and Emily hissed while she tried to pry her friend's claws off her.

"He just asked for my phone number," said Allison.

"Yeah, I was here. It was literally two seconds ago."

"Do you think he's going to call?" Allison asked suddenly.

"Yeah, Allison, I do," replied Emily.

Allison went up on her toes and Emily believed Allison was the happiest person in the world. Allison slid her arm through the crook of Emily's and the two of them locked arms before walking away. They went a different direction from Jeremy even though it was out of the way. They didn't want him to think they were following him after all.

CHAPTER 10

A NEW CHALLENGER APPROACHES

"WATCH MY MOVEMENTS," said Aunt Elaine.

It was Sunday, and Emily and her aunt were back in the training room standing parallel to one another. Her aunt stood with her legs shoulder-width apart and her knees bent. Her hands were balled into fists and resting at her waist with her fingers facing up. She took a slow step forward and brought her right hand up in a calculated movement. Her fist turned and the movement changed into the slowest punch ever. Emily emulated the movement, but it was clunky whereas her aunt's movements were smoother.

"No," said Aunt Elaine. "Do you see where you messed up there?"

"It wasn't as clean as yours," replied Emily.

"Yes," said Aunt Elaine. "What else?"

Emily played the movement back in her head and tried to imagine what Aunt Elaine had just done too. "I don't know."

"Your form was weak," said Aunt Elaine. "You have to bend your knees more. Your legs are your foundation. Try again."

Emily and Aunt Elaine took their positions and Aunt Elaine started her motion again. Emily followed along after her aunt and did her best to copy what her aunt was doing. Aunt Elaine frowned at Emily's movements, but she let Emily continue with the rest of the maneuver. She did this until they had finished it completely and then she stood up straight.

"Okay, show it to me," said Aunt Elaine. Emily started and only got three motions in before her aunt said, "Stop."

She stepped toward Emily, corrected her posture, and showed her the right angle for the punch.

"Try again," said Aunt Elaine. Emily performed the move the way her aunt had corrected but her aunt stopped her again. "Your back leg is too straight. Bend it more. If you're standing up too straight there's no foundation. Bent knees allow for more movement, more options, and more explosiveness. It's like how runners start in their position. Do you understand?"

Emily shut her eyes and took a deep breath. "Yes."

"Try again."

Emily started again and got only a little farther in before her aunt stopped to correct her.

"No," said her aunt, frustration evident in her voice. "Wrong again."

A groan exploded from Emily that was just as frustrated as Aunt Elaine's voice. These training sessions were already wearing on her physically, but now they were starting to grate on her mentally too. It was difficult to appreciate what her aunt was trying to do when she kept nitpicking at everything Emily did.

"Maybe," said Emily before Aunt Elaine could tell her what she was doing wrong, "we can try something else."

Aunt Elaine folded her arms across her chest and there was disappointment in her posture. "Emily, we're not doing anything else until you get this right."

"No, not that." She glanced down at the ground and played with the ring on her finger. "Maybe, Meihua could show me."

Aunt Elaine's eyes widened and something in Emily's mind came to life. It was like when she was in a crowd or when she was focusing intently on something and she would swear she heard her name despite no one saying it.

"Maybe just this once. To see how it goes. If Meihua can... or wants to."

I would be happy to, said Meihua.

"She said she would," said Emily to Aunt Elaine. "So, how do I like... let her?"

Her aunt smiled. "You just let her. Talk to her. Tell her she can take control for what you want her to do, and then give control to her."

"I don't get it," said Emily.

"Just trust me," said Aunt Elaine. "And her. And yourself."

"Okay..." said Emily. She thought that Meihua could show her how to do this one technique and that was it. Emily let her body relax.

A warm sensation filled her body. It started in her head then cascaded down her body like syrup. And then suddenly she was slowly moving in the same way that Aunt Elaine had tried to show Emily. Emily's body shifted and it was weird having it move on its own. It was like she was on cruise control. Like when someone throws a ball at you and your body just reacts on its own to catch it.

Meihua controlled Emily's body through the first step of the maneuver so Emily could understand it and then stopped.

Got it? asked Meihua.

Yes, said Emily.

Her body started again through the next step, and that was the process for the next minute or two. Emily wasn't sure how much time had passed. Meihua took Emily's body step-by-step until she had finished it.

That's it, said Meihua.

And then Emily's body shuddered for a second and it was hers again. She stood up straight and held her hands up in front of her. She wiggled her fingers and watched them. Then she turned her attention back to Aunt Elaine who had a passive expression on her face.

"Want to give it another try?" she asked.

"Yeah," said Emily with a distant voice, like she was thinking about something else entirely.

She stood in front of her aunt and then Emily did what Meihua had shown her. She moved her arms and legs, and it was still clunky, but she could remember how it felt to be in the right position. When she did something wrong, she corrected it herself without her aunt having to say something. She finished, turned back toward her aunt, and bowed.

"Better, but still not perfect. Let's keep practicing."

"Okay," said Emily. And then they stood parallel to one another and started over again; only this time they moved at the same time instead of Emily following her aunt.

A few attempts later and Emily had done the maneuver

three times in a row without a mistake. Pride formed on her aunt's face and Emily's whole mood inflated.

"Think we can go onto the next one?" asked Emily.

"For now. We'll come back to it later. We have to drill the maneuvers in your head so you can do them without thinking."

"Okay," said Emily.

"So, I'll show you the next one, and then we'll keep working on them over and over, got it?"

"Yeah," said Emily. "Do you think Meihua could show me how to do the next one too?"

"Yeah," said Aunt Elaine with a smile on her face. "I think that would be fine."

A couple of hours later Emily emerged from her room in sweats and drying her hair with a towel. She had managed to learn three more moves from her aunt and Meihua had helped her with all of them. She had finally made progress. It had only been a week, but she hadn't been making any progress before. The things her aunt tried to teach her just didn't stick or they were complicated. Meihua had made them easy though, like she had been doing it all her life but had just forgotten how to do it. It was like riding a bike.

She couldn't help but feel happy that her martial arts training was going well. And now she had time to get ready to hang out with Allison. She couldn't tell Allison about any of it and that frustrated her to no end, but she needed to celebrate the little things while she could.

"Thank you, Meihua," said Emily aloud to the open air.

You're welcome, replied Meihua. *I am glad I was able to help.*

"It just kind of feels like everything is going right all of a sudden," she said. "Like nothing can go wrong."

I know the feeling, said Meihua. *I am happy for you.*

Joy spread inside her and she started moving toward the sound of voices with a spring in her step. Her aunt and parents were talking in the living room. A fourth voice she didn't recognize joined in and Emily stopped in her tracks. It was a man's voice.

Emily leaned against the wall beside the stairs as silently as she could and listened.

"Where is she?" said the new voice. His voice was rough, angry, and had an impatient edge to it.

Stephen? said Meihua. *What is he doing here?*

"Who's Stephen?" whispered Emily.

Your father and aunt's cousin, replied Meihua.

"Cousin?" repeated Emily.

"She was taking a shower," said Aunt Elaine with a much calmer voice. "Calm down, Stephen. We had no idea you were coming."

"How long does a shower take?" spat the man.

"As long as she wants," her mother said. She sounded heated too, but more protective than combative.

"What are you even doing here?" asked Dad. "All these years. You've never visited. You've never called. Why now?"

"You know why I am here," said the mystery man.

Emily decided it was finally time to reveal that mystery and stepped onto the stairway.

The first thing she noticed was that there were two visitors, not just one. There was a man pacing around the living room with his hands on his hips. His gaze swept up the staircase immediately after Emily stepped out and he hit her with the most venomous glare she could remember having ever received in her life. He wore slacks, a button-up shirt, and a sweater over that.

The other visitor was around Emily's age or maybe a little older. He had a much softer face compared to the angry man. All-in-all, he was just less severe in every regard. He was wearing dark jeans and a light blue T-shirt. He had darker skin than Emily and her family had, and his hair was wavy and had to be held in place by a fair share of pomade.

Emily turned to her parents and then her aunt before directing her attention back to the man who seemed to hate her just for taking a shower. She descended the stairs as slowly as she could and casually dried her hair with the towel.

"Emily," said Aunt Elaine. "This is Stephen. He's your dad's and my cousin. So, I guess your uncle. That is his son, Bryan. Your cousin."

The boy waved at Emily. His eyes were muted, almost glazed over, and Emily got the idea that he didn't really want to be there. Emily had never heard of either of them in all her life. Her dad hadn't really kept her up to date with their family.

"Hello." Emily walked up to Stephen and held her hand out to shake his.

Stephen's eyes shifted to her hand and pure disgust erupted on his face. Emily checked to make sure she didn't have anything weird on her hand. There was nothing there, but there had to be a reason for her "Uncle" Stephen's reaction. The only thing on her hand was the ring.

Stephen looked over Emily completely, ignoring her and focusing his attention on Aunt Elaine. "You've done it already."

"Yes," said Aunt Elaine.

"Excuse me," said Emily's dad. He stepped forward and pulled Emily back, so she was behind him. "What's your problem, Stephen? You can't just show up here and act like this. My daughter's done nothing to deserve it."

"This doesn't concern you," said Stephen. "You left the family."

"If this concerns my daughter, it concerns me," snarled Dad. He stepped up toward Stephen until they were inches apart.

Stephen laughed. "Please. You don't scare me anymore."

"Yeah?" said Dad. "Maybe I just need to help you remember why you were afraid."

"Christopher," breathed out Mom.

"Enough," said Aunt Elaine. "What do you want, Stephen?"

Stephen's eyes shifted toward Emily one more time and then he scoffed. He stepped away from the four Laus so his back was facing them and rested a hand on his son's shoulder. Bryan regarded his father for a second but Stephen didn't turn. "Bryan."

The boy stood up and crossed the room so he was standing in front of Emily. Her dad stepped in front of him but Bryan had already stopped a couple feet away. He raised both his hands up, his right in a fist and his left hand blanketing his right, and then he bowed to them.

"Emily Lau," said Bryan in a deeper voice than she had expected. "I challenge you to a duel for Meihua."

CHAPTER 11

FAMILY HISTORY

"WHAT?" said Emily.

There was really nothing else for her to say. She knew she must have had more family, but she had never met or spoken to them until today. They just showed up out of the blue. And then not only did her uncle hate her for no reason whatsoever, but also his son was challenging Emily for Meihua. Was that even possible?

"I'm challenging you to a duel for Meihua," repeated Bryan.

Emily spun to face her aunt. "Can he do that?"

Her aunt was glaring at Stephen, but when she turned to Emily the anger transitioned into disappointment. "Technically, you can challenge anyone to a duel. He cannot challenge you for Meihua though."

"Actually, he can," broke in Stephen. He spun to face them all and had a self-righteous expression.

He moved to stand next to his son and rested his hand on Bryan's shoulder. "I looked it up. A member of the family can challenge the current guardian of Meihua for the sword.

The duel must be fought, but it is still up to Meihua to choose who will be her guardian."

"Meihua chose," said Emily. "She chose me."

"She chose wrong," spat Stephen. "Bryan is a much better candidate. He is part of our world. He is more skilled. He should have been Meihua's guardian. The duel will show that."

"Why?" asked Aunt Elaine again. "Emily is right. Meihua made a choice."

"She chose wrong!" yelled Stephen again. His face flushed crimson and there was a small vein that Emily swore was pulsing. "Bryan was the only choice. You had no children."

He turned to Emily again.

"She," he spat, "was never a candidate. Should never have been. She was never there."

Emily's heart plummeted. She knew that the man didn't like her from what she heard while she was coming downstairs, but there was still a small vestige of hope burning inside her when she learned he was related to her. That little flame had been snuffed out now as hatred seethed off him. What had she done to deserve this? He didn't even know her.

"Just because you can't see something doesn't mean it doesn't exist," said Aunt Elaine. "You may have never seen Emily, but that doesn't mean she wasn't a candidate."

Stephen grunted. "My son should have been chosen."

Aunt Elaine turned to Bryan who had just sort of blended into the background like a wallflower at a party. "Do you even want this?"

Emily turned and saw that Bryan was staring at her. There was a strange wistfulness in his eyes that Emily felt in her heart. She had wanted so badly to meet her family. To know them. She dreamt of cousins and visiting family.

Bryan stepped forward and opened his mouth to speak. He glanced at his father who did not acknowledge his son, and Emily watched his eyes harden.

"I've challenged her. It's done."

And just like that the dream inside her died.

She nearly collapsed onto the couch beside her but managed to make it look like she meant to sit. Or at least she hoped she did.

"She can say no," said Mom. Everyone turned to her and there was surprise on everyone's face, including hers. "She can say no, right?"

"Not really," said Aunt Elaine. "Duels are important in our world."

"I'm not saying no." The words had come out before she realized she said them. Anger burned in Emily's chest and she glared at Stephen. Bryan was the one she was going to have to fight. But it was Stephen who had challenged her, he who had said she was unworthy. "I'll fight for Meihua."

Stephen smiled then, a triumphant smile that Emily would have liked to smack off his smug face. It was like he saw Emily as a real person for the first time. "Good." He clapped his son's back. "This should be over quickly."

"Not now," said Aunt Elaine suddenly. Stephen's face spun toward Aunt Elaine. "You can't show up out of the blue and issue a challenge. We need some time to prepare."

Stephen's face bristled like he had just swallowed something particularly bitter. "How much time?"

"Two weeks."

He sneered at Emily then Aunt Elaine. "Done." He held his hand out toward her and the two of them shook. He gestured at Bryan with his head, a silent order that said, "let's go," and made his way to the front door. He didn't try to get out of anyone's way, instead attempting to walk through them so Emily and her dad had to move. Bryan rolled his eyes and started to follow his father out. He stopped next to Emily and his face was apologetic.

"I'm sorry about this," he whispered.

"Bryan!" yelled Stephen from the door.

Bryan opened his mouth to say something but stopped himself before he followed his dad out the door. Emily's mother followed quickly behind them and slammed the door shut. She slinked back into the living room and Emily could see her shaking in the doorway.

"What an ass," said Mom. Everyone turned to her with shock on their faces. Dad was standing by the window closest to Mom while Aunt Elaine was across the room behind Emily. "His son seemed pleasant. But what happened to Stephen to make him... such an ass?"

"Stephen trained with us when we were younger," said Aunt Elaine.

"He was considered a candidate to inherit Meihua too," added Dad.

"But our dad was Meihua's guardian," said Aunt Elaine. "Which kind of meant that while he was considered, he really wasn't."

"And he's probably a little upset about that still," said Emily's dad.

"So, this duel is all because he's mad that he didn't get Meihua?" asked Emily.

"Probably," said her dad.

"That doesn't make any sense. Why not just challenge me himself?" asked Emily.

Aunt Elaine sat down on the closest chair and pinched the bridge of her nose. "Because that wouldn't be honorable."

Emily's parents both sat down on the couch and her dad started rubbing his chin. "You see there's this unwritten code between martial artists. Like a set of guidelines everyone follows. He can't challenge you. He's close to being a master; you're pretty much a novice. But his son is around your age and is allowed to challenge you."

"And duels are pretty sacred in the world of martial arts," said Aunt Elaine. "People duel all the time over honor or what not. And Stephen is right, Bryan is totally within his rights to challenge you for Meihua. It's still kind of a sleazy thing to do."

"Why's that?" asked Emily.

"Well, for one thing," started Aunt Elaine, "Bryan has been training in martial arts for a lot longer than you. Everything I've just started teaching you, he's been learning for years. Which means we have a lot of work to do."

"I can still go out tonight with Allison though, right?"

Emily watched the pained expression on her aunt's face form and her hopes were crushed under the weight of her aunt's withering gaze.

"Emily, I don't think it's the best time," said Aunt Elaine. "You have two weeks to learn how to defend yourself. Bryan's been training with qi for years. If you can't put up some sort of defense, he'll crush you. He could really hurt you. I think we need to start training again."

"Wait," said Emily. "Could he really take Meihua away from me? Like if he wins the duel, do I lose Meihua?"

"Not necessarily," said Aunt Elaine. "But it's still a possibility. Meihua chose you, but she can change her mind. There's precedence."

Emily noted how silent Meihua had been. She slid her phone out of her pocket.

"What are you doing?" asked her mom.

"Texting Allison," replied Emily. "I have to tell her I won't be able to hang out. Again."

"So, what are we going to do now?" asked Emily. "More maneuvers?"

They were back in the demesne. Emily wore her same sweats and Aunt Elaine paced back and forth in a short line.

"Yes," said Aunt Elaine. "Sort of. This is going to be a little more intense."

"How?

"You know how we let Meihua move your body to show you the maneuver? We're going to do the same, except she's going to practice for you. She's going to manipulate your qi for you. That way you can feel it, see how it moves, what it can do. Then you will try to do it yourself afterward."

"That doesn't sound too bad," admitted Emily.

"This is going to exhaust you, Emily," said Aunt Elaine. "Your body isn't used to using qi. It's not used to having qi being moved. We're going to force something. It's going to be like when you work out and lift heavy weights. Like high weight, low rep. We're doing the equivalent of tearing your muscles so they can become stronger."

"I think I get it," said Emily. She had her right arm across her chest and her left arm holding it in place so she could stretch it. "We're just going to work out really hard."

Aunt Elaine stopped pacing and turned to face Emily. "No. You're not really going to be doing the work. I mean you are, but Meihua is going to be moving your body. Moving your qi. It's like someone else is going to exercise your body for you. And then you get your body back."

"I mean that sounds kind of awesome," said Emily. "All the benefits and rewards without doing the work."

"Except your body is *actually* doing it," said Aunt Elaine. "Meihua isn't going to feel the aftereffects of it. You are. You're the one who's going to be in pain. You're the one that's going to be tired. You're the one that has to bear it. Do you understand?"

"Yeah," said Emily, though she wasn't so sure.

Aunt Elaine studied her for a moment, then shook her head. "You don't, but you will. Are you ready?"

Emily took a deep breath. "Yes."

"Meihua, go easy on her."

She let her body relax, inhaled a deep breath, and let it go. Her body went slack, and then Meihua took over. It was comforting, like the warm embrace of a blanket in the morning. Her legs spread into a wider stance and her knees bent ever so slightly. Her arms started moving and it was like someone was gently pushing them for her.

Are you okay? asked Meihua.

Yes, replied Emily. *It's still a little weird, but I'm getting used to it.*

It's going to get worse from here, said Meihua. *But I'll do my best to protect you from the worst of it.*

Her body started moving in complex forms she had never tried before. There was no resistance, no tension. She was the water in the river and Meihua was the current. Then it was over. Emily let out another deep breath, but she wasn't sure if it was her or Meihua who did it.

And then her body started again. It was the same form as before but there was something different this time. A shimmer of warmth appeared in her body. It was soft, like a candle flickering in the wind, but it was there.

That is your qi, said Meihua. *You can feel it, right?*

Yes, replied Emily.

I'm going to use it and move it along with your body, said Meihua. *Pay attention to how it feels.*

Meihua shifted Emily's body over and over in the same way, and each time she did it the warmth in her body grew. It spread over her like she had submerged herself into a warm bath. Emily wasn't sure how many times they did it, or how long it had been.

I'm going to let go now, said Meihua. *Get ready.*

For what? asked Emily.

The backlash, said Meihua.

Her body went slack for a moment and she started to fall. She caught herself as she was about to lose her balance, then steadied herself with her hands. Her shirt clung to her skin and rivulets of sweat slipped down the sides of her face. Her arms glistened with it, and she felt the uncomfortable tickle of sweat behind her knees too.

Emily's world rocked and she tilted forward. Aunt Elaine

rushed forward and caught Emily by her arm and helped her stay on her feet. Her whole body became heavy like the day after her very first workout.

"Are you all right?" asked Aunt Elaine.

"Yeah," lied Emily. "I just need a second."

"Deep breaths," said Aunt Elaine. "Take it slow. You have no idea how much your body just went through."

She let herself fall against Aunt Elaine and they just stood there, Emily cradled in her aunt's arms, until Emily could stand again. A few minutes, or years later, she stood up. She was still unsteady and her knees rocked and rattled. "I'm okay."

"You're not," said Aunt Elaine. "But you don't have time to not be okay right now." She stepped back and gave Emily some space. She was still close though. Probably just in case she needed to dash forward and catch Emily again. "Do you remember what she taught you? Do you remember how the qi felt inside your body?"

Emily nodded slowly.

"Can you show me?"

Emily got into the starting position that Meihua had shown her, and then her body started like it was preprogrammed. It was like she was on a ride at an amusement park. Emily could feel the warmth that Meihua had said was her qi. It wasn't as strong as when Meihua had made it, but it was there.

Her body was getting weaker and weaker with every motion, but she persisted. She reached the end of the form, brought her hands up, and bowed to her aunt. Then she forced herself to keep standing.

"That was amazing," said Aunt Elaine. There was a genuine smile on her face. "Let's get some food in you, and then straight to bed."

Emily was on cruise control for the rest of the night. She couldn't remember the last time she was this tired. She had rinsed off in the shower, and her aunt had made Emily's mom stand outside the bathroom door "just in case." Then she went downstairs for dinner. Her aunt and father had been in a muted, but heated, discussion, but they both fell silent when Emily walked in the room. Her aunt crossed the room and shoved a mug of steaming tea into Emily's hands.

"Drink this," she said. "It'll help."

Emily drank the tea slowly and it did start to help. Some energy returned to her limbs and mind when she had finished the mug. She wasn't a zombie anymore, more like an exhausted athlete after a game.

After she had finished eating dinner, she moved to the couch and just rested until she decided to go to bed. She curled into her bed and brought her phone out. She had no new messages. She hadn't even heard from Allison after she called to tell her she couldn't go out anymore. There was this gap between her and Allison now. She opened her conversation with Allison and saw the last message she had sent her.

I'm sorry.

And just below that a single word that meant so much more than it actually did: *Read.*

Emily started typing another text to her best friend, but the words wouldn't come out. There was so much she wanted to say. So much she couldn't. In the end all she managed to type out was "I'm sorry" again. But she couldn't muster the strength to send it. There was this feeling inside her that she could only describe as wanting to go back to the way things were, but that was a lie.

She wanted this. She wanted Meihua. She wanted the adventure that Meihua and her aunt had teased her with. She wanted to be more than she was. The weight of the ring around her finger was suddenly tangible. The tug of attention in the back of her mind. What was Meihua costing her? Maybe a normal life. Definitely her friendship right now.

In the end she did send the apology to Allison, and she had said she would talk to her tomorrow. She hoped Allison would want to talk to her.

She set the phone down on the nightstand and had just settled into bed when someone knocked on her door. She turned over just as her dad stepped inside her room.

"Hey," said her dad with a soft voice. "How are you feeling?"

"Tired," said Emily. "But better."

"Yeah, I remember what it feels like. I came to see if I could help."

"I think I just need to sleep, Dad," said Emily.

"Right, humor me though." He grabbed the chair from Emily's desk and sat beside her bed. "Turn over on your side, so your back is to me."

Emily shifted as requested.

"Now, I didn't really keep up with all the martial arts," said her father. "But I've never stopped meditating. Take a deep breath. Good. Now exhale. Right, just like that. Don't think about breathing. Be just like a baby. Just breathe and be. Clear your mind."

Her father became silent, but she could still sense his presence looming just behind her. Clearing her mind was easier now than before. She was dead tired and even her mind wanted rest. She breathed in and out like there was nothing else to do in the world except breathe and be right where she was.

He spoke to her intermittently to give additional instructions. His voice was soft and gentle, so when he did speak, he didn't break her concentration. Warmth spread through her abdomen and Emily recognized it as her qi. It was comforting feeling it there.

Her dad spoke a few more times before finally telling her to stop and wiggle her fingers and toes.

"Good job," he said. "This is how you should always meditate. Now, go to sleep."

Her father put the chair back and left the room. She closed her eyes again and let sleep take her.

CHAPTER 12

EYES OPEN

EMILY COULD USUALLY tell when she was dreaming. A fog muddied the details around her, and there was an edge like a constant threat that if she did the wrong thing, she might wake up. But dreams with Meihua were different.

They had clarity and things looked and felt just as real as they would if she were awake. That was simultaneously pleasant and worrying to Emily. She wondered if she would be able to wake herself up if she wanted to.

She was seated on a cushion on the floor in the middle of a room. A low table was in front of her. A tea set lay in the center of the table between Emily and Meihua.

Meihua was pouring tea into the two cups while Emily watched. Meihua's clothing had changed. She still wore a *hanfu*, but now it was red with gold accents.

The floor and table were made up of dark wood, but the rest of the room was shrouded in darkness.

"Where are we?" asked Emily.

Meihua finished pouring the tea and set the teapot down onto a tray on the table. She pushed a cup of tea toward Emily and took her own. Emily lifted the cup. Heat permeated through it and warmed her hands. She took a sip and tasted jasmine tea. She didn't want to think about how she could taste the tea in a dream. She was sure that would lead to a headache.

"This is where I show off my memories," said Meihua.

Emily studied the shadows all around her. It hung thick in the air, like humidity, and pressed against her.

"Nice place," said Emily. "Not at all creepy."

Meihua smiled at Emily and took a sip of tea.

"Why did you bring me here?" asked Emily.

"I thought we should talk," said Meihua.

"About what?"

"What do you think we should talk about?"

Emily wasn't sure what to say, and then she was. "Could you pick him?" She bit her lip when Meihua didn't answer. "Like if we fight and I lose. Would you leave for him?"

Meihua set the cup down on the table. *"I don't know."*

"What do you mean you don't know?" asked Emily.

"It's the future," said Meihua. *"It hasn't happened yet. How could I tell you what I will do in the future? There's a phrase for it. How did it go again?"* Meihua's eyes shifted up for a brief moment and then settled back down on Emily. *"Que será, será. What will be will be. I can tell you right now that I chose you. For now, that is all that matters."*

"No, it's not," cried Emily.

"Emily," said Meihua. There was steel in her voice that stopped Emily from continuing. And then she softened. It was

a kindness after the rebuke in her voice a moment ago. *"I chose you. I am helping you. And I am here for you. That matters."*

Emily wasn't sure what to say. She had just been given the sword and the promise of a new life full of adventure and magic, and now it could be taken away from her. She couldn't help but feel like it was monumentally unfair. She didn't even know Stephen or Bryan. Why were they doing this to her? Why couldn't they just be her family? She opened her mouth to speak, but Meihua held up a hand to stop her.

"Your aunt is going to teach you how to fight," said Meihua.

"I know how to fight," said Emily defensively.

"No, you know how to punch and kick," said Meihua. *"Your aunt will show you the difference. She's going to use me to help."*

Meihua snapped her fingers and the darkness disappeared. It was like all the light in the world was situated on just them, and then a curtain was pulled back and the illuminated area grew and grew revealing cream colored walls adorned with weapons of every kind. Swords, hammers, spears, shields, staves, and weapons she couldn't name surrounded her.

"What is this?" asked Emily.

"These," said Meihua, *"are all my former guardians."*

"What?"

"This is my armory," said Meihua. She stood up and as she did the weapons came off the walls and started to slowly spin all around them. *"All of my guardians' fighting styles, my memories of them, are stored in these weapons."*

She held out a hand and a long staff floated toward her. *"This guardian was strong and supple. She struck fast and hard. She was a master of many weapons and fighting styles."*

Meihua let the staff go and turned in a different direction.

She held up her left hand this time and a hammer floated to it. *"This one was all strength and brute force in a fight. Yet he had one of the gentlest souls I've ever encountered. Loved dogs."*

She let go of the hammer and it joined the other weapons in the slow-moving maelstrom.

"Your aunt is going to train you how to fight. You're going to have to decide what kind of weapon you are going to be. What do you think?"

Meihua gestured to the swirl of weapons all around them. Emily watched. They all moved in concert, like the world's deadliest school of fish, swimming around her. There were too many to focus on and the whole scene was starting to make her dizzy.

"Which one is my aunt?" asked Emily.

Meihua held a hand out to her right and a sword floated toward the two of them. It was not a *jian* like Meihua was. It had one curved edge and resembled a scimitar.

"A dao," said Meihua. *"General of all weapons. Your aunt was a leader. A trailblazer."*

Emily studied the curved blade and wondered what kind of weapon Meihua thought Emily was. Meihua chose the forms that these memories took based on their personalities and Emily couldn't figure out what weapon her personality would make her. She wondered if there was an online quiz she could take to find out. Like the ones to figure out what kind of donut you are or what group you belonged to from books.

She opened her mouth to ask when something caught her attention. It was there, in the corner of her eye, near the pinnacle of the storm. A sheathed sword, except it wasn't anything like the others. She watched it swirl around and around like she was watching the blades of a fan.

Every weapon in the turtle-paced tornado was pristine and clean except for this one. This sword was wrong. The handle and sheath were decayed and covered in grime like they had been left in a fetid pool for too long and it had rusted. And then after that someone had doused the sword in oil and lit it on fire and left it charred black. Finally, a pristine chain with eight golden locks was wrapped all around the sword.

"What's that?" asked Emily. She pointed up at the black-ened sword.

Meihua turned to where Emily had pointed and froze. She actually froze. Emily couldn't tell if she was even breathing, and then suddenly Meihua waved her hand in the air. The shadows returned and all the weapons went flying in different directions to be hidden again. Emily tried to follow the path of the chained sword but she lost it in the scramble.

"Hey," said Emily. She swung her head back to Meihua and found her grimacing at the ground. She was hugging her arms close to her chest and shivering like she was out in the snow. Emily reached a hand out toward Meihua. "Are you okay?"

Meihua didn't answer. She took three more deep breaths and then raised her head so their eyes met.

"We all have our secrets, Emily," said Meihua. And then she stood up straight as if nothing had happened. *"I think it's time for you to wake up."*

Emily opened her eyes, sat up, and blinked until her vision became crisp again. Fresh daylight was spilling in through the blinds onto the floor and her desk. Emily held her hand up to glower at the plum blossom ring on her finger. It glinted once at her, a ring's equivalent of a wink maybe, and Emily couldn't help but feel like she had been robbed of something important.

"Hey Meihua," said Emily. "What was that sword?"

She waited for a response, but none was forthcoming.

"Umm... Meihua?"

Still nothing.

Emily's phone started ringing next to her and she nearly jumped in surprise. She reached over and her alarm was going off, telling her it was time to get up. She let out a groan and threw the covers off herself so she could get ready for school.

While she was brushing her teeth and showering, she kept thinking of the sword wrapped in chains. She couldn't get it out of her head while eating breakfast. And to make matters worse her aunt had decided to sleep in so Emily couldn't ask her about it before she left for school.

The sword was still on her mind when Allison barreled into her while she was emptying her backpack into her locker.

"Hey!" said Emily after she peeled herself off the locker wall. "What was that for?"

"Um, for bailing on me?" said Allison. "What was that?"

"Oh, sorry," said Emily. She dropped another book into her locker and thought about what to say. "My uncle and cousin came over."

Allison's face was full of confusion.

"Your aunt's married?" asked Allison.

"What? No," said Emily quickly. "It's my dad's cousin. So, I guess he's like what? My first cousin, once removed? His name is Stephen and he's an asshole."

"I didn't know your dad had any cousins," said Allison while she was rummaging through her locker.

"I mean I knew he did," said Emily. "I just didn't think I'd ever meet any of them."

"And the cousin? He's Stephen's kid?"

"Yeah, his name is Bryan," replied Emily. "He's actually pretty nice."

"What'd they come over for?" asked Allison.

Emily shut her locker door and spun around to lean against it. She watched the students walking by and mulled over what she should say to Allison versus what she wanted to say. She wanted to just tell her everything going on now. That would make it easier. She wouldn't have to lie or hide or write down her lies so she'd remember them all. Meihua was right, everyone had their secrets. But it was her choice to share it or not. And today she was thinking it was time to tell Allison what was really going on.

Emily... came Meihua's voice in her head.

"Oh, now you have something to say," said Emily.

"Excuse me?" said Allison indignantly.

"What?" said Emily. She glanced over at Allison and saw the scorn on her face. "No, not you."

"Who were you talking to then?"

The idea of telling her the truth came up again. Only this time it was accompanied with other thoughts. What would Allison think? How would she react? What would Emily even tell her? *Oh, just talking to the voice in my head. Aha, by the way the voice is a sword. Oh wait, that sword is a spirit that looks like a Chinese princess.* Yeah, that would go over well.

And then there was the chance that Allison might believe

her. What then? She would have to explain to Allison why she hadn't told her. Why she didn't trust her. No, she couldn't do that.

So, Emily didn't say anything.

"Right," said Allison. "Bye."

Allison grabbed her backpack, slammed her locker so hard that it opened again, and started walking away.

"Allison, wait!" cried Emily.

Her best friend stopped for a moment, and then walked away. Emily wondered what Allison was thinking about at that moment. Did she think about staying? What did she think was going on in Emily's life? Emily watched her friend leave. Tears built up in her eyes and one trailed down the side of her face just as she became aware of someone staring at her.

Jeremy was standing a few feet away to her left. He watched Allison storm off, and then turned to Emily. "Hey, you okay?"

Emily sniffled and wiped the tear away from her eye. "Yeah, I'm fine." She shut Allison's locker and spun the dial on it. She pulled at the latch a couple times to make sure it was locked, and when she turned around, she expected Jeremy to be gone. Only, he was still there.

"You know she's worried about you, right?" he said.

Emily's insides boiled. What gave him the right to tell Emily that? Of course, he was probably talking to Allison more than Emily was now.

"Yeah, well, she's got nothing to worry about," said Emily.

"That's not what it looks like," said Jeremy.

Emily couldn't meet his eyes. "What do you know?"

And before he could answer, she grabbed her backpack and started walking toward her class.

"So, we've been fast-forwarding your qi training with Meihua," said Aunt Elaine. "Now, it's time to teach you how to fight."

"Meihua said that would be next," replied Emily.

"You guys are talking more? That's good," said Aunt Elaine with surprise in her voice.

"Not really," admitted Emily. "She pulled me into a dream last night and showed me a bunch of weapons."

"Oh, the armory!" said Aunt Elaine with an excited gleam in her eye. "Did she show you me?"

"Yeah," said Emily.

"How was I? What kind of weapon?"

"You were a dao," said Emily.

"Nice," said Aunt Elaine. "That's a good one."

"There was another sword there," blurted out Emily now that she had a chance to talk to her aunt. "It looked like a *jian*, but it was... wrong."

Emily watched her aunt for any sign of recognition but there was none.

"What do you mean wrong?" asked Aunt Elaine.

"It was black and crusted over," said Emily. "Like it'd been left somewhere to rot. Literally. And there were chains with locks all over it. Does that sound familiar?"

Aunt Elaine scratched her head. "Hmm... I don't remember seeing anything like that. Did you ask Meihua about it?"

"Yeah, that's the crazy part," said Emily. "She sent all the weapons away and I lost sight of it. She was shaking like she was scared. I asked her if she was okay and she just said 'we all have our secrets' and hasn't said anything to me about it all day, even when I ask and I *know* she can hear me right now."

Aunt Elaine started stretching her arms and stared at

Emily like she was trying to decide if Emily was telling the truth or not.

"I'm not lying," said Emily.

"I didn't say you were," replied Aunt Elaine while switching arms. "She's right though. Everyone's entitled to their secrets. Including Meihua. If it were important, she'd tell you. Here."

Her aunt stopped stretching to pick up a plastic bag and tossed it to Emily. "Try those on."

Emily opened the bag and found a set of padded fingerless gloves, a mouth guard, and headgear.

"What's all this?" asked Emily.

"I told you," said Aunt Elaine while pulling out a pair of big, red gloves from another bag. "I'm going to teach you how to fight. Well, me and Meihua are."

Emily dropped the bag. "I don't know if I want Meihua's help today."

Her aunt sighed. "Listen, Emily. Your whole life you're going to have to work with people you might be upset with. If you're going to get mad every time you don't get along with someone, then you won't make or keep very many friends. Got it?"

"Yeah," said Emily, and then without trying to hide it. "I won't keep many friends by lying to them either."

Aunt Elaine started pulling a glove on and glanced up at Emily. "Trouble with Allison?" Emily nodded. "We'll have to deal with that later."

"Seems like my life always gets pushed to later," muttered Emily under her breath. Her aunt must have heard her because she gave Emily a dour face.

"This duel with Bryan is important. You don't want to lose Meihua, do you?"

Emily thought about it for a second, and her aunt raised an eyebrow at the pause. "No."

"Good. Is Meihua okay working with you right now?"

I am, said Meihua.

"Yeah," said Emily.

"All right, let's get to work."

Aunt Elaine spent the next few minutes explaining what they were going to do while Emily put on all her gear. Apparently, they were going to be sparring in rounds and each round they would alternate who was in control. The first round would be Emily alone, then the second round Meihua would be given some control to help Emily, and so forth. Each round was going to be three minutes long.

"How come I have more gear than you?" asked Emily. "And my gloves are thinner."

"Because the chances of you hurting me are slim, even with Meihua's help," replied Aunt Elaine like she hadn't meant to insult Emily. It still stung. "And the chances of me hurting you are very high."

Emily had a sarcastic remark ready, but then she remembered that the last time they fought, her aunt had taken her phone out to check emails and still mopped the floor with Emily. This time would be different though. Emily had been training, and she had Meihua.

The two of them bowed to one another after Emily had put in her mouthpiece. Emily took a stance with her weight on her right leg behind her, and her left hand stretched forward in a fist. Her right fist was pulled back, close to her face.

"All right," said her aunt. "First things first. You're going to learn how to take a punch."

"Whadh?" blurted Emily through her mouth guard.

In the second it took Emily to say that word, her aunt had closed the distance between the two of them. Her aunt's gloved fist flew toward Emily's face and Emily closed her eyes, bracing for an impact.

Emily waited for one agonizing second, and then another, but nothing happened. She opened her eyes. Her aunt's piercing gaze was just above Emily's glove.

"You closed your eyes," said Aunt Elaine. She stepped back, put her weight on her right side, and rested her hand on her hip. Then she pointed at Emily with her left fist. "That's the first thing we're going to have to work on. Keeping your eyes open even as something is flying toward you. It's going to be difficult. It's instinct to close your eyes to protect them. But if you close your eyes, you can't fight. You can't respond. You can't block, you can't dodge, and you can't counter. You can only get hit. And if your eyes are closed, you won't even see where you're going to get hit. Now, hands up."

Emily put her hands up in the same position as before. Her aunt advanced on her slowly. She threw soft jabs at Emily that were fast but just slow enough for Emily to keep up with.

"Good," said her aunt. "I'm going to speed up now, okay?"

Emily was about to answer when her aunt burst forward just as she had before. She came in fast with a left jab that Emily got her hands up in time to block. She was not ready for her aunt's right fist though. Emily tried to slide a hand over, but she wasn't going to be able to block it in time and she shut her eyes again.

WHAM! Aunt Elaine's fist slammed into the side of Emily's head and she went stumbling back. She tripped over her own feet and fell onto the mat. A shadow loomed and Aunt Elaine stood over her, hands on her hips, striking a menacing figure.

"You all right?" she asked.

"Yeah."

"Good." She offered Emily a gloved hand to help her. "Get up then."

Emily took her aunt's hand and let herself be pulled to her feet. She took up her stance again, despite being rattled. She was pretty sure her aunt had pulled her punch, but she was still glad for the headgear and mouth guard. Aunt Elaine slammed her fists together. The sound of the impact was like a thunderclap and Emily's body flinched on instinct.

"Remember," said Aunt Elaine. "Eyes open."

CHAPTER 13

THE DUEL

TWO WEEKS PASSED more quickly than Emily could have ever imagined and now she found herself sitting in her kitchen surrounded by her family. Her breakfast sat in front of her largely untouched. Emily couldn't find the will to eat. She had tried but she only managed to eat a couple bites of toast, and she was fighting to even keep that down. She might not win the fight against Bryan, but she was determined to win the fight against her nerves and stomach.

Waves of anxiety mixed with nausea hit her intermittently. She sat at the kitchen island and rapped her fingers on the counter impatiently. She checked her phone for what must have been the fifth time in fifteen minutes. The phone read 11:57. So the fifth time in the last two minutes, actually.

Her thumb lingered over the little bubble icon on her phone. She tapped it idly, out of habit, and opened Allison's thread. The messages they had sent one another had become sparse over the last two weeks. Her impending duel with Bryan had been a thorn in Emily's side in more ways than one.

At first Allison's messages had become frequent again after Emily had to cancel on their last plans. But then they had the fight. She wanted to text her now, but she couldn't afford to lose what little focus she had left. She let out a groan and reached for her earbuds.

She slid them into her ears and picked one of her favorite songs to try to drown out her thoughts. A song that was perfect for this exact moment.

"Just keep breathing…" she sang quietly to herself.

There was a noise and a tap on her shoulder. She turned and Aunt Elaine was there. Emily pulled an earbud out and realized the music was blaring out louder than she expected.

"I didn't whisper that, did I?" asked Emily.

"No," said Aunt Elaine. "But good advice. Do you know what you're going to do?"

Emily nodded.

"Good," said Aunt Elaine. "Just stay calm. Keep breathing."

Her aunt left Emily to herself and Emily put the earbud back into her ear. She turned the volume down and stretched her arms back. Her eyes swept across the room. Her dad stood at the kitchen sink. He had been doing the dishes for the last few minutes, and judging by the empty dish rack next to him, Emily guessed he had been washing the same dish the entire time. Her mother stood next to him, drinking something warm from a mug. Emily watched the steam rise. She followed the trail up until she met her mother's eyes. They both gave one another weak smiles and then Emily turned away. She started breathing like her father had taught her. She managed a few breaths before a hand jolted her from her reverie. Her aunt was standing over her with a grave expression. Emily took her earbuds out again.

"They're here." Aunt Elaine's eyes and voice were tinged with sadness.

Emily turned. A red SUV was parked in their driveway. Bryan exited the car and then Stephen stepped out from the driver's side.

She spun away so she wouldn't have to look at her "uncle." A moment or two later there was a knock at the door and Emily's body tensed. No one in her family moved and silence filled the house in the space of time it took for Stephen to knock again. Bryan must have knocked initially. It had been a polite knock; cordial even. The second knock had been loud and aggressive. Stephen had practically pounded on the door.

"Oh, for heaven's sake," said Emily's mom. She glowered at all of them. "What are we all scared of?"

Emily wasn't scared. She just had this terrible feeling building up inside her that made her want to explode.

Her mother crossed the room and opened the door.

"Finally," Emily heard Stephen say. "What took so long?"

"Dad," Bryan admonished.

"What?" Stephen snapped. "They knew we would be coming."

"Just come in," said her mom. Emily could tell from her mom's voice that she had lost her patience. And that was saying something because her mom liked everyone.

The three of them walked into the kitchen. Stephen strode in first. He scanned the room and then his eyes rested on Emily. His face gave nothing away, but his eyes were gloating.

Emily wanted nothing more than to knock that look off his face. But to do that she would have to go through…

Bryan.

Bryan stepped through after his father and the only thing that came to mind was how different he was. She hardly knew either of them except for their first impressions, but Stephen was serious, dour, and arrogant. Bryan was everything Emily wanted in a cousin. He was quick to smile, happy, and sympathetic. That could have been because he believed he was going to win and get Meihua, but Emily thought that he was happy to have a cousin. Emily was happy to have one too, but she had to bury that happiness. This cousin was here to fight her and try to take Meihua away from her.

There was a moment of everyone just staring at one another and then Aunt Elaine clapped her hands. "Right. Let's get started."

Everyone followed Aunt Elaine out of the kitchen and to the hallway. Neither Stephen nor Bryan were confused when Aunt Elaine stopped in front of the closet, and it didn't faze them when that closet door opened to show off a room bigger than the house.

They walked inside and Emily found that a mat had been laid out in the center of the room like usual, but this mat had a ring on it. The ring was about fifteen feet in diameter. Not a lot of room for movement there. They stopped right at the mat and Aunt Elaine turned to Emily. She held out her hand. "Meihua, please."

"Oh, right," said Emily.

Meihua had been quiet all morning. They had a short conversation the night before, and Meihua still refused to tell Emily who she was going to pick. The conversation had grown awkward, so they silently agreed not to talk at all. Now that it was time to take Meihua off, to maybe lose her, Emily found herself hesitant to do it. There were so many things she should have told Meihua. The silence had spoken volumes, but now she thought she had said too little.

I'm sorry, Meihua.

You have nothing to be sorry for, replied Meihua. *Good luck.*

Emily took a deep breath. She slipped the ring off her finger and the ring turned into a sword. Emily held the sword out for her aunt who took it in her right hand.

In that instant all the anxiety that had been coursing through her veins turned up to an eleven. The safety blanket that Meihua had provided her was gone now and she was feeling the full force of everything that was about to happen pressed down on her. She forced herself to breathe like her aunt and father had taught her. One breath after the other. She did her best to not think about what was going to happen and to instead focus on what was happening in the present moment.

Emily stood in front of her aunt, flanked by her parents. Bryan waited next to her with a few feet of separation. Stephen glowered on the far side of his son. Aunt Elaine held Meihua out in front of her with both hands. She eyed Bryan and then Emily.

"Bryan Lee has challenged Emily Lau to a duel for Meihua," she said. "The victor of this duel will not determine Meihua's guardian though. This is just a showcase. Meihua will still choose her own guardian. Is that understood?"

"Yes," said Bryan.

"Yeah," said Emily when her aunt turned to her.

"Good." Aunt Elaine gestured to the mat with her hand. "Get your gear on and get ready. Gloves and headgear."

Emily turned and walked to her left. She wanted her aunt with her, but Aunt Elaine was the judge now. She couldn't be with Emily in her corner. Instead, her parents walked with her and stood in silent vigil while Emily began rummaging through her bag. She pulled out her gloves and headgear. She was fishing for the little case that held her mouth guard when her dad stepped up beside her.

"Are you ready for this?" he asked.

"As ready as I'll ever be." She found the case and pulled it out. She set it down beside her and picked up her headgear. Emily pulled the foam helmet over her head and pulled her ponytail out of the back of it. She set the Velcro strap and tapped the sides of the helmet to make sure it fit.

Her dad held up the case with her mouthguard and Emily opened it. She pulled out the guard and slipped it in her mouth while her dad leaned down to be eye level with her. "Stephen was always a patient person. Cautious even. He taught his son how to fight so Bryan's going to be the same. You're the unknown here. He's going to come at you slowly to test you, got it?"

"Yeah," said Emily with a breathy voice. She had forgotten that her dad had lived this kind of life. That her dad was meant to inherit Meihua. He had grown up with Stephen. She stretched her fingers out and her dad grabbed her by the forearms to settle her. Their eyes met without flinching or blinking. He let go of her arms and held his fists out.

"You've got this," he said.

She slapped her fists down on his. "Yeah, I've got this."

Emily turned toward Bryan. He looked taller somehow. He had removed his hoodie to reveal a skintight shirt that Emily recognized from athletes in commercials. His whole body seemed to ripple when he moved. He flexed his fists and slammed them together much like Aunt Elaine had during training. It still sounded like thunder, but it was less threatening than her aunt's had been.

The kindness was gone. He might have been a cousin before but now his face was hardened with purpose. He stepped onto the mat and waited.

Emily's insides churned like a turbulent sea and she forced her eyes to look down at her own bare feet. She was inches away from the mat but couldn't bring herself to step onto it. She wiggled her toes and leaned back on her heels. She had the overwhelming urge to start running, moving, do anything to make it stop. Her mind was racing, showing her everything that could go wrong. Her body tensed and she was about to turn around when someone came up behind her and placed their hands gently on her shoulders. Her mom was standing behind her.

"Hey," she said. "Take a breath."

She inhaled glorious air and then breathed out normally.

"Good," said her mom. "Everything's going to be okay. This is just like all those other times you sparred. Just remember, the only way out is through."

"Right." There was no running from this. Emily would have liked to say that she steeled herself and the nerves just went away, but this wasn't like her books. Fear wouldn't disappear because Emily wanted it to. She closed her eyes and took a few grounding breaths. She clenched her toes against the cold concrete floor, took one more breath, and stepped onto the mat.

There was a change then. The mat was maybe a couple of inches thick, but she felt like she and Bryan towered over the other three people who were not on the mat. It was like they were raised on a pedestal. The lights above her were brighter than before. Like only the ring mattered and all the ground past it had crumbled. The light was heavy on her shoulders. She kept stepping forward, and each step made the next one easier.

She and Bryan met at the center of the ring where Aunt Elaine stood. Both Emily and Bryan turned and bowed to her.

"All right," said Aunt Elaine. "This duel will be decided by submission, being knocked out of the ring, or when I decide it is over. Got it?"

"Yes," said Bryan.

"Yeah," added Emily.

The two of them turned to one another. They bowed and took their stances. Bryan had stepped back with his right foot so his left faced forward. His right hand closed into a fist and he let it rest at his right hip. He raised his left fist, turned it so it was vertical, and pointed it at Emily. Emily stepped back with her right foot and put her hands up in the stance she was most comfortable in.

The two of them just stood there in perfect silence, statuesque except for their breathing. And then Bryan rushed forward.

Emily retreated a step in surprise but managed to stop herself after that one step. She couldn't run from this. She couldn't retreat. She had to fight. Emily launched herself forward and met Bryan head on.

She deflected his first punch and countered with her own. Surprise etched itself on his face at her counter, but his body moved independently of his surprise. He countered her counter and Emily moved to respond. They met each other in a flurry of strikes that surprised Emily too. It was like her body was moving on its own and she was actually keeping up, and that was when she slipped.

Bryan deflected one of Emily's punches, his arms snaked around hers, and he pulled her into a hold. Emily's panic rose again and she shifted her body sideways and kicked Bryan in the torso. The blow pushed her away and her arm slipped from Bryan's grasp.

They both stumbled back and took up defensive stances. Emily's breath was pounding in her lungs while Bryan didn't appear to be winded at all, despite the kick to the chest.

"Wow," said Bryan.

Emily furrowed her brow. "What?"

"You're better than I thought you'd be," said Bryan.

"What are you doing!" screamed Stephen. "Attack her!"

Bryan shot a disapproving look at his father, and when he turned back to Emily he was dejected. "Don't mind him. He's just really invested."

"I can tell," said Emily. And this time she attacked.

She came in fast with a palm strike aimed at Bryan's face. He hopped back slightly to avoid the blow, but Emily was hoping he was going to do that. She couldn't beat Bryan in an extended fight, so she was going to try to end this as quickly as possible. Emily stomped hard on the ground and pressed forward with her qi. She sped up in a burst and lowered her shoulder.

Emily collided with Bryan sending him stumbling back. He grabbed her by the waist and dug his heels into the mat. He slid back a few inches, but he stopped before Emily could move him far enough. He twisted his body and spun Emily to try and throw her, but she grabbed him by the forearms and held onto them like a vice grip. She came down hard and pulled at him, using the momentum from his own throw to try and throw him.

Bryan shifted his stance again with a little stutter step and Emily couldn't get him to budge. She was stuck in an awkward position where she tried to throw him, and it didn't work, so he took advantage. Bryan pulled Emily toward him and kicked her.

Emily tumbled backward but turned her fall into a roll so she was able to jump up just in time to meet Bryan's new rush. He came at her strike after strike, but Emily met each one of them head on. She deflected, blocked, and countered, but her breaths were getting heavier. Bryan, on the other hand, was speeding up. It was like his engine had just warmed up and his tempo was increasing. He was a metronome and each one of his strikes was a tick.

He pressed her and Emily was forced to give ground, until she realized she was getting closer and closer to the ring. The edge of the ring pressed against her like the precipice of a cliff. She met Bryan's charge head on and shoved him back. She hopped on her toes and tried to dash past Bryan, but he recovered and cut her off.

He came at her fast, but deliberately. Each move calculated to take something from her. Emily was just trying to survive, to show what martial arts she had learned, and Bryan was playing chess with her while striking. Emily was losing pieces every second and she couldn't even see the board. She kept giving ground, inch by inch, as Bryan herded her to the edge. She glanced over her shoulder and saw she was inches away. It was less than a second but when she turned back Bryan had launched a strike at her body. She moved but not in time and he scored a hit on her left cheek.

She was about to fall out of the ring, but she stomped her right foot down hard, willing it to be an anchor. Fear came up fresh in her mind, but she ignored it. This was no time for fear. This was a time to move, to act, to attack, and take what was hers.

She let out a cry from somewhere deep inside her belly and launched herself at Bryan. She came swinging with her right arm determined to knock his head gear off.

Wham! She connected! And then there was another impact and Emily's breath exploded out of her. She started to stumble back, but Bryan caught her. The blow forced her to hunch over just in time to witness Bryan's fist pulling away from her stomach. Panic erupted in her body and she started hyperventilating. She was struggling, grasping, and clawing for air with her lungs, but nothing was coming in. Her eyes began to water. She clutched her stomach. Bryan put his arm on her shoulder and clutched the back of her head with his hand, so she was forced to meet his eyes.

"You're okay, calm down," he said. "You got the wind knocked out of you. Just slow down, catch your breath."

"What are you doing!" yelled Stephen. "Finish her!"

Bryan turned his head toward his father and Emily saw the tail end of the face he made.

Disapproving.

But he turned back to Emily with sorrow in his eyes. "Sorry about this."

He moved his hand from her head to her shoulder and started to gently usher her out of the ring.

NO! screamed Emily. Or she tried but only a choking sound came out. She dug her heels in and pushed against Bryan, but with no breath to back her up, she was like a child throwing a tantrum.

But she fought anyway. She threw punch after punch at his head, but his arms came up in an instant protecting him from the worst of it. She switched to body shots and hit him in his torso as hard as she could. She finally managed to catch a breath and hit him hard in the stomach. He grunted and his body jolted. She tried to rip herself from his grasp, but he swept his leg out low, sweeping one of her feet up. She clawed at him and clung to him as she fell but he kept his balance. He leaned over and dropped Emily gently on to the mat. Outside of the ring.

There was deafening silence, and then there was Aunt Elaine.

"The duel is over. Bryan Lee is the winner."

Chapter 14

The Aftermath

SILENCE.

It was the moment after thunder. That space of time where everything just waits in awe and fear of what nature has wrought, of what was coming next. Then there was movement.

Her parents started moving toward her, and Stephen was cheering like a yapping dog. She sat up and didn't move. She wasn't sure what to do. All she felt was this bottomless pit of just... emptiness. A void had been carved out of her soul. And then she started to feel again. A profound sadness she had scarcely felt before. There were only a few times in her life when she had felt like this. When she was a child, and her aunt would leave without saying when she would be back. When the lion died in a stampede of wildebeest and his son was forced to run. When Allison turned her back on Emily and walked away. The sadness changed and shame and anger rolled over her like waves on rocks. A hand appeared in front of her, and she raised her head. Bryan was standing over her.

"That was a great duel," he said.

She ignored his hand and got up on her own. She bowed to Bryan and he returned the gesture with worry on his face. No, not worry. Hurt. The pain etched on his face sent new waves of shame cascading over her. She ignored that too and turned toward her parents just as Stephen walked past her and put an arm around his son.

"Well done," Stephen said. "The sword is ours!"

"I'm sorry," said Emily when her parents came up and hugged her. Tears welled up in her eyes. "I couldn't win."

"Don't be sorry," said her mom. She squeezed Emily tight. "We're so proud of you."

"So proud," repeated her dad. "You did so well. I had no idea you could fight like that. You must have trained so hard."

"Emily, Bryan," called out Aunt Elaine. Everyone turned to face her. She was standing at the center of the ring holding Meihua out in front of her like some sort of offering. "Come here please."

Bryan stepped away from his father and walked toward Aunt Elaine. Emily slid out of her parents' embrace to join him. They stood side-by-side in front of Aunt Elaine. She had to muster up enough strength to look up.

"Bryan won the duel," said Aunt Elaine. "And now it's time to see if Meihua has chosen him." She offered the sword to him. "Try to draw her."

Bryan stepped forward and took the sword from Aunt Elaine.

In that moment Emily's life flashed before her eyes. Not what had happened, but what could have been and what she could do now. The life of adventure that had been promised to her was gone. She knew her aunt would continue to train her if that was what Emily wanted. She couldn't go back to it though, not anymore, it was too painful. She had been promised her dreams turned reality, and now that promise was broken.

But she could find some solace in the fact that there would be no more lies with Allison. No more training to get in the way. She could go back to the way things had been. To normal. And that didn't sound so bad to her.

Bryan turned Meihua over in his hands and studied her for a little while. The same urge that had coursed through Emily's veins when her mom tried to draw Meihua that first night welled up inside her. She wanted to cry out, to attack, to pry the sword out of Bryan's hands and run away with her. But she couldn't. She had lost, and this was the result.

He turned to his father and Emily glanced over her shoulder. Stephen was smiling at his son, pride plastered on his face, and there was this hungry, almost desperate, gleam in his eyes. He nodded to Bryan, and Emily thought that this might just be the happiest day of her "uncle's" life. And the worst day of hers.

She turned back to Bryan. He lifted the sword up, so it was horizontal and just below his face. He grabbed the handle with his right hand, took a deep breath, and pulled.

Meihua didn't budge.

He pulled once more, twice more, but still nothing. Then he shrugged and offered the sword to Emily.

Emily reached out slowly, as if Meihua was made of smoke and might disappear at her touch. Her hand stretched forward, and she noticed it was shaking. She took Meihua. The solidness of the hilt, the weight. It was just right. She grabbed the sheath with her other hand, took her own deep breath, and pulled.

Meihua slid free from her sheathe and rang out in the air.

She watched the smile form on her face in the reflection of the blade. "Welcome back," she whispered low enough just for her and Meihua.

Glad to be back, said Meihua.

And then chaos broke loose. Stephen let out a guttural howl, a frantic and somehow wordless outburst that made everyone in the room look at him. He yelled, practically screamed, and advanced quickly toward Aunt Elaine. He spouted sounds more than words, and Emily expected he was trying to talk, but he was in such disbelief that he couldn't articulate. Emily sheathed Meihua and stepped back so she could get away from his tirade.

She collapsed on the mat and set the sword down beside her. Then, as if there was nothing else in the world to do, Emily leaned back on her hands and watched while her parents, aunt, and Stephen talked. An impish grin grew on her face as Stephen turned a particularly bright shade of red. He was starting to resemble a pink Skittle.

"Mind if I join you?" Bryan collapsed onto the mat next to her and watched his father. "Sorry about him. I guess he's a bit broken up about it."

"And you're not?"

He took his gloves off and tossed them aside. "Not really." He tilted his head toward Emily and shrugged. "I didn't really care all that much."

"Why did you do it then?" she asked. "I mean, it would have saved me a lot of trouble."

Bryan chuckled, more a pity laugh than anything. "I did it for my dad. He was pretty... uh... pissed off when Aunt Elaine came by and said she was going to give the sword to you. He said it wasn't right. He said you didn't even know about the world we live in. He said I was the clear choice. I had been trained by him, by her. I'd been around Meihua my entire life."

He scratched his head. "Aunt Elaine told him no again, so he went and started researching ways to overturn her decision. He talked me into challenging you. I mean I kind of had to do it. He's my dad. Plus, I knew Meihua wouldn't pick me."

"How?" asked Emily.

The argument had gotten louder by now and they were all making aggressive hand gestures in the air.

"I didn't really want Meihua," said Bryan.

"What? Why not?"

He shrugged. "I mean, Meihua was around me. All the reasons my dad said it should have been me, Aunt Elaine and Meihua had to know them too. If Aunt Elaine wanted to pick me, I figure she would have actually picked me. But they both picked you. And I told my dad that, but he wouldn't listen. He really started to act weird about it. Like I *had* to fight you and I *had* to get the sword. He got a little obsessive about it."

Emily snorted. "Yeah, I can tell."

Bryan gave Emily another apologetic face. "So, how long have you been training?"

"Just a few weeks, maybe a month." Bryan gave her a deadpan look and she added, "What?"

"You're joking, right?"

"Well, I've taken karate all my life," said Emily. "My dad

signed me up at a local dojo. But I've only been training with Aunt Elaine for a little while."

"And your dad didn't teach you anything?" he asked.

"No," said Emily with a laugh.

"Why are you laughing?"

Emily opened her mouth to answer but stopped herself. She was confused by the seriousness in Bryan's voice. She turned to study her dad who was glaring daggers at Stephen. His arms were crossed, and Emily took this time to really study him. He was definitely in shape, but she had never thought of him as a fighter. He had taught her how to play basketball, watched Laker games with her, and had been there for every one of her competitions. His competitive edge, however, fell short at actually participating. She had never even seen him play basketball competitively, and he had never shown a love for martial arts. In her head there was no way her dad had a dangerous side.

"I don't know," admitted Emily. "He never really took part in my lessons. He was supportive, watched some of my lessons, but that was it."

"Huh," said Bryan. He turned to Emily's dad and frowned. "That's weird."

"What is?" asked Emily.

"Well, my dad talked about your dad like he was the greatest fighter he's ever seen," said Bryan. "I mean they grew up together. I think my dad kind of looked up to your dad. And he was a little jealous. I think he always felt like he was the odd man out. I mean your grandpa was Meihua's guardian, and everyone knew your dad was going to be chosen. Until Meihua picked your aunt, that is. Your dad was that good I guess."

"That's what they told me," said Emily. "But I guess I didn't believe it. Sometimes you have to see something to believe it, you know?"

"Yeah," said Bryan. "Don't worry about my dad. He'll get over it eventually. He doesn't have a choice anymore, actually. Maybe now he'll finally let this all go. Move on."

"I don't know." Emily bobbed her head in his direction. "He doesn't look like he's going to let it go."

Bryan waved his hand at his dad like he was dismissing him entirely. "Like I said, he'll get over it." He leaned back until he was resting on the ground and crossed his hands behind his head. "I'm already over it."

Emily and Bryan sat on the floor talking to one another for another fifteen minutes before her parents and Aunt Elaine had managed to calm Stephen down. They had made their way back to the house where Stephen spent an inordinate amount of time pleading his case again. Mom had extricated herself from the argument that was going on in the living room and had started making lunch. The two actual combatants were sitting at the kitchen island eating turkey sandwiches.

"If you need someone to spar or train with, I'd be happy to help," Bryan said suddenly.

"Seriously?" She put down the glass of water she had just picked up because she didn't believe what she heard.

"Yeah," replied Bryan. "I mean, I don't know how Uncle Chris and Aunt Elaine train you, but I think it'd be fun."

"Uncle Chris?" repeated Emily.

"Well, he is my uncle, right?"

"Not really. More like a second cousin or something."

"It's an Asian thing," added Bryan. "Anyone who's older

than you that isn't your parent or grandparent is an aunt or uncle. You know what I mean."

"I guess," said Emily. "I don't really know any of my family."

"Well, you know me now." He pushed the plate in front of him and gestured toward her phone. "Let me give you my number. That way if you ever need someone to talk to you can always call or text me. We don't have to just train. We can just hang out."

"Are you staying in town?" asked Emily.

"For a while I think," he replied. "We didn't really make a lot of plans. My dad rented a house. I think he thought I would have the sword."

Emily's eyes narrowed on Stephen and she thought back to what Bryan had said earlier. "I don't have to call him Uncle Stephen, do I?"

Bryan laughed. "No. I don't think he'd want you to, either."

"So, why'd you pick me?" asked Emily.

She was finally alone in the solace of her room. She had closed the door when she came in and locked it. Now Emily was lying on her bed and letting gravity bear down on her. She spoke the words to the empty room and let them linger in the air while she waited for the answer that was coming.

Why wouldn't I?

Emily shrugged, then felt weird for shrugging to nothing. "Bryan was better than me. He actually won the fight."

He won the duel, came Meihua's reply. *But you don't win*

my loyalty just because you win a fight. You can't win a person. They make a choice.

"And winning a fight doesn't mean you earned something?" asked Emily.

No. Meihua's voice was ice in Emily's mind and chills shivered up her arms. *Martial arts isn't about winning fights. Martial arts reveals character. It tells you what a person is like. Winning a duel means that at that exact moment, you were a better fighter than someone. It doesn't mean you're a better person.*

Emily let the words resonate in her and swirled them around in the confines of her head. She hadn't expected Meihua to be so grand in her thought process. She was a little embarrassed too. She liked to think she was a good person, but a good person didn't think they were a good person. They just were.

"So why me?" she asked again.

Silence. The awkward kind. Emily followed a single fan blade on her ceiling fan spin round and round. She traced lines with her eyes. She cleared her throat. She waited.

You were your aunt's choice, said Meihua. Her voice was soft. *I saw you when she saw you. I saw how you were raised. I saw how you grew up. I saw you when you thought no one was watching. You were always going to inherit me. The only question was when.*

"Thank you," whispered Emily. "I hope I live up to your expectations. Both of yours."

You don't have to live up to anyone, said Meihua. *Don't live for someone else. Live for yourself. Be great because you choose to be.*

Another question burned inside her, but she wasn't sure she should ask it.

What is it, Emily?

Of course, Meihua could sense it. She could basically read Emily's mind. She had no reason to hold it back now.

"Why didn't you pick my dad?"

What do you mean?

"Everyone said that *yeye* was going to pick my dad. But then you picked Aunt Elaine. What happened? Was he not your pick?"

Meihua was quiet and Emily could feel her thinking. It was a peculiar feeling. Like when she was on the phone and the person on the other end went quiet to think about their answer. There was this silence that she could feel.

He was, said Meihua finally. *But that changed after your grandpa was hurt. I could see the hatred in your dad's eyes. All the rage and anger. I knew if I went to him then he would use me to do something unforgivable. I couldn't let him do that. Not to me, and not to him.*

"So, you chose my aunt to save my dad?" asked Emily.

Yes, said Meihua. *To keep him from going down a dark path. To save him from himself.*

CHAPTER 15

BETTER TODAY
THAN YESTERDAY

A WEEK PASSED and Emily found herself walking to her locker on Friday with the feeling that she wasn't alone. Of course, she wasn't literally alone. She was surrounded by hundreds of other students and classmates, and she had her parents and aunt, and she had Meihua. But there was more. She had a *cousin*. She had an uncle, too, and she wasn't so sure about that, but she had family. Someone who actually cared about her wellbeing and wanted to be her cousin. It was a happy feeling. She had been happy before and it's not like she had been particularly unhappy since she was given a magic sword, but the secrets she had to keep had forged a gap between her and her friends. So now, with Bryan at least on her side, Emily was fulfilled in a way she hadn't been before.

She was smiling at her feet when she got close to her locker. She raised her head and froze like a deer caught in headlights. Allison was standing at her locker, just as frozen as Emily. She shut her locker quickly, picked up her bag, muttered something that sounded like "sorry," and started to walk away.

"Wait!" cried Emily.

Allison stopped mid step and slowly turned to face Emily. Lost in all the training and preparation for the duel was that Emily had gone almost three weeks without talking to her best friend. They had avoided each other at their lockers, had sat close to one another at lunch, but still apart, and that separation had grown with each passing day. She hated it. Allison waited.

"Yeah?" she finally said.

She wasn't sure what to say. So much had changed now and their argument felt like it had been a lifetime ago. And then finally, Emily said, "I hate this!"

"What?" said Allison.

"I hate this," Emily repeated. "You and me not talking. I have so much to tell you. So much I want to tell you."

Tears were welling up in her best friend's eyes. "Me too."

"Can we hang out?" Emily asked. "Like tonight?"

"I can't tonight," said Allison, pain in her voice. "I have to sing the national anthem at the basketball game."

"I'll be there," said Emily. "Then you can come over after?"

"I'll ask my parents," she said between sniffs. "But yes."

"I need a break," said Emily after she blocked a punch from her aunt.

"A break?" Aunt Elaine pulled her arm back and aimed a kick at Emily's forehead. Emily deftly jumped back to dodge and landed in a crouch.

"Yeah, a break," said Emily. "The duel's over. Meihua is mine. I think I deserve a break."

"Oh?" said Aunt Elaine. Her aunt rushed forward and threw a new series of strikes at Emily that she either deflected or dodged. "And what would you do on this break?"

Emily hopped back again and then came in with her own attack pattern that Meihua had shown her. "I would go see a basketball game tonight. Allison is singing the national anthem. Then after that she's coming over."

"You already invited her over?" asked Aunt Elaine. She caught one of Emily's punches and pulled her off balance. She tried to trip Emily, but Emily dove into a roll to dodge it.

"Yup," she replied. "Mom and Dad said yes already. You're the only one left to convince."

She was about to launch herself into another attack, but Aunt Elaine held up a hand to stop her. "And you think you deserve a break?"

"Yes," said Emily.

"Really?" asked Aunt Elaine. "Tell me. How did you feel when you lost the duel to Bryan?"

Emily thought back to the duel. She remembered the pit, the shame, the anger, and the triumph on Stephen's face. "Angry. Sad."

"Yeah, those are pretty much what everyone feels when they lose," said Aunt Elaine. "Are you okay with feeling that way?"

"No," said Emily.

"Good," said Aunt Elaine. "No one likes losing. What's your favorite sport?"

"Basketball," said Emily.

"Favorite team?"

"Lakers."

"Of course," said Aunt Elaine. "Favorite player?"

"Kobe," said Emily like it was the stupidest question in the world.

"Kobe Bryant," said Aunt Elaine. "Do you think he took breaks after a loss?"

"No," replied Emily. Of course, he wouldn't. He would probably be training the same day.

"This isn't a game, Emily," said Aunt Elaine. "You have to really want this. The world you're entering is dangerous. You just don't know it yet. You have to always want to improve. Be the best version of yourself. Try to be better today than you were yesterday. Do you think you can handle that?"

"Yes," said Emily.

"Do you still want a break?" asked her aunt.

"Yes," replied Emily. "I want to see Allison sing tonight. And hang out with her."

Her aunt held up a hand and gestured for Emily to come at her. "Convince me you deserve one then."

An hour later Emily found herself walking into her high school's gym. Her body was tired and sore, but she was there. The Foothill cheerleaders were seated in a large group that took up multiple rows of bleachers. The boys' basketball team was split into lines in the middle of a layup drill while the opposing team did the same thing but were shooting jump shots. The band was seated at the far end of the gym in the top row. They were all warming up individually, so it sounded like a riled-up aviary at a zoo.

Emily walked between the bottom row of bleachers and the sideline of the court. She stopped at the first set of stairs and started searching for Allison, but neither her nor her parents were in sight. She started to survey the rest of the gym to find her when Meihua spoke.

There. On the left. Far side of the court, said Meihua.

Emily focused on where Meihua had indicated. Allison was waving at her from beside the scorer's table. She was holding a mic in her hand and pointed at it before she pointed up at the clock. Emily turned. The scoreboard was lit up on the wall and the countdown had less than a minute left before the horn would blare and the game would start. She sat down in the first row of the bleachers and made a movement with her hands that she hoped indicated that she would wait for Allison there.

"Thanks for your help," said Emily.

You're welcome, said Meihua.

"How'd you know where she was?"

I see what you see, said Meihua. *I just notice more than you. I saw her on the way in and knew where she was.*

"Neat trick," said Emily. "Can you help me on my math test?"

No, that would be cheating, said Meihua. *Also, I hate math.*

Emily snorted and started to laugh, drawing the attention of some people standing near her. Color rushed to her cheeks and she cleared her throat before sinking into herself. "So, I'm not the first person to try and get you to do math?"

No, said Meihua. *I see you when you do it and it's like a foreign language to me.*

"Me too."

The horn blared and both teams walked to their benches. The cheerleaders lined up at the baseline facing the wall with the flag on it.

"Ladies and gentlemen, welcome to Foothill High for tonight's game featuring the Tillers of Tustin High School and your Foothill Knights." There was a smattering of applause from the crowd. The announcer introduced both teams and then they all lined up on the court.

"Now, please rise for the singing of our national anthem, sung tonight by Allison Walker."

Emily stood with everyone else and put her right hand over her heart. Her best friend stepped out onto the court with the microphone in her hand. She closed her eyes, took a breath, and then brought the mic to her mouth.

"*Oh say, can you see…* "

Allison gave the mic back to someone at the table and started power walking past the Foothill bench. People applauded and she sort of waved and mouthed her thanks. Allison turned and there was an awkward, uncomfortable smile on her face. Allison didn't really like being the recipient of praise. She usually just froze when people complimented her. Her walk had become rigid after she passed a trio of cheerleaders so Emily guessed they must have said something to her. She sped up her walk and Emily stood up to meet her best friend as she arrived.

"Hey," said Emily.

"Hey," replied Allison. "Let's not sit this close."

Emily followed Allison up the wooden steps and then leaned back against the bleachers. She did her best to get comfortable, but there are just some things that can't be done.

"Good job by the way," said Emily.

"Thanks," said Allison. "I thought I messed up a bit."

"I didn't notice it. Don't think anyone else did either. I mean they cheered louder for you than they did the starting line ups."

"I heard," Allison said with a cringe.

"Why do you sing if you don't like being told how good you are?"

"Do you do karate so other people know how good a fighter you are?"

"No," said Emily. This conversation was starting to sound familiar. She could imagine Meihua smirking at Emily saying "*I told you so*" in her head.

"I sing for me," said Allison. "I do it because it makes me happy. Because I feel like I can express myself through singing. And because I have fun doing it."

I like her, said Meihua.

Allison turned to Emily and nudged her with her elbow. "So, what's new with you?"

"Lots," said Emily. "Remember the cousin I told you about?" Allison nodded. "Totally cool. Turns out he and his considerably-less-cool dad are sticking around for a while. He wants to actually be my cousin."

"What's with all your family visiting all of a sudden?"

"I don't know," lied Emily. "It's nice though. Having family around."

"Yeah, my cousins are all pretty cool too," said Allison. Her voice trailed off at the end and her eyes were gazing into the distance. Emily turned. Jeremy had just walked into the gym with a couple friends. He waved at Allison and she waved back.

"So," said Emily with inflection.

"What?" asked Allison.

Emily gestured toward Jeremy with her head while he was turned away. "What's going on with him?"

"Nothing," said Allison. She focused her attention on the court, but she couldn't hide the color rising to her cheeks.

"Uh huh," said Emily. "He tried to talk to me about you."

"What?" Her head spun back to Emily so fast that Emily got whiplash. "When?"

"Two weeks ago or so," said Emily. "Like right after our…"

"Oh," said Allison. "I'm really sorry—"

Emily bumped Allison with her shoulder. "Stop. You don't have to be. You're sorry. I'm sorry. Let's just stop being sorry and just be us, okay?"

"Okay."

"Great, now do we really have to stay for the game?"

CHAPTER 16

THE NIGHT
THINGS CHANGED

E MILY AND ALLISON left the game when they realized
they didn't really care who won and cared more about
spending time together. They opted to go to Emily's
house and just relax. They had no idea what they were going
to do. They might watch a movie, or Emily might play a
game while Allison watched. Maybe they'd watch one of their
favorite streamers. They just wanted to spend time together,
and the possibilities were endless.

They crossed through the parking lot under trees that
had been there long before they were born. Streetlights illuminated the parking lot, so they weren't walking in complete
darkness. And even then, the moon was shining high above
them, basking them in a soft light.

Emily looked up at the moon between the trees and the
leaves and thought of how lucky she was. She had a loving
family, a cousin who actually cared about her, and now she had

her best friend back. Emily rested her hands on the back of her head while she walked. She stood close to Allison because she would warn Emily if she was about to walk into anything.

They lived in the city so starlight didn't show as well as it might have if they lived in the country, but specks of stars still made themselves known in the night sky. They were like tiny gemstones in dark purple and blue velvet.

"What are you looking at?" asked Allison.

"The stars," replied Emily. "You can actually see them a little tonight."

Allison tilted her head back. "Yeah, you can."

"Makes you think, doesn't it?"

"About what?" asked Allison.

Emily thought for a second and then just shrugged. "All the things I'm thankful for. Things that make me happy."

She took a deep breath of cold night air and the two of them walked in silence until they made it to the street. They walked on the sidewalk alongside a fence with the high school track on the other side. The track was made of dirt and once a month they had to run the mile on it. Luckily, Allison was in her P.E. class and they just walked the entire mile. She wasn't sure how they managed to take a full class period to walk one mile, but they did it. It was like magic.

"So, how are rehearsals going?" asked Emily.

"Good!" declared Allison. "I really like the theater it's going to be at."

"It's not going to be at the multi-purpose room?" Emily kicked a stone on the sidewalk out of the way and into the street.

"No, it's going to be at this theater at Beckman."

"Oh, that's a really nice school."

"Yeah," replied Allison. "It's like an actual theater."

"I can't wait to see it."

"You're going to come?" asked Allison. The pitch of her voice was questioning, unsure, and a little embarrassed. "You've just been so busy lately."

"I know," admitted Emily. "But I promise you I will come see your show. I haven't missed any yet, have I?"

"No," said Allison.

"And I won't start now," said Emily.

They were silent then, taking in the crisp night air and enjoying the feeling of being with one another, with nothing but friendship to worry about. Emily took a deep breath and closed her eyes so she could fully appreciate the moment. It felt nice that she wasn't alone in the universe. That there were people who cared about her and wanted to spend time with her. It was at that moment that she believed in her bones that everything would be okay.

And then the bushes in front of them shook.

Emily and Allison screamed, and it broke the silence like a dropped glass in a crowded room. A dog stepped out of the brush and stared them down. Emily and Allison froze, clutching each other. The dog stood ten feet away on the sidewalk. At least, Emily thought it was a dog. Its ears were pointier, and its tail was bushy. It was roughly two feet tall and longer than she expected a dog to be. It had tawny fur mixed with gray that Emily could just barely make out in the streetlight.

"Just a stray?" whispered Allison.

"I think it's a coyote actually," said Emily.

The coyote yelped at them. It was a throaty, high-pitched yowl that made both Emily and Allison jump and scream again.

"What do we do?" asked Allison.

"I mean it's more scared of us than we are of it, right?" said Emily.

"I don't know about that," said Allison with a shaky voice.

Maintain eye contact, said Meihua suddenly. Emily jumped a little again and Allison did too.

"What was that?" asked Allison.

"Sorry," said Emily.

Don't turn your back on it. Don't run. Try yelling at it to scare it off.

"Okay, we're going to yell at it," said Emily. "Together."

"Will that work?"

"It should."

"We just screamed at it."

"I know, but let's try again. On three."

"OK."

"One, two—"

"You should run," said the coyote in a heavy, gravelly voice.

Emily and Allison froze. They turned to one another in disbelief. The coyote let out a growl that sounded like distant thunder and forced their attention back to it. It took a step forward and its claws scraped against the concrete. Its golden yellow eyes began to glow in the night. The coyote's body shuddered, and then impossibly, it began to grow. It grew and grew until it was the size of a horse. It scowled down at the two of them with malice in its golden eyes and let out another howl.

The high-pitched yowl from before was replaced by something far deeper and primal. Emily's body jolted from the weight of it. The coyote fixed its glowing eyes on Emily and hot breath poured out of its maw as fog. The coyote snarled and its lips pulled back to reveal fleshy gums and a row of sharp teeth.

Allison stumbled back and fell. "What the hell is that?" she asked in a panicked whisper.

Emily didn't turn to face Allison. She didn't dare. All her teachers had told her to avoid fights. To only fight as a last resort. And Emily had only learned how to fight against a person. She had no idea what to do against this, against a monster.

It took a small step forward and Emily stepped back on reflex. Her hands shook when it took another step. The coyote's lip curled up, baring its teeth even more, and Emily heard a whimper from behind her.

And that was when Emily realized she couldn't run. Allison couldn't protect herself. Emily could, somewhat. And she had a magic sword. She was Allison's only chance to escape. She balled her hands into fists hoping they would stop shaking. They didn't.

"Meihua," said Emily and she was ashamed that her voice was quivering even with Meihua's protection.

I am here, came Meihua's reply. *I am with you.*

"Allison, run to my house," said Emily.

"What?" asked Allison.

"I need you to stand up and run to my house. I'll keep it distracted."

"What are you talking about?" spat Allison. Emily heard the fear in Allison's voice. Allison clutched at Emily's arm and tried to pull her away. Emily ripped herself free of her friend's grip and held her hand out. Light flashed and the ring on her finger changed into a sword.

She glanced over her shoulder at Allison who was gaping at her.

"Go!" said Emily with all the force that she could muster. Her voice was hard with an edge as sharp as Meihua's. It broke Allison from her reverie. Emily leveled her best friend with the most reassuring gaze that she could muster, even though she wasn't sure about any of it. "I'll be right behind you."

Allison stared at Emily in disbelief, but she turned and started running. The coyote watched Allison go and Emily swore it was smiling as it spoke again. "I love it when they run."

"Hey!" yelled Emily.

The coyote whipped its head back to Emily and she pointed the sword at it. It was the first time she had taken the sword out with the intention to actually use it. She had never learned how to use a sword. She wished her hands would stop shaking. Her mind raced with fleeting ideas of everything that could go wrong, but then she remembered that Allison was running for her life. "Meihua, help me."

Always.

The coyote's eyes flashed with murder and it lunged forward with its jaws spread wide. Emily slipped control to Meihua and her body reacted as soon as the monster moved. She thrust the sword out and up into the coyote's mouth. Resistance pressed against her arm and then the sword pierced through flesh. The coyote reared back and howled in pain. The howl crashed into Emily's ears and she stumbled back from the sheer volume of it.

You have to move, Emily! screamed Meihua.

She spun on her feet and sprinted past the coyote.

The howls stopped and the coyote lunged at Emily as she dove by. Her body became lighter, and she practically flew past it. She glanced behind her. The coyote was charging after her. Bloody saliva flailed out of its mouth as it ran and panted. Claws tore into the street, ripping up concrete in the chase. Emily sprinted toward the closing gate of her neighborhood. Allison was on the other side of the gate watching Emily.

"GO!" screamed Emily. She ran as fast as she could toward the gate, but it was going to close before she could get to it.

Jump! yelled Meihua.

Emily did as she was told and jumped. She soared higher than should have been possible for her and jumped clear over the fence. She landed in a roll and Allison pulled her to her feet. They both started sprinting toward Emily's house.

A heavy crash behind her told her that the coyote had jumped over the fence as well. They weren't close to her house yet, so Emily pushed Allison forward and spun on her heels to face the monster head on.

"Go!" yelled Emily again.

The coyote dove at her and lashed out with tooth and claw. Emily jumped to the side while it was still in midair and then lunged towards its hindquarters while it landed. She thrust the sword deep into the coyote's leg. The blade slipped through and the monster howled out in pain.

The coyote snapped its jaws at Emily, but she had already jumped back. As soon as she landed, she lunged forward and kicked the coyote under its lower jaw, snapping it shut. Her leg rattled with the impact and pain exploded in her toes. And then as quickly as the pain came, it was gone. She silently thanked Meihua for existing.

The coyote shook its head and lunged forward. It swiped a massive paw at Emily who tried to dodge, but her legs wouldn't move like she wanted them to. Fatigue was already starting to settle in. Meihua moved Emily into the attack. The claws were behind her, but the paw collided with her body and sent her tumbling across the street.

Her skin burned where it scraped across the concrete. Pain flared in her head and something trickled down her temple. Emily wiped at it with the back of her hand. Blood, her blood, smeared across her hand when she pulled it back. Her head spun and her stomach turned as the blood slid down her hand and onto her forearm.

The coyote stalked toward her in deliberate steps. Emily was screaming at her body to move and she knew that Meihua was trying to force her body to move too, but it just wouldn't respond. Her legs wobbled and then the rest of her body started to shake. The coyote licked its lips and let out a low growl that sounded like rocks rolling down a hill.

Emily stabbed the sword down and used it to push herself up. The coyote stopped and watched her. Emily lifted the sword up slowly and held it out in front of her, tears streaking down her face, intermingled with blood. All her lessons with her aunt and dad had taught her how to react, how to fight, but nothing had prepared her for this. What use was martial arts against this?

"EMILY!" someone screamed.

Both Emily and the monstrous coyote veered their heads toward the sound. Aunt Elaine was sprinting toward them carrying a long bo staff in her right hand. She jumped and launched herself at the coyote. She soared through the air and the monster leapt back from her lunging attack. The staff connected with the ground and punched through. Aunt Elaine lifted the staff up and tore out chunks of concrete. She stepped between Emily and the coyote.

"Are you all right?" she asked.

"Yes," croaked Emily.

"Stay behind me," her aunt said.

Aunt Elaine charged forward with the staff. The coyote lunged toward her and they met each other in a fury of attacks. The monster tore at Aunt Elaine but she dodged with ease. She used the staff to knock the monster off its path and to thrust at its body. It stumbled back from each impact, but it didn't deter the monster.

She watched her aunt move like a graceful cat. She wasted no energy, moving only enough to make sure she wouldn't get hit. Every move brought her some sort of advantage, and Emily was watching her so intently that she started noticing that the coyote's violent attacks were getting closer.

Sweat glistened off her aunt's skin, and her body heaved with heavy, labored breaths. Her movements became more ragged, and dodges became near misses. The monster must have realized it too because it began to press its attacks even more. There was a feral gleam in its eyes, as it realized it was beginning to win. It was the intense gaze of a predator wearing down its prey.

The coyote snapped its jaws at Aunt Elaine, and she jumped back just in time, but she doubled over suddenly. She clutched at her abdomen like she had been stabbed and then coughed. It was a dry heave and her body wracked with the weight of it. The coyote didn't let its opportunity slip and lunged forward.

Emily started moving the second her aunt doubled over. Something inside her tore open and she charged forward with Meihua. The coyote's eye swiveled toward Emily and she saw her own reflection in its golden eye. The sword dipped forward and pierced through the eye with a sickening crunch. The coyote howled in pain and started shaking its head wildly. Emily refused to let go of the sword, but the coyote's thrashing dislodged it and Emily was sent tumbling. She toppled onto the ground next to her aunt.

The sound of footsteps from behind made Emily turn. New light poured over them as two people carrying flashlights came running into view.

"Emily?" yelled her dad. "Elaine?"

The coyote growled again and swept its eyes from Emily to her aunt to the two newcomers. Then, deciding against attacking, the coyote turned and ran away into the cold night.

CHAPTER 17

CALLS FOR HELP

"I NEED MY PHONE!" yelled Aunt Elaine as the four Laus burst into the house.

Her dad carried Emily straight into the living room. Aunt Elaine hobbled in, despite no obvious injury and Emily's mom brought up the rear and shut the door behind them. Allison was standing in a corner, face white as snow, with her hands covering her mouth.

"Oh my God! Emily! Is she okay?" screamed Allison.

Aunt Elaine brushed past Allison and started throwing things around the room. Books, cushions, anything that her phone could have been under, Emily guessed. "Where is my phone?"

"I'll call it," said Mom.

Emily didn't understand why her aunt wanted a phone. She was pretty sure she needed a hospital, considering she couldn't move.

That's me, said Meihua. *I'm not letting go of you until your aunt says so.*

Her dad lay Emily on the couch and she could move her eyes and head, but she felt so weak.

I had to do a lot of things we haven't practiced yet, said Meihua. *Use qi in new ways. Your body isn't used to it. If I let go now, you're going to be in a lot of pain.*

Is there any way you can let me move? asked Emily in her head.

Yes, said Meihua. *But you can't move too much. Try not to move at all if you can help it.*

Emily was suddenly more aware of her limbs. She could wiggle her fingers and toes, but that was about it. There was a heavy weight on her body when she tried to lift her arms and legs, like she was buried in sand. Her body was exhausted. She would have bet that she could have fallen asleep right then and there if not for all the noise and movement going on around her. Something rang under her and her dad reached between two cushions and pulled out a phone.

"Here it is."

Aunt Elaine snatched it from him and called someone. There was a brief pause and then Aunt Elaine spun toward Emily.

"Henry, I need you now," she said. There was another slight pause where Emily assumed Henry was talking. "Henry, this is an emergency. My niece and her friend were attacked by a monster. My niece used too much qi." Another pause and then Aunt Elaine gave Henry their address before hanging up the phone.

"Jessica, a man will be here in a couple of minutes to help. He'll need hot water in a kettle. Best to make a lot."

"On it," said Emily's mom and she disappeared into the kitchen.

"Why isn't she moving?" asked Allison. Emily raised her head. Allison breathed a sigh of relief when Emily moved, and she tried to give Allison some sort of sign that she was all right but she barely mustered a smile. "What's wrong with her? What happened?"

"Allison," said Aunt Elaine.

Allison jumped but Aunt Elaine caught her attention. "Everything's going to be fine. Can you go help in the kitchen?"

Allison had an unconvinced expression on her face but disappeared from the room.

Emily's dad was kneeling next to Emily holding her hand. He rested a hand on her head. "Is she going to be okay?" Emily squeezed his hand to affirm for him. "She's burning up."

"Meihua probably took control," said Aunt Elaine. "Had to do things Emily couldn't do on her own. She hasn't given control back because if she does things will get worse. She'll be fine."

Her aunt turned away and made another call. "Stephen. Emily was just attacked. I don't know where it started, but it ended outside the house. Can you try to track it?" A pause. "Thank you. Be careful. It was big and mean."

She hung up the phone and directed her attention to Emily. There was pain and worry and Emily thought there were tears at the corners of her aunt's eyes. Then there was a knock at the door.

"I've got it," said Aunt Elaine. She practically sprinted to the door and opened it in a hurry. "Henry!" Her voice sounded relieved. "Thanks for coming so fast."

"Where is she?" a man asked.

"This way, in the living room."

There were hurried but light footfalls, and then a stranger came into view.

Henry was not what she had expected. He was an elderly man with graying hair that still had a little color to it. He had a pair of thin-framed, rectangular glasses. He was carrying a brown doctor's bag. It was old and reminded Emily of something Mary Poppins would carry. And then he was wearing pajamas. Flannel pajamas. He had a tartan robe over the pajamas and bedroom slippers to complete the ensemble.

"Here she is," said Aunt Elaine.

Aunt Elaine gestured to Emily and the man crossed the room. He sat down on the coffee table and began to study Emily carefully. Now that he was closer Emily could see that he wasn't as old as she first thought he was. He was old, sure, but his face was lived in. He had wrinkles at the corner of his eyes from smiling. His eyes were wild and youthful, like he refused to be old. He rested the back of his hand against her forehead and his skin was cool to the touch. His eyes met Emily's and she could have sworn they twinkled. He gave her a warm smile, grandfatherly and kind.

"Hello," he said. "My name is Henry Black. I'm a friend of your aunt."

"Hello," croaked Emily.

"I've heard you've used up a lot of qi," said Henry.

Emily nodded.

"Wait, you know what qi is?" asked Emily. Her mom and Allison walked back into the room, her mom carrying a tray with a teapot and three mugs on it.

Henry chuckled. "Of course, I know what qi is."

"But you're white," said Emily.

"Emily!" cried her mom, but Henry started laughing loudly.

"That I am," he said. "But I wouldn't be a very good wizard if I didn't know about qi."

Emily's eyes went wide. "You're a wizard?"

"Yes, I am," he said. "Is that hot water for me?"

Emily's mom set the tray down on the table.

"Thank you," said Henry.

He pulled his bag toward himself and opened it. He started picking out small glass bottles and jars and laying them on the table. He studied a couple and then pulled one of the mugs toward himself. He twisted the top off a glass jar and pinched his fingers inside. He sprinkled something like glitter into one of the cups. Then he grabbed a tiny bottle and poured a purple liquid into the mug. Finally, he grabbed the teapot and poured steaming water into the mug before offering it to Emily's dad with a spoon.

"Mix this for her. Stir clockwise seven times, counter-clockwise three times, and then have her blow on it five times. Then she can drink it."

Her father took the mug, and hesitated before asking, "What will it do?"

"Help," he said. Henry turned and pulled a plastic box out of his bag and set it down on the table. It was a first aid kit. He grabbed a few items from inside and went to work on Emily. He cleaned the cut on her head and started mumbling softly to himself. Emily's mom helped her out of her jacket and then Henry just sort of studied Emily's face. He put a hand on her forehead, whispered to himself, and closed his eyes.

A moment later, he opened them and put a hand on

Emily's back. Warmth bled through her clothes and into her body. He moved his hands slowly along her shoulder and then suddenly the warmth was gone. "There, that should do it."

Then he turned his attention to Allison. She had taken a seat in one of the lounge chairs in the living room and was staring at Emily. She was hugging her legs, holding her knees to her chest. She was pale and shaking a little bit. Emily thought she was going to be sick. Henry reached out and rested a hand on her arm. She jumped at his touch and turned to face him.

"Hello," said Henry with a soft voice, like someone talking to a frightened child or animal. "What's your name?"

"Allison," she whispered.

Emily's dad handed the mug to Emily and she took it.

"Remember, blow five times," he said.

Emily took the mug and blew on it the requisite number of times then took a sip. It tasted like cinnamon and oranges. Henry was rummaging through his bag again. He pulled out a thin purple, paper pouch and ripped it open. He pulled a tea bag out of the pouch, placed it in one of the empty mugs, and poured hot water into it. Then he grabbed a third jar that had something red inside it. He sprinkled it over the cup and red flakes fell into it. He offered the cup to Allison and she jerked back from it.

"It's okay," said Henry. "It's tea. Chamomile lavender. To help calm your nerves." He showed her the paper he pulled the teabag out of and offered her the mug again. This time Allison accepted the mug and took a sip, and then another. "Can you tell me what happened?"

Allison set her legs down, took another sip of tea, and then let it rest in her hands in her lap.

"We were walking home," said Allison. "Then this dog came out. No, Emily said it wasn't a dog."

"It looked like a coyote," offered Emily.

"Yeah," said Allison, like she remembered something important. "We were deciding what to do when it spoke."

"It spoke?" repeated Henry.

"Yeah," said Allison with a yawn. "The coyote spoke. It said something to Emily and then…" She yawned again. Her head lulled and she lurched forward. The mug was about to fall, but Henry made a quick motion with his hand and it started floating. Allison stopped mid-fall too and her body slowly leaned back into the chair. The mug floated into Henry's hand and he set it down on the table.

"Allison!" yelled Emily. She turned to face Henry. "What did you do to her!"

"Sleeping draught," said Henry. "Your friend is kind and young. She saw something traumatic that could leave her with deep scars. The best thing for her right now is sleep. Her mind isn't protected like yours."

As if on cue, Allison started moving in her sleep. Her peace was broken, and she started having a fit. Henry leaned forward and rested a hand on her forehead. There was a dim purple glow under his hand and Allison stopped fidgeting. Her breathing slowed and she drifted into a calm sleep again.

"She's been through a lot," said Henry finally.

"Can you do it?" asked Aunt Elaine.

"Yes," he remarked, "but it will cost you."

"How much?"

The elderly man held up a hand to stop her. "Nothing like that. A favor."

"Fine," said her aunt. Her face had morphed into a grimace like she had eaten something sour or rotten.

Henry reached down by his feet, pulled up his bag, and rested it on the table in front of him. He popped it open and started rummaging inside.

"What's he going to do?" Emily asked her aunt.

"I'm right here," said the man without turning.

"Sorry," said Emily. "What are you going to do?"

"I'm going to blanket her memories of tonight. I'll need some peace and quiet. Is there a different room I could take her to?"

"There's a guest room upstairs," said Mom. "Chris can carry her up."

"That won't be necessary," said Henry. He lifted his hand and Allison rose into the air.

"That's useful," said Mom. "Follow me."

Emily watched her mom, Henry, and her floating best friend leave the room and go upstairs. That left Emily alone with her aunt and father. That and the memory of a monstrous coyote chasing her down the street.

There was another knock at the door and Aunt Elaine left the room to answer it. A moment later she returned with Stephen and Bryan in tow. Bryan was carrying a pair of hook swords, but he went straight to Emily. He set his weapons down on the floor and knelt beside her.

"Are you okay?" he asked.

"Yes," said Emily quickly with a whisper, but she was focused on Aunt Elaine and Stephen. They spoke quietly to one another but then Aunt Elaine held up a hand to stop Stephen.

"We might as well tell everyone," said Aunt Elaine. "Emily deserves to know. So does Chris."

Stephen glared at Emily one more time, but he relented. "Very well."

Bryan picked up his weapons and sat down in the chair that Allison had recently vacated while Emily made room for her dad on the couch. Aunt Elaine and Stephen elected to remain standing.

"We rushed over as soon as you called," said Stephen. "We were actually pretty close. We picked up the trail from outside the house and followed it as far as we could, but the trail just vanished."

"What do you mean vanished?" asked Aunt Elaine.

"I mean what I said," said Stephen defensively. "The trail just disappeared. It was there one second, and literally the next step it wasn't."

"It was like a ghost," added Bryan. "Just poof! Gone."

"Thank you for that," said Stephen. "We circled the area around where the trail disappeared just in case it picked up again, but there was nothing." Stephen turned to Emily now and bowed his head just slightly to her. "I'm sorry."

"It's fine." She wasn't sure how to react. Everything about Stephen had led her to believe that he didn't care about her wellbeing at all. Maybe she was wrong about him.

Aunt Elaine raised her right hand and started rubbing the sides of her head like she had a headache. "All right. Thank you for trying, Stephen."

"You're welcome," said Stephen. "We're staying for a little while longer. Turns out Bryan wants to see some of Southern California."

Bryan shrugged. "Don't come down here very often."

"Right, Elaine, if you need anything else don't hesitate to call," said Stephen. Then he turned and started leaving the house.

Bryan stood up and bowed to Aunt Elaine, picked up his hook swords, and turned to Emily. "I'm glad you're all right. Like he said, call if you need any help."

Aunt Elaine followed Bryan and let the two of them out. Snatches of conversation made their way through the door until they were too far away to be heard. Her dad was silent and his face set in determined lines. Emily nudged him with a foot.

"Hey, you okay?" she asked.

He turned to her, sputtered out a sound that tried to be a cough and leveled her with an incredulous look. "You get attacked by a monster tonight and you're asking me if I'm okay?"

She wasn't sure what to say. She didn't understand why she was fine, like it hadn't just happened. Or she did understand. It was Meihua, but it was weird. Like it didn't matter, like it barely happened or instead of just happening it happened months ago. She was saved from having to answer her dad when Aunt Elaine walked back in with Henry in tow.

"That should do it," said Henry. "She'll sleep through the night and won't recall the monster. She'll just think they made it here and she fell asleep."

"Thank you, Henry," said Aunt Elaine. She held out a hand to him and he shook it.

"Where's my mom?" asked Emily.

"Upstairs," said Henry. "Just making sure your friend is all right." He crossed the room until he stood in front of Emily. "Now, you need some rest too. Finish the drink I gave you. It will help you sleep and heal your wounds. The best thing that you can do is get a good night's sleep, like your friend."

"Okay," said Emily. She made to get up and she could tell Meihua was helping her move, but her dad helped her up anyway. He pulled her in for a tight hug and after a moment relinquished her. Something wet dripped off her cheek, except she wasn't crying.

"I love you, Dad," she said.

"I love you more," he replied.

They let go of one another and Emily bowed to Henry. "Thank you for all your help."

"You're welcome," said Henry. "Sleep well, child."

Emily walked out of the living room with her dad's help. Her aunt gave her shoulder a firm squeeze as she walked by. She made her way slowly up the stairs and listened to her aunt talk to Henry.

"Can you do anything about her injuries?" she asked.

"I already did," said Henry. "The tea has some healing herbs in it. And from what I've learned about you and that sword, the sword will help a lot with the healing process. She's probably already started healing."

"Oh, thank you. Now about that favor," she said. Her voice was trailing off as Emily climbed the stairs and her own weariness came down on her. "You know I might not be able to do it...."

They reached the top of the stairs and turned toward her room. Her curiosity was gone now. All that was left was an intense need to sleep. Her dad opened the door to Emily's room and helped her onto her bed. She didn't change into her pajamas. She just slept on top of her bedspread. There would be no dreams or conversations with Meihua tonight. At least, she didn't want any. All she wanted was a heavy bout of uninterrupted sleep.

But she did dream. She dreamt of monsters. Of teeth and claws and blood. And worse, she heard her best friend scream. Again, and again, and again.

CHAPTER 18

THE DIFFERENCE BETWEEN KNOWING AND KNOWING

"SORRY I FELL asleep so early," Allison said. There was a look of embarrassment on her face as she rubbed her eyes. "I can't believe how tired I was."

"Don't worry about it." Emily gave her friend as kind a face as she could at the moment. The night before weighed heavily on her mind. How close she had been to being hurt. And worse, how close her best friend had been to being hurt. Here Allison was, less than twelve hours later, perfectly fine. She had no memory of it. She was as happy now as she had been last night at the basketball game. "You've been really busy lately. It probably just caught up to you."

"Yeah," admitted her friend. She moved in and hugged Emily suddenly. Emily didn't move at first, but slowly she put her arms around her friend and squeezed her just as tight. Allison let out a sharp intake of breath and pulled away. "Sorry."

"For what?" asked Emily.

"I don't know," said Allison. "I just had this weird urge to hug you. To thank you for something. Maybe because I ruined our night and you're just forgiving me so easily."

"No," said Emily quickly, and then she muttered, "Trust me, you didn't ruin anything."

Emily's mom walked into the hall carrying her purse. "Ready to go?"

"Yeah, thanks for giving me a ride home, Mrs. Lau." Allison turned to Emily again. "I'll talk to you later, okay?"

Emily couldn't say anything. She gave Allison a weak smile while a pit formed in her stomach. She didn't dare try to speak. She was worried she would say something she shouldn't. She would cry or do something wrong. She hated this. Where did it come from? This idea that just talking to her friend would make everything worse.

She slid into view beside the window and watched them get in the car. It was hard to describe the inner turmoil in her mind. She was sad that Allison was leaving, mad that she had been put in danger, and happy that she was all right.

Emily couldn't help being confused about herself. She had nightmares last night, but eventually the dreams left and she was able to sleep. She believed that Meihua had been to thank for that. But there was something wrong, something missing. Voices in the kitchen drew her attention and she made her way there. She found her dad, Aunt Elaine, and Henry arrayed around the island.

"Good morning," said Henry when Emily entered the room.

"Good morning," she said back.

The strong scent of coffee wafted in the air and clawed at

Emily's insides. She went to the refrigerator and pulled out a carton of orange juice though. Coffee was a lie to her. It smelled amazing and she loved the scent, but it tasted awful.

"How did you sleep?" asked her dad, worry evident in his voice.

"Fine," lied Emily.

Henry crossed the room and put a hand on her forehead. The same warmth from the night before was there, but it was less pronounced this time. "Your body is healing well. The cut's already gone. You'll probably have some bruises but not for very long. I bet you'll be fully healed in a day or so. That sword of yours is amazing. Well, the sword and my magic. That tea helped too. Qi really is so wondrous."

"That tea," Emily said. "Was it like a potion?"

"Hmm," said Henry mulling it over. "In a way, yes, but also no. I knew that your qi would help with the healing process. I just added some ingredients to the tea that would help it along. I've done a lot of research into all sorts of medicine."

"And then turning clockwise, counterclockwise, and blowing on it five times?" asked Emily. "Where did you learn that?"

"Ah," said Henry. "That was made up."

"What?" asked Emily.

Henry shrugged. "It was a show. You knew I was a wizard. Magic is all about believing. I put a little flare into preparing the magic medicine and it gave it more meaning to you. You believed it would work and it did."

"That's cheating," said Emily.

"No, that's magic," said Henry with a mischievous smile. He turned to Aunt Elaine and Emily's dad. "I really should be going. It was lovely to meet you all, though I wish it had been on happier terms."

"Wait!" called out Emily. She walked up to Henry and stood next to him. "Did you really erase her memory?"

"No," replied the elderly man.

"But she doesn't remember," said Emily.

"I blanketed her memory. There's a difference. Erasing someone's memory is dangerous. I just kind of blocked the memory out and suggested she fall asleep. Deep down the memory is still there, but I am good at what I do. She won't remember it. She might dream about it occasionally but that's it."

"Oh," said Emily.

"Any other questions?" asked Henry.

"No."

He stood up and held his hand out for Emily to shake. He covered her hand with his other hand and gave it a gentle squeeze. "You'll be all right, Emily."

"Thanks," she said.

"Thanks again," said Emily's dad.

He walked over and shook Henry's hand. Aunt Elaine hugged him, and then Henry turned to Emily again. "Take care of yourself."

"Thank you," said Emily.

"Wait, Henry!" yelled Aunt Elaine when he made his way toward the front door. He stopped and turned to her. "It's daytime. I think the backyard might be best. Unless you're planning on walking until no one sees you."

"Ah, right you are," said Henry. Emily and her dad followed Aunt Elaine when she led Henry through the back door.

He walked into the backyard and took a quick spin to make sure there were no nosy neighbors peeking over the walls or through windows. Then he whispered something, and a wispy blue orb appeared in the air in front of him.

It was about the size of a tennis ball but then it grew. That was the wrong way to describe it. It just stretched until there was a circle roughly Henry-length in diameter. Through the circle was a room. There were wooden bookshelves filled to the brim and a few lounge chairs. It was probably a study or an office. There was a desk with a light lit and a boy sitting. The boy was holding a pen and writing something but raised his head. Their eyes met and they held each other's stare long enough for it to feel awkward. Emily waved at the boy. His face sort of scrunched up and then, evidently deciding that this wasn't very interesting, he focused on whatever was on the desk.

Emily was about to ask who he was when Henry stepped through the portal. After he was through, he turned, waved a hand, and the portal disappeared.

"Henry Black. He's got style," said Aunt Elaine. "So how are you feeling? Want to get a little training in?"

"No," said Emily quickly. Her aunt had a surprised face because of Emily's fast and forceful answer. "It's just... I'm really tired. I think I'm just going to play basketball for a little bit. Clear my head."

"Okay," said her aunt. She retreated into the house, but her dad stayed outside while Emily ran inside and grabbed a basketball. He was still standing in the same spot when she returned. He was peering up into the sky when Emily came back outside.

He turned when Emily started dribbling. "Hey."

"What's up?" asked Emily.

"Mind if I shoot around with you?" he asked.

"Nope," said Emily. She passed the ball to him and he caught it with one hand and started dribbling.

They didn't say much for the first few minutes. They just took turns dribbling and shooting. Emily would rebound for him, and him for her. The sun was warm overhead but not so warm that they were uncomfortable. Emily found herself getting lost in the rhythm of the dribbling and the shots. She couldn't remember how many she had made and missed, she just liked the idea of doing something normal. She shot a jump shot and watched it bounce around the rim before falling through the net. Her dad caught the ball and held it.

"It's been a while since we've done this," said her dad while passing the ball to her.

"Yeah."

"Are you really all right?" he asked. "You can talk to me."

Emily tossed the ball with a spin so it would bounce back toward her and stepped into another shot. This one went in smoothly, no rim rattling. "Yeah." He tossed the ball back to her. "I don't know."

Another shot; this one she missed. Her dad jumped up and caught it and moved around the backyard so he could shoot while Emily moved in to rebound.

"We should talk about it," he said when he passed her. "All of us. Once your mom gets home."

He shot and missed badly. Emily ran after the ball and as she did her mom's car pulled into the driveway.

"I guess that's now," she said.

"Last shot then," said her dad.

Emily dribbled once, twice, and then pulled up for a jump shot. "Kobe," she called, and the ball soared through the air and splashed through the net.

Her dad had collected her mom and Aunt Elaine and soon enough they were all seated back in the living room in the same spots they were in the night before.

"We need to have a talk," said Dad. "About what happened last night."

"Okay," said Aunt Elaine. She sounded wary, on guard.

There was a pit in Emily's stomach again. She hadn't spoken to Meihua since the night before, and Meihua hadn't said anything to her. There was this agreed silence between them. It was like when Emily and Allison got into an argument and didn't speak to one another but still ran into each other at school. Something had happened. It changed everything. And Emily didn't want to talk about it. Not with Meihua.

"Are you all right, Emily?" asked Aunt Elaine.

She realized everyone was staring at her. Emily traced the ring around her finger. The magic ring. No, the magic sword that Emily had wanted so badly. The promise of adventure.

"I don't know," said Emily finally. "I mean I shouldn't be, right? I got attacked last night. By a monster. A coyote came out of nowhere and talked to us. Then it grew until it was the size of a horse and attacked us. It chased me and my best friend down. I had to protect her. I had to put myself between a monster and Allison and keep her safe. Give her time to get away. I was about to sacrifice myself for her."

She paused to take a breath and swallow the buildup at the back of her throat.

"I stabbed it. I called up Meihua, not as a ring, but as a sword. I stabbed that thing in its eye. I tried to hurt it. I stabbed a living thing. I shouldn't be okay. How am I okay?"

"Oh, thank God," said Emily's mom.

Everyone turned to her. She was sitting in one of the lounge chairs leaning toward her husband. They were holding hands and their eyes were on Emily like they were afraid she was going to break. "I'm sorry. It's just... Your dad and I were talking, and we were worried about how okay you were with it. Knowing that you're not—it's like a weight off my chest. Now, we can really talk about what happened last night."

"What do you mean?" asked Aunt Elaine.

Emily's dad turned to his sister and he appeared to be having a hard time choosing his words. "You don't get it, Elaine. This is the life you lived. You promised Emily a life of adventure and wonder and magic, and then you just kind of tossed everything else in there at the end." He turned to Emily and his stare bored into her. "Did she tell you about the danger? The monsters? You remember, right?"

"Yes, I told her," said Aunt Elaine. "It was one of the first things I said."

"I know," said Dad. "We know. She knows. But there's a difference between knowing and *knowing*. Before monsters were a possibility, after last night they're real. Realer than real. They're here."

"What even happened last night?" asked Emily suddenly. "Why did that happen, I mean? Do we know what that thing was?"

"I called Stephen to compare notes this morning," said Aunt Elaine. "We know it was big, and that it came after you. I don't know why."

"I was never attacked by a monster before," said Emily. "What's different now?" She lifted her hand and brushed a strand of hair out of her eyes and in that motion, she saw the ring. "Oh."

"What?" said Aunt Elaine.

Emily showed off her hand. "This. This is the difference. I was never attacked by monsters before. I'd never even seen one. Then I get this, and I get attacked. It's Meihua, isn't it?"

Aunt Elaine had the decency to be ashamed. "I can't say for sure, but it's possible. I don't know how or why, but it could have tracked onto you because of the sword. Some monsters are attracted to power. That coyote could have been around here for ages. He could be the apex predator of this region and he felt like the sword was a threat. Monsters in power don't like threats to their own."

It was a lot of information to take in all at once. She had thought that Meihua was the answer to her boring life. She thought she was going to become a hero like the ones in all the books she read. She thought she was going to have an adventure. She was going to fight monsters. She never thought about how real an adventure would be. How real the monsters would be. And was her life really that boring? She had been perfectly happy with it before her aunt showed up and offered her something new and wondrous and enticing. How could Emily say no to that? How could she say yes to it now?

If it wasn't for Meihua, she wouldn't have these problems with her best friend. She wouldn't have been attacked by a monster. She wouldn't have put her friend in danger. She wouldn't have nearly died.

Emily—

She took the ring off and it turned into a sword again. It was beautiful still, but now she saw it for what it was. She saw the burden, the danger, and she saw her best friend screaming in terror the night before all over again.

"I don't want it," said Emily. "Take it back."

Her aunt nodded solemnly. "Of course. I never meant for this to happen. I need you all to understand. I never intended for Emily to be put in danger. I'll take her."

She reached her hand out and Emily handed the sword to her. Her aunt's fingers closed around it and she pulled it from Emily, only Emily's hands wouldn't let it go.

"Emily?" said her aunt. She pulled harder and Emily tried to let go of the sword, but her fingers wouldn't budge an inch. "What are you doing?"

"I don't know," said Emily.

"Emily, just let go," said her mother.

"I can't!" said Emily. Then on a whim she said, "Meihua, what are you doing?"

No, said Meihua. Her voice was ice and steel. *I will not leave. I will not go back to her. I can't.*

"Why not?" cried Emily. "You were Aunt Elaine's sword before. Why can't you be her sword again?"

NO! screamed Meihua in Emily's mind. Pain flashed across the side of her head and she flinched from the feeling of it. It was like a rolling pain had just gone across the side of her head, like a headache that dissipated after a second. *I will not kill her!*

"What are you talking about? What do you mean kill her?" asked Emily.

Images and memories flew through Emily's mind like a photo reel. There was a doctor visit with a muted conversation. A grim face. Pamphlets with words blurred out. A night of crying in a bed that wasn't hers. Then there was a time where Emily tried to unsheathe the sword, but it wasn't her hands. They weren't her hands.

Emily didn't recognize any of these images.

Then she remembered Aunt Elaine fighting the night before and falling, clutching her abdomen. Hobbling into the house despite not getting hit. Talking to Henry, telling him she might not be able to make up that favor.

Tears streamed down the side of Emily's face, but she hadn't been the one to start crying. She wasn't the one who felt this sadness. A pit formed in her stomach, deeper than any before.

Dad rushed to her side and so did her mom. "What's wrong, Emily?"

"What are you talking about, Meihua? What is this?"

Ask her, said Meihua. *Ask her why I left her. Why I didn't let her draw me.*

"Aunt Elaine," said Emily. "Did Meihua stop working for you?"

Aunt Elaine looked away, a new shame on her face. The room grew eerily quiet before Aunt Elaine finally whispered, "Yes."

"Why?" asked Emily. The images played through her head again.

Her aunt choked back a response. She took a deep

breath, and there were tears falling down her face. "Because I'm dying."

Tears still streamed down Emily's face, but now they were hers. Emily had always thought her aunt and parents were invincible. Immutable objects like mountains. Things unaffected by time. Deep down she knew that people didn't live forever. She knew that people would die, but it was something that wouldn't happen to her family. And now she really understood the difference between knowing, and *knowing*.

CHAPTER 19

WHAT WE DO NOW

THE WORDS STRUCK the noise from the room. There was nothing but the silence and the ringing that silence becomes. The clock on the mantle that usually ticked seemed to take up a moment of silence too, despite its moving hands. Emily held her breath and watched her aunt squirm. Emily turned slowly to find some sort of solace in her parents, but she found none. Her mom had a hand up covering her mouth. Her dad stared at his sister in stunned silence. A cold sadness washed over Emily.

Her father broke the silence first.

"What do you mean you're dying?" he said.

Aunt Elaine wiped a tear from her face and laughed flimsily at her brother. "I mean, I think it's pretty obvious."

"No. It's not," he said. "We're all dying. Living is dying. What do you *mean* you're dying?"

Aunt Elaine nodded as if she finally understood what he was asking, then sat down in one of the chairs. She buried her face in her hands and wiped away whatever tears were left on her face. Emily's mom grabbed a box of tissues and handed it to her.

"Thank you," said Aunt Elaine. She wiped at her eyes and nose. She didn't pay attention to everyone else. It wasn't like she held their attention like a mother holds a newborn. "I have cancer."

Stunned silence continued through the room so she continued.

"They found it a few months ago," she said. "I was fine. Then suddenly I wasn't. I visited every doctor I could. I could afford the best, but everyone said the same thing. Terminal."

"How long do you have?" whispered Dad.

"Could be months, could be years. It's just coming for me. This monster in my own life that I can't fight."

"You can fight it," said Dad. "There has to be treatments."

"Nothing that would cure me," said Aunt Elaine. "And nothing that wouldn't take away what makes me, me."

"I don't understand," said Dad. "You're what makes you, you. What could medicine take from you that isn't worth it?"

"You wouldn't understand," said Aunt Elaine.

"Then explain it to us!" yelled her dad. He stood up now and advanced on his sister. "How could you not tell us? How could you not tell me?"

"How could I?" whispered Aunt Elaine harshly. "I hardly ever see you." She gestured toward Meihua. "I took your dream from you. I took everything from you. How could I just come and ruin your life again?"

Her father stalked toward his sister, his breathing hard and heavy, and Emily thought he might attack Aunt Elaine, but he fell to his knees and pulled his sister into an embrace.

"You have never ruined anything," he whispered. Emily only heard it because of how deathly quiet the rest of the room was. "You took my dream from me?" He released his sister and gestured to Emily and his wife. "What did you take from me? I have everything I ever wanted right here. This is the dream. The only thing missing is you."

He hugged her again and Aunt Elaine put her arms around him. They were quiet at first, but then the tears started coming down her aunt's face again. Her father's back heaved before the sobs started leaving his body. She wanted to do something, anything, but she was just stuck. A hand rested on her shoulder and she turned. Her mother's tear-stained face waited for her. Her mom gestured that they should leave, and Emily followed her out of the room.

Once they were in the kitchen, her mom pulled Emily into a hug. She hugged her hard, refusing to let go, and then Emily squeezed her mother just as hard. They sobbed as quietly as they could, but they took this moment to be sad together.

Then, before they had finished crying their tears, her mother pulled herself away. She held Emily by her shoulders, so they were eye-to-eye, tears still falling down her face. "It's not fair, but I need you to be strong right now. Just for a little while. Your dad and your aunt need some time to talk. I'm going to stay down here and wait for them. Can you go upstairs? Just for a little bit?"

Emily wiped tears away from her face and nose. "Sure, Mom."

"That's my brave girl," said Mom. She kissed Emily's forehead and left her in the kitchen.

Emily made her way out of the kitchen and slowly up the stairs. She walked to her room listening to the sound of crying coming from below. Her aunt and her father were both apologizing to one another over and over, intermingled with heavy sobs. She stepped inside her room, slid the door shut behind her and the sound of other people crying drifted away until the only crying she heard was her own.

She leaned her back against the door and just slid down until she was sitting on the floor, hugging the sword to her chest. She cried until her eyes dried out and then she cried some more. She squeezed the sword so tight the muscles in her hand started to burn, but that was preferable to the hole that was spreading inside her.

Emily? said Meihua. *Are you okay?*

Meihua had been so quiet that Emily had forgotten that the sword she was carrying was basically a person. A thinking person. Someone who knew about Aunt Elaine all along and hadn't told any of them.

"Why didn't you tell us?" whispered Emily, and then she croaked, "Why didn't you tell me?"

Meihua was quiet for a moment, but Emily could tell she was thinking. She couldn't explain how. It was like how she could get to all her classes but couldn't remember the classroom numbers. *It wasn't my secret to tell.*

Emily suddenly remembered something.

"That first time we met in the dream," she started, "you said all the flowers were former guardians. There was one that was wilting. That was Aunt Elaine, wasn't it?"

Yes, said Meihua.

"What happened?"

She got sick. It happened so slowly we had no idea what was happening until it was too late.

"That can't be right," said Emily. "There's a whole world of monsters out there and my aunt gets sick? How is that even fair?"

Life is hardly ever fair. The fairness is that it is unfair to everyone.

"So, you're telling me that there's magic and miracles, and there's nothing that can be done for my aunt?" said Emily.

Nothing we found, said Meihua.

"Does it hurt her?" Emily asked in a whisper.

There was a slight pause before Meihua said, *Not always.*

They were quiet then, basking in the silence and the sunlight breaking through her blinds. Tears trickled down the side of her face again. She sobbed into her arms and kept rubbing at her eyes with her sleeve to wipe the tears away. Meihua was quiet the entire time, allowing Emily to feel the depth of her sadness. She didn't know how long she cried for, but she finally managed some control over herself.

"Did that monster really come after me because of you?" she asked when she had finished crying.

I can't say for certain, but if I had to guess, yes.

"And you won't go back to Aunt Elaine."

I can't go back to Elaine, said Meihua.

"I didn't ask for this," said Emily.

No, you didn't.

She stood up and collapsed onto her bed. She lay there with her face turned toward the door. She held the sword in her right hand and let it rest on the bed with her, so it was in her line of sight.

"Why did you leave Aunt Elaine?" asked Emily.

She is dying.

"That doesn't answer my question," said Emily. "Why did you force her to pick me?"

You were always her choice. I just forced my way to you sooner. I had no other choice. Using me, using qi, taxing her body, it hurts her. The life she chose, it would kill her faster. Leaving her was the only kindness I could offer. It was the only thing I could do for her.

When I first refused to let her draw me, she was hurt. She was angry. I told her it was time to choose a successor. She thought I was abandoning her. You can't fathom how much that hurt. I love every one of my guardians. It burned my soul to have her think that.

And then I told her I wanted to go to you. She said no at first, but I gave her no choice. We've both known for years that it was going to be you. But this time, when I suggested it, she argued against it. Your aunt is a good person. She would give up her own life if it meant she could save someone else's.

The words hung thick in the air like the last echoing notes of a song. The dying embers of a fire before it burns out.

Your aunt is a hero. She can't be anything else. She would take me back in a heartbeat if it meant saving you from danger. She would rather die than put you at risk. She would endure pain and agony before she let you get hurt. She loves you that much. I won't be the reason she dies. Neither should you.

Emily's body began to shake as a flurry of emotions struck her. Anger, sadness, resentment. She wasn't sure what to do.

I know it's hard, Emily. I didn't expect this to be easy, but I didn't expect things to get bad like this.

"So what?" asked Emily. "It was my destiny to inherit you? My destiny to face off against monsters?"

You're scared, but you have to make a choice. Humans are funny. They talk about destiny like it's some grand design or something that's been planned for years when really destiny is made up of small moments. One after the other that leads up to one big moment. Just one moment where you make a choice. That and the courage to follow through. So, Emily, what are you going to do?

Sometime later there was a knock at her door.

"Yeah," called Emily.

The door opened and her entire family appeared. Her dad walked in first, followed by her mom, and then Aunt Elaine. They all settled into different places around the room and Emily guessed that it was time for the family discussion.

"Hey," said Emily.

They all remained quiet. They just waited, everyone deciding who should speak first without actually speaking. Finally, Aunt Elaine cleared her throat and sat on Emily's bed next to her. She opened her mouth to speak but stopped herself, then tried again. She sniffed once and wiped at the corner of her eyes.

"I'm sorry I didn't tell you," she said. "I should have told you all sooner. I just wanted to spend time with my family before... you know."

Dying. That's what she meant. The pit in her stomach started to form again and threatened to take over but Emily focused on her breath. She focused on the tiny space of time between an inhale and an exhale.

"I can't change the fact that I didn't tell you all," said

Aunt Elaine. "But I can fix something I've already done. Give Meihua to me. Tell her to come back. If you give her to me willingly, she might come with me."

Emily lowered her eyes to the sword. This was exactly what she had wanted earlier, but she had questions now.

"I have a few questions," said Emily.

Her aunt's brow furrowed with confusion. "Sure."

"Do Stephen and Bryan know?" she asked.

"No," said Aunt Elaine. "I just told them I planned on retiring, then left. No reason why."

"Don't you think they have a right to know?" asked Emily.

"Yes. I talked about this with your mom and dad already. I'm going to call them later."

"Okay, good. Just one more question then." Aunt Elaine waited for Emily to ask but the question stopped itself in Emily's throat. She wasn't sure she wanted the answer to this question. "How much does it hurt?"

Confusion crept on Aunt Elaine's face. She glanced at Emily's parents before turning back to Emily. "Excuse me?"

"How much does it hurt?" repeated Emily but with more emphasis on her words. "Meihua told me. She said that when you exert yourself and use qi it hurts you more. How much does it hurt?"

"Emily—"

"What is she talking about?" Dad interrupted. "Emily, what are you talking about?"

"I talked to Meihua a lot while I was by myself," said Emily. "She said you know that using qi makes you sicker. She said it hurts you. I want you to tell me how much it hurts."

Aunt Elaine turned away, shame evident on her face again,

like a teacher had read her note to the entire class. "Emily, it's fine."

"She said that you know this, and you do it anyway. She said that you can't help yourself. She told me that you'd try to take her back after this. If I give Meihua to you, what are you going to do? Go back to helping people? Are you really going to kill yourself faster?"

"Emily, I can handle a little pain," said Aunt Elaine.

"A little pain?" repeated Emily. "Meihua showed me a memory of you writhing on the ground, screaming."

Her aunt was crying again. "You don't have to do this."

"I know I don't have to do this," said Emily. "But I think I should."

CHAPTER 20

GROUNDED

"What?" said Mom and Dad at the same time.

"It's the same as before, right?" said Emily. "I don't have to use her, but I can keep her. The only thing that's changed is there's a monster out looking for me."

Her aunt cleared her throat. "Emily—"

"You'd really do it, wouldn't you?" asked Emily, cutting her off. "You'd die for me."

"Yes," whispered Aunt Elaine.

"Well, I think I can live for you," said Emily. "Now, what do we do about this monster?"

Aunt Elaine opened her mouth to speak but nothing came out. She shot nervous glances at Emily's parents, but they didn't have a response either. Emily had made up her mind. She couldn't back down now, though it would have been too easy to say no, to run away. But if she started now, when would she stop?

"*We* are doing nothing," said Aunt Elaine finally. "I don't agree with your decision, and I'm sure your parents don't either."

"We don't," said Mom quickly.

"But like it or not I can't force you to change your mind," said Aunt Elaine. "And you seem set in this decision."

"I am," said Emily.

"Emily, you can't be—"

"I am, Mom," interrupted Emily, only realizing after she spoke over her mother and how much trouble she was probably going to be in for that. "I can't let Aunt Elaine die. Not if I can save her."

Her mother was on the verge of tears. "Emily..."

"You might be taking control of the Meihua situation, but I'm still running the monster side of things," said Aunt Elaine. "I'm grounding you. I mean, if it's okay with your parents."

"What!" cried out Emily. "What for?"

Emily's parents used their parental power to communicate without words. Emily's dad was the first to break the silent conversation.

"Depends, what are you grounding her for?" he asked.

"Well, there's still this monster out there," said Aunt Elaine. "We don't know anything about it other than it came after Emily. I don't like unknowns. Until we either catch and kill this monster, or find out more, I think Emily shouldn't expose herself any more than she has to."

"Meaning?" asked Mom.

"Meaning no going out unsupervised," said Aunt Elaine. "She goes to school and back. She trains. She does everything with either me, Bryan, or Stephen there."

"Stephen?" cried Emily.

"Uncle Stephen," corrected Aunt Elaine.

"Never calling him that," said Emily.

The sound of whispers came from the corner and Emily turned. Her mom and dad were whispering to one another and she didn't like their grave expressions.

"We agree," said Mom.

"WHAT?" said Emily "This isn't fair. I didn't do anything!"

"You're not really grounded," said her dad. "We're just trying to keep you safe."

"This isn't fair," said Emily again.

"Life's not fair," said Aunt Elaine. "This isn't permanent. Just give me, Stephen, and Bryan time to find the monster. Trust us. This is what we do."

Emily was about to storm out of the room but she realized she was in her own room. Where else was she going to go? So, she pulled her legs up to her chest and pouted into her knees.

"Wait," she said suddenly. "What about this weekend? It's Allison's musical. I always go see her show."

"She does. We can't keep her from her friends," said Mom.

"Well, if we catch and handle the monster by then it won't be a problem," said Aunt Elaine.

"And if you don't?" asked Emily.

Her aunt shrugged. "We'll talk."

Emily was back in the demesne after school the following Monday. Her aunt took the rest of the weekend off so she and Emily could heal fully, but now they were back to business. She was holding two wooden poles with handguards on them. They were obviously meant to be swords. She tossed one to Emily and she caught it by the "blade." She held it by the handle and tested the weight of it. She swung it a couple times and then thrust it forward. It was the exact weight and length of Meihua.

"What's this?" asked Emily.

"It's your practice sword," said Aunt Elaine. "Up until now I haven't trained you with any weapons. That's about to change."

"Why?" asked Emily.

"Now, there's a monster," replied Aunt Elaine. "Now, there's a reason for you to be able to defend yourself fully. You need every tool and trick in the book to do this. So, I'm going to teach you how to fight with a sword."

"Oh," said Emily.

"You already know how much of a burden a sword is," said Aunt Elaine. "You talked about it with the monster. A sword can cut. It can injure easily. It's something used to kill, but it doesn't have to be. You are not a sword, you are a person, and you decide how a weapon is used. Got it?"

"Yeah," said Emily.

"Good," replied her aunt. "Now we're going to do something a little different."

"How so?" asked Emily.

"We normally have Meihua take over fully, but now I want the two of you to learn how to work together."

Emily frowned at her aunt. "Haven't we been doing that?"

"Yes," said Aunt Elaine, "but we're going to go further. I want you and Meihua to really work together. I want you to walk on the edge of control so Meihua can take over at a moment's notice to move for you. To maneuver. To act. The two of you working together like that. It'll reduce the stress that Meihua puts on your body and keep you in the fight longer."

"So, kind of like only trying half the time?" asked Emily. "You want me to take it easy?"

"Not take it easy," said Aunt Elaine. "Just don't show all your cards until you have to. Keep it as a trump card. Your enemy doesn't know how skilled you are or aren't. Having Meihua surprise them could make a difference in a fight. When Meihua takes over and does everything for you, it leaves you exhausted. This way you get the most out of using her without weakening yourself too much. Get it?"

"Yes."

"Let's get to it then."

They practiced for an hour with Meihua showing Emily how to do something, Aunt Elaine explaining what it was for, and then Emily practicing it over and over until she was able to do it on her own. After that they started sparring with each other. This was where Aunt Elaine had Emily keep Meihua in the back of her mind. It was awkward and they stumbled more than once. She couldn't let Meihua take control effortlessly in the thick of combat. It always took a second too long. Aunt Elaine was patient though.

She waited for Emily to readjust and she offered advice when she could. They attacked one another over and over, her aunt performing the perfect counter to what Emily attempted to do each time. It was like she was in Emily's head and could predict every move she was going to do. And it didn't help that Emily kept making mistakes even with Meihua's help. She was sloppy, and her aunt took advantage every time.

Finally, her aunt stopped the session and threw Emily to the ground.

"What is going on with you?" asked Aunt Elaine. "You're awful today."

Emily rolled over and sat up, sweat glistening off her body. She glowered at her aunt and couldn't tell if she should be angry or sad, and that was the problem. Tears threatened to show themselves and she wiped her forehead of sweat to hide them. Her aunt was glaring down at her with her hands on her hips.

"Well?"

"Well, what?" asked Emily.

"What is wrong with you?" asked Aunt Elaine.

"Wrong with me? What's wrong with you?" asked Emily. "You're dying and we're just going to train like that's not happening? Like things are just normal? Like everything's fine?"

Her aunt inhaled. "Ah, right."

"Yeah," sneered Emily.

Her aunt sat down in front of Emily and fell silent. Emily brushed at her arms nervously while her aunt tried to speak. She opened her mouth a couple of times and stopped.

"Things aren't normal, Emily," said Aunt Elaine. "They can't be. There's no way. But I can't just sit here and wait to die. I have too much living left to do. And that means I am going to take as much time as I can with my family. But I also have a responsibility to you and to Meihua. You might not want to use the sword anymore, but eventually you're going to have to give the sword to someone. To pass down the mantle. And I want you to be ready. Ready for the fights that might happen. Ready to teach someone someday. A person is more than what they do, they're what they leave behind too. You're part of my legacy, Emily. When it comes time for you to leave your own legacy, I want you to be able to leave a good one."

Emily stayed quiet. Her head was tilted forward, and she was twisting the knuckle of her thumb into the mat trying to drill a hole in it. Sweat had trickled off her and dripped onto it. She swiped at a drop with her hand and then raised her head. Her aunt was smiling. Emily was ashamed. She wasn't the one dying. She wasn't the one who had a timer counting down. But she was the one wallowing in pity.

"I'm sorry," she said suddenly. She jumped up to her feet and held a hand out for her aunt. "I'm ready now."

Her aunt's smile widened, and she took Emily's hand. "Good."

Emily lifted Aunt Elaine up and they started sparring again.

Emily had grown uneasy and impatient as the week progressed. Stephen, Bryan, and her aunt had not been able to find or catch the monster. As a result, Emily was sort of dodging conversations with Allison about her show all week. Allison had asked her twice now how many tickets she would need to save for her, but Emily had to tell her she didn't have an answer yet. She had lied to her, saying her parents were still figuring out their schedules. And now it was Friday, the day of the show, and Emily still didn't have an answer.

When she had asked her aunt about it that morning her aunt had told her there was still no news, and that made Emily believe she wouldn't be able to go.

"So, how many tickets are you going to need?" asked Allison at lunch. "I have to tell them today if I want to save any tickets."

"Honestly, I don't know if I'll be able to go. My parents said that we might have to go to some work event for my mom."

"Oh," said Allison. There was surprise on her face. "It's fine." And then there was sadness. "It's fine."

"It's not," said Emily. "I really want to go, Allison. I just don't know if they'll let me."

"Why wouldn't they let you?" asked Allison.

"The work thing," said Emily a little too quickly. It even sounded like a lie to Emily when she said it and she regretted having said it at all.

"Right," said Allison.

"Just give me two tickets," said Emily resolutely. "I'm coming."

"Really?" said Allison like she didn't believe her.

"Yes," said Emily. "I'm not missing this even if I get grounded for the rest of my life. Two tickets."

Emily left Allison and headed to fifth period wondering how she was going to swing this. Her family had been adamant all week about how she needed to be protected. She had only been allowed to go to school and back. She was taken to school and picked up by a combination of her aunt and one of her parents. She wasn't allowed to leave the house to go anywhere. Allison had asked to hang out once and Emily had to tell her no. It had been a rough week. She had basically been a prisoner in her own home and she was going stir crazy. She had to go to this show tonight. She just had to convince her parents and aunt that she was going.

Emily waited at the junior parking lot gate for a car she recognized to come into view. Her mom's car turned the corner of the parking lot and Emily let out an internal cheer. Her mom was the parent she was hoping would pick her up today because she was the most likely to side with Emily when she brought up the musical.

"Hey Emily!" yelled someone from behind her. She turned and saw her friend Marina walking toward her. "Are you going to the show tonight?"

"I hope so," said Emily. "Allison left me tickets. Just have to get permission from my parents."

"Let me know if you need a ride," she said. "My older sister is taking me."

"Okay, thanks," said Emily.

She started walking toward the car and jumped into the back seat since her aunt was sitting shotgun in the front.

"Hey, honey," said her mom. "How was your day?"

"Good," said Emily. "My teachers didn't give out very much homework, so I won't have much over the weekend."

"That's good," said her mom.

"I thought so too," said Emily. "Have you had any luck catching the monster, Aunt Elaine?"

"Not yet." There was frustration in her voice but Emily knew it wasn't directed at her. Since Aunt Elaine was in charge of teaching Emily she was usually not involved in the actual search for the monster. She had been upset at the lack of progress from Stephen and Bryan. So was Emily.

"Oh," said Emily, a little crestfallen. A small part of her had hoped she wouldn't have to ask to go to the musical with a monster still on the loose, but now she was going to have to face that fear. "So, I was wondering…"

She trailed off and let the words linger in the air. Her mom's eyes darted to her rearview mirror and she raised an eyebrow. "Yes?"

"So, remember Allison's musical? Well, it's tonight… I was really hoping I could go," said Emily.

Her mom's eyes shifted to Aunt Elaine. Aunt Elaine hadn't moved at all. She just stared out the window with her arm resting along the door. "We still haven't caught the monster."

"Yeah, but I was hoping you or Bryan could come with me," said Emily. "She's leaving me two tickets."

"Bryan and I are both going to be hunting for the monster tonight," said Aunt Elaine. "Stephen called me this morning. He was upset because he hadn't caught the monster yet either and he suggested that the three of us get together and then split up to look for the monster."

"Okay, so Mom or Dad comes with me," said Emily.

"No," said Aunt Elaine. "What happens if we're out looking for the monster and it comes looking for you? We need you safe at home."

"How am I safe at home if you're all out?" asked Emily.

"Stephen has put protective charms around the house," said Aunt Elaine. "And homes have a protection of their own. You can't just attack a house or enter it without leaving some of your power behind. Nothing will be able to get to you as long as you stay inside the house."

"Great, so I'm stuck inside the house again tonight?" asked Emily. "Mom, please."

"What if we go straight there and back?" asked her mom. "There would be a crowd. The monster wouldn't attack the show."

"Yeah, but what about on the way there or on the way back?" asked Aunt Elaine. "I'm sorry, Emily, but we can't take the risk."

Emily was sitting in the confines of her room working on homework that didn't need to be worked on. She had also read one of the fantasy books she had already read, and she had played a video game for a while. Now, time was inching closer and closer to the musical and Emily was still stuck.

"Ugh!" she groaned. "This is so unfair!"

It is, said Meihua. *I am sorry.*

"It's not your fault," said Emily.

It kind of is.

"Yeah, but I'm still willing to let it slide," said Emily. "It's not like you asked for a monster to attack me and to take over my whole life."

Her aunt had left after depositing Emily at home with her mom and was supposedly out trying to hunt the monster down right now with Stephen and Bryan. She hadn't heard from Aunt Elaine or Bryan, so she assumed that meant the monster was still on the loose. The dream of her aunt catching the monster by now and Emily being able to go at the last second was being dashed.

"I could always sneak out," said Emily all of a sudden. And then, the idea took hold. What if she snuck out? It was just a few hours. There had been no trace of the monster since that attack the week before. Maybe it was gone. "Meihua, I could sneak out."

We could, said Meihua. *I don't know if it's a good idea.*

"Yeah, but I really want to see that musical."

What is a musical?

"What?" asked Emily aloud.

A musical, what is it?

Emily thought about what Meihua meant. A musical was obvious to Emily but Meihua had belonged to warriors her entire life. She may have never seen a musical.

"A musical is like a play, but with lots of singing in it too. The characters sing to tell the story."

Ah, like a xiqu.

Emily had no idea what the word meant but images flooded her head like distant memories. It was a theatrical presentation full of music, singing, dancing, acrobatics, and martial arts.

"Exactly, sort of," she replied. "Though less acrobatic usually. Allison is in a musical called *Beauty and the Beast*. Have you ever seen it?"

No, I have never seen it. What is it about?

"It's about a girl whose father gets kidnapped by a monstrous beast. She takes his place and I'm not going to say anymore because then I'd be spoiling it for you."

It sounds interesting. Who is Allison playing?

"Belle. The main character. One of them at least."

Is she a good singer?

"The best singer I know," replied Emily. "She's going to be great. She sings songs from that movie all the time."

Movie? repeated Meihua. *I thought it was a musical.*

Emily scratched her head. "Well, Allison's in a musical, but *Beauty and the Beast* is also a movie."

I don't understand.

"It was a movie first and then they made a musical. I think. We should watch the movie sometime," remarked Emily.

I think I would like that, said Meihua. *I think we should sneak out.*

Emily tried not to grin. She and Meihua had a better connection now, a deeper one at least. And she was all for Emily sneaking out. Emily was starting to think less like she was being intruded upon and more like Meihua was a friend.

She grabbed her phone and sent a text to Marina asking her to pick her up outside the gate. Marina texted back almost immediately and Emily rushed to get ready. Then once she was dressed and ready to go, she slid open her bedroom window, and slipped out into the setting sun.

CHAPTER 21

BEAUTY AND THE BEAST

A S PROMISED, MARINA and her older sister picked Emily up outside of her neighborhood and drove her to Beckman High School. They went their separate ways after they realized their tickets weren't close to one another, but Emily agreed to meet up with them in the lobby after the show. She stood outside the theater searching the crowd. She spotted Allison talking to a group of people and sped off toward her best friend.

"Allison!" she called when she was a few feet away.

Allison spun and her face lit up when their eyes met. Emily ran up to her best friend and they threw their arms around one another.

"You came!" said Allison.

"Of course," said Emily. "I've never missed a show and I'm not about to start now."

"Yeah, but the way you were talking earlier, I thought you were busy."

"Not busy enough to miss this," she added.

The group of people Allison had been talking to before wandered off, evidently not wanting to stand there awkwardly. Allison was in a white and blue frock that Emily recognized from both *Beauty and the Beast* movies. Her hair was tied back in a bun, and she had a thin layer of makeup on her face.

A woman's voice called out Allison's name in the distance. A middle-aged woman with frizzy hair was waving at her from a door by the entrance. Allison turned back to Emily.

"Gotta go," she said. "I'll see you after the show? Our usual after-show stop?"

"Of course," replied Emily. "I got a ride here so I might need a ride with you."

"Yeah sure!" called Allison behind her. She had already started running back toward the theater.

Emily turned and started making her way into the auditorium now since there was no reason to stay outside. The inside of the theater had a lot to take in. Foothill didn't have anything like this. Rows of seats sloped down towards the stage. The seats themselves were something she expected to see in an actual theater or stadium. They were cushioned with the type of seats that only stayed down when you sat in them. The stage was a light, laminated wood with a blood red curtain. The theater was way too nice for a high school. It was more like a professional theater.

She took her seat on the aisle and folded the program in her lap. A constant chatter milled through the air as people talked to one another and moved to their seats. People dressed all in black moved about along the rows of seats and a few spotlights were being tested. Emily started thumbing through the program to pass the time until the show started.

This is a bigger deal than I thought it was going to be, said Meihua.

"Yeah, I didn't expect this," replied Emily.

In my experience, it's more the performers than the place it is performed at. A good xiqu will be good whether it's played indoors or outdoors.

"Oh, you've seen a lot of shows like this?" asked Emily.

A few, said Meihua. *Most of my previous guardians didn't appreciate the arts. They didn't like sitting still long enough. It became worse as time went on. It's like art disappeared in the minds of people.*

"What? People would rather fight with a sword than appreciate a sword?" mused Emily.

Meihua made a sound like a disgusted scoff. *Are you forgetting that it's called martial arts? Focus on the* arts. *Martial arts used to be about bettering yourself and finding balance. There is no balance in only fighting. There's no art or beauty in it. You can't just survive life, you have to live it.*

A rush of emotions and thoughts sprang up inside her. She wanted to say something, to ask more, to debate, but her thoughts were hushed by the dimming lights. Everyone around them quieted as well and the last few stragglers made their way to their seats in a hurry. She bit her lip, still wanting to say something, and Meihua must have sensed it.

Shhh... We'll talk later. I want to see this.

Emily smiled despite her curiosity and settled into her seat. The lights dimmed until the large, expansive theater was almost completely dark except for the lights along the stage, the aisles, and the rows of seats. Music thrummed from speakers all around them and then a woman's voice began narrating.

"Once upon a time a handsome young prince lived in a beautiful castle...." the woman said. She spoke of how the prince was selfish, and despite outward appearances he was ugly on the inside. There was a crash of cymbals and a new character appeared on the stage. She wore a paper mache mask that gave her an ugly appearance. She had only wanted a place to stay but the prince refused her. The student tore the mask off to reveal a fresh-faced young woman with curling blonde locks.

"True beauty is found within," said the girl. She cursed the prince into the form of a monstrous beast; cursed his castle and all who served him. They were forgotten as the enchantress erased all memories of them. The last thing she said before she left the stage was that the only way to break the curse was for him to learn to love another and earn their love in return. The music drifted off into silence until the narrator was the only sound left in the darkness.

"Or else he would be a monster forever."

The words resonated in the dim until the music started again. The music was lighter, happier, not as harsh, and then the curtains drifted apart. On the far left of the stage was a makeshift house that had obviously been put together by the students or parents. It was good, but it still had that arts-and-craft feel to it. A flimsy door swung open, and then Allison stepped out.

She was wearing the same blue-and-white dress. Her hair was tied back in a bun with a blue ribbon holding it together. She swung a basket in her arms and walked down the steps onto the stage like she wasn't about to sing in front of a crowd of people. It was like she didn't have a care in the world. And then she started to sing.

"Little town, it's a quiet village..."

Her voice was beautiful and carried through the theater. Emily shivered at the strength and the sound of it.

She's wonderful, said Meihua's voice in her head.

She agreed silently. Moments like these had been rare since Emily had been given Meihua. She didn't often get to sit back and enjoy herself. So she sunk into her chair and just watched.

Your friend is amazing, said Meihua while Emily stood in line for the sink in the restroom.

"Honestly, I think she's meant for this," said Emily. "She's been singing songs from it her entire life. That first song? She would start singing it randomly when we were younger. She'd try and get me to sing too but I was terrible, so she'd just sing every part on her own. She'd change her voice and everything."

The person using the sink in front of Emily raised her head to get a look at Emily through the mirror. She must have been wondering who Emily was talking to since there was no one else in the restroom.

A fresh wave of embarrassment washed over her.

"Sorry," said Emily, taking a step back. "Talking to myself."

The woman eyed Emily for another second before she turned off the faucet and grabbed a paper towel. Emily stood in the same spot, not daring to move, until the woman left the restroom. She let out a sigh of relief when the door closed.

Emily washed her hands and made her way out of the bathroom into a near-empty lobby. There were a few ushers talking to one another, and then someone walked into the lobby from outside. Emily stretched, yawned, and started walking toward the door to get to her seat.

"Hello, Meihua," said the man who had just walked into the lobby.

Ice erupted in her veins, her breath caught in her throat, and Emily stopped mid stride. She watched in horror as the ushers who were standing in the lobby disappeared inside the theater, leaving Emily alone. She turned slowly, still holding her breath, and took a step back from the stranger.

He was tall, but not much taller than Emily. He wore a heavy-set jacket with a hood over his head that hid his face. The inside of the man's hood was dark. Literally dark. Everything from just above the man's mouth and up was shrouded in shadow.

It was the deepest black she had ever seen. It was suffocating and somehow alluring. Her eyes were drawn to it like moths to a flame and suddenly there was this pressure in her chest. It was like the depths of shadows at night. The long expanse of a dark hallway. The kind of blackness in the middle of the night where Emily got the urge to ask who's there. The darkness that stares back.

"Who are you?" asked Emily.

"Oh, it took you a while to ask the important question, didn't it?" the man said. "You're a little slow on the uptake. Have you even noticed that we're not speaking English?"

"What?"

He's right, said Meihua. *He's speaking Mandarin. I'm translating it for you and translating you for him.*

"Who are you?" asked Emily again.

"Meihua knows who *we* are." His voice was different now, echoed, like multiple people were speaking. And Emily wasn't even sure they were people's voices.

Yuansou.

"Yuansou?" repeated Emily.

"You remember us? We are touched," came the echoed reply.

Emily tensed up and hugged herself. Chills shivered up her flesh like thousands of insects were crawling up and down her. She shuddered and stepped back.

"Now, now. No need to be so frightened. I only want to talk. Why don't you and I go for a walk?"

No! shouted Meihua in Emily's head.

"No," repeated Emily.

"Oh, don't be like that," he replied. "If you don't come nicely, I might get upset. Who knows what I'd do to everyone here if that happened."

"Who is he?" Emily asked Meihua.

He is an old enemy of mine, said Meihua. *A sorcerer. A summoner. He calls on monsters and demons to do his bidding. It all makes sense now. He must be the one behind the coyote.*

Emily shifted defensively. Anxiety washed over her mind sending jitters down her body. And that was new. Meihua took the edge off for Emily in situations like this. She wasn't supposed to feel like this. Why did she feel so scared?

"There's no need for things to get unpleasant. I only want to talk to you. I will not harm you or anyone else here if you just step outside with me."

Emily took another step back. She turned her head and peeked through one of the windows on the doors. Allison was in a flowing gold dress, descending a staircase, and then walking into a grand dining room. Classmates, families, and friends all sat in their seats unaware of the danger that was present. Could she stop this man if he did something? Could she save everyone? She felt the fear in her mind, in her body, and then she asked herself the only question that mattered. What if she couldn't?

"Walk with me and I will answer your questions for you, since that sword evidently has not."

Do not trust him.

Emily's eyes swept behind her toward the crowd again and she played with the band on her finger.

"You promise not to do anything to anyone here?" asked Emily.

"I promise I will not harm anyone here," exclaimed Yuansou, his voice like a knife in the dark. He moved back toward the door and held it open for Emily. The cold night air shifted in, but it almost warmed her. She walked past Yuansou and shivered again when she did. He followed her out and stepped up, so they were walking next to one another.

He took even steps, keeping pace with her, and he moved with a quiet purpose. Like he was holding himself back, tempering his movements, pretending to be human. They walked in silence for less than a minute until they were a decent distance away from the theater. Emily held up her hand, and after a flash of light she was holding Meihua. She shifted into a defensive stance and backed away from Yuansou.

He sneered at her. "Feel better?"

"What do you want?" spat Emily.

Attack him, said Meihua. *He's a threat. Get rid of him and all our problems are gone.*

The thought had occurred to Emily, too. She could lash out, get rid of him, but the way he stood so calmly unnerved her. It was like he didn't view Emily as a threat, even with Meihua in her hands.

"I know what you're thinking," he said. "Or, I should say, I know what the sword is thinking. Get rid of me. Get rid of all your problems. Well, I have an alternative." Emily didn't answer but she took another step back and brandished the sword out in front of her.

"Give me the sword."

"*What?*"

"You heard me," replied Yuansou. "All I want is the sword. Give it to me and I will leave you, your friends, and your family alone."

He stepped toward Emily but stopped when she tensed up.

"It's a good offer. Did they tell you what would happen if you took the sword? Did they tell you the danger you would be in? Did they give you a choice? I am. I'm here offering to take this awful burden off your back. All you have to do is give it to me."

For a second Emily imagined giving him the sword, letting him walk away with her, and living a normal life again. She wouldn't have to hide or lie to Allison anymore. She could have time to herself. She could just relax and live the life she had always imagined.

Except, a normal life wasn't the one she had always imagined. She had dreamt of being a hero. She had imagined living a life like her aunt. Travelling the world, being more than just some girl.

And worst of all, Yuansou had called Meihua "it."

"I don't think so," replied Emily.

Yuansou glowered. The confidence on his face disappeared

and was replaced with scorn. The air around him seethed. Her body tensed up as a wave of something she could only describe as danger emanated from him and she took another two steps back.

And then all at once it was gone. He took a step back and clasped his hands behind him. "Very well. We'll just have to take it from you."

"You can try," growled Emily. "Wait—*we?*"

A dark mass dropped from above and landed between Emily and Yuansou. Emily hopped back and held the sword out in front of her. The shape was huddled over and had impossibly long arms. It had armor of some kind and there were a pair of swords strapped to its back. It reached up with its arms and pulled two broad, curved swords from its back that Emily recognized as dao. Its arms were covered in fur the color of sand on a dull day. Its face was leathery and much darker than its fur. A long tail stretched out behind the creature. It twirled the swords in its hands and glared impassively at Emily. All she could do was gape at the monkey standing before her.

"We did say we wouldn't harm you," Yuansou said while inspecting his fingernails. "He didn't though."

The monkey shrieked at Emily and charged.

It came at Emily faster than any enemy she'd faced in her limited experience, but she was ready with Meihua in hand. The monkey slashed down at her with both dao and Emily brought Meihua up to meet the charge. The monstrous monkey had thin limbs, but its strength shoved Emily back all the same. It pressed down with its blades and kicked up from the ground, flying over Emily in a somersault. It lashed out with both swords one after the other. Emily parried the first, but something hot flashed against her shoulder. She cried out and fell to the ground.

Tentatively, she reached behind her and touched her shoulder. It came away slick and when she brought it around there was blood on her fingers.

The monkey studied her briefly. "You're not as good as I thought you'd be."

Emily was stunned. "You can talk?"

The monkey snorted. "That's what surprised you?"

"I guess it shouldn't have. Nothing should surprise me now."

"Give up the sword. You can't win. I'd rather not kill a little girl," said the monkey.

Emily hefted Meihua in response and charged. The monkey shrugged, jumped high, and placed both dao back into their scabbards. He climbed up the wall until he was on the roof of the building and stood there patiently.

"Meihua, can you help me?" Emily asked.

Always.

Relaxing her body was odd and difficult for her mind to do considering everything that was happening, but she somehow managed to achieve a level of clarity. She bent her knees and Meihua slipped in and helped her jump. She jumped higher than she ever had before. She landed against the wall with her feet and then kicked off lightly, sending herself up even higher until she too was on the roof.

The monkey grunted and they both lunged. Emily dodged and parried its first two blows and then lashed out with Meihua. One dao came up and slapped her thrust aside and countered with its own. She twisted her sword down and sent the monster's thrust aside, spinning while doing so. She lashed out with a kick, but the monkey balanced itself on one hand and caught her kick with his foot. He grunted again and threw both swords into the air. He shoved her leg away and she stumbled back. As she was falling, he jumped up, grabbed the two swords, and came down with both in another downward slash.

Emily rolled back out of the way and sprang up with a slash of her own. The monkey parried the blow and came at her again. The next sequence was a flurry of slashes, parries, and thrusts so fast that Emily couldn't remember performing half the maneuvers. Meihua was helping her, but Emily's breath was growing heavier with each movement. The monkey finally slipped through her defenses by dropping one sword, catching it with his foot, and stabbing it toward Emily's leg. She had stepped back reflexively and the monkey countered by punching her hard in the gut.

She tumbled back and the air in her lungs exploded through her. She held Meihua out in front of her while holding her stomach with her left hand.

"You're getting tired," remarked someone from behind.

She spun around.

Yuansou stood there as if he didn't have a care in the world. "It seems you're just not ready for the sword."

"Shut up!" Emily dove for him and unleashed an enraged slash.

Something heavy landed on top of her before she could reach him and her body collapsed on itself. She was pressed face down on the roof. She was still clutching Meihua, but her hand was pinned. She managed to turn her head. The monkey was sitting on her back, his limbs restricting her movements.

"Well done," said Yuansou. "Disarm her."

The monkey shifted his weight and position over Emily and tried to pry Meihua out of her hand, except Emily wouldn't let go. She clung to the sword. If she let go, it would probably mean the end of her life. She strained against the strength of the monkey, but neither of them budged. He slammed her hand against the roof and the roof bit into her skin. It raked and burned and blood was sliding down her arm. The monkey slammed her hand down again, but she still clung to the sword. She realized now it must have been because of Meihua because if it was up to her, she would have let Meihua go already.

"She won't let go," said the monkey.

"Disarm her. Literally," ordered Yuansou.

The sound of metal grating against metal broke Emily's struggles and drew her attention to her opponent. The monkey let the cool steel blade rest on her hand. He caressed Emily's skin with the sword, a silent promise that something bad was going to happen. The monkey locked eyes with Emily.

"Last chance to let go of the sword."

"Screw you," spat Emily.

The monkey shrugged, raised his hand up, and let it come flying down. Two things happened at that moment. The glint of light off the sword came down like lightning, and then another shape came flying in and collided with the monkey. The weight off her back was released so fast that Emily almost forgot that she was free. Almost.

She jumped up and brandished Meihua in front of her

again with the edge pointed toward Yuansou. There was the sound of a scuffle, and Emily forced herself to look. Her aunt was fighting the monkey. Somehow, she had taken one of the dao from him and they were slashing at one another. They were locked in a dance of blades, which left Yuansou to Emily and Meihua.

Emily shifted her attention back on him and advanced. She came in quick with a downward slash moving from right to left. Yuansou dodged it deftly. His lip curved into a frown.

"We are at a disadvantage," he said matter-of-factly. "We promised not to harm anyone here tonight." He let out a distraught sigh. "Let us take our leave."

"No!" cried out Emily. She lunged at him again, but he jumped high into the air, which all in all was a stupid decision to Emily. She positioned herself under where he would land and got ready to thrust Meihua up and stab him.

A dark shape flew in from her right and blocked her line of sight. It passed quickly and when it did, Yuansou was gone. Emily searched the night sky and found a giant bird flying away with Yuansou standing on its back. He waved a hand and then the monkey disappeared in a cloud of inky, black smoke.

CHAPTER 22

PLUM BLOSSOM ELEGY

EMILY RETURNED HOME injured from a monster attack for the second time in a month and she was tired of it. Her aunt helped her into the house and held her up from her uninjured shoulder. "Chris! Get the leather pouch from my room! It's on the dresser!"

"What happened?" screamed her mom.

Aunt Elaine and Emily made their way into the kitchen and were followed by Mom. Dad came into view holding the aforementioned pouch and set it down on the island. Emily leaned against the island while her mom and aunt pulled her jacket off her. Her mom gasped and then someone's hands touched her shoulder.

Emily's shoulder had seared with pain earlier but now with Meihua helping, the pain was more like a dull ache. She was cut, but she couldn't tell how bad it was. She barely felt her aunt's fingers touching it.

Her aunt opened the pouch and pulled out a little jar that looked like it was for hair wax. She spun the top off and scooped a thick glob of white cream with two of her fingers. She started swabbing it on Emily's cut and a cool sensation spread over her shoulder and the pain dulled even more.

"It's shallow and short," said Aunt Elaine. "You were lucky."

"I dodged most of it," said Emily.

"Not enough of it," replied Aunt Elaine. "I think it's just skin deep. Maybe he was going easy on you."

"What happened?" asked Emily's mom again.

Aunt Elaine wiped her hands off and then pulled out some bandages from the pouch. Her eyes darted to Emily's mom and then back to Emily with anger and disappointment in her eyes.

"Why don't you ask your daughter?" said Aunt Elaine. "I told her to stay home."

"I just wanted to see Allison's show." Emily hissed through her teeth as her aunt applied pressure and a bandage to the cut on her shoulder. "It was intermission and some guy walked in. He said Meihua's name, and then he threatened everyone in the theater if I didn't walk out with him."

"What?" said Aunt Elaine. "A man came up to you? And he knew about Meihua? What did he look like?"

"He had a hood over his face, and it was crazy," said Emily. "The shadows inside his hood stretched out to cover his face. I couldn't see anything above his mouth. But his voice was the creepiest thing I've ever heard. He had more than one. And Meihua knew him too."

"Meihua knew him?" said her dad. "How is that even possible?"

Emily shrugged. "He said his name was Yuansou or something."

Emily felt her aunt's hands freeze just above her shoulder and there was a sharp intake of breath. Her father went deathly still in front of her. Emily glanced over her shoulder. Aunt Elaine's hands were shaking. Emily turned back to her dad. His head was tilted down at the ground and he was biting his lip. Emily turned to her mother, but she just had a confused expression on her face.

"Yuansou?" whispered Aunt Elaine.

"Yeah, that's it," said Emily.

"Are you sure?" asked her dad. "Absolutely positive?"

"Yes," said Emily. "Who is Yuansou?"

Her dad ignored her and addressed Aunt Elaine. "How can that be? He's real?"

"I don't know," replied Aunt Elaine.

"You saw him, too?" her dad asked. Aunt Elaine nodded. "I thought he was just a story."

"What are you talking about?" asked Emily.

"You're sure he said his name was Yuansou?" asked her dad.

"Positive. Meihua hated him," said Emily. "She wanted me to attack him."

Emily replayed the moment Yuansou identified himself. She recalled the ice in his voice but thinking back she remembered the absolute venom in Meihua's. But there had been something else in her voice, too. A quiet quiver. Something that Emily had in her own voice when he appeared in front of her. Why was Meihua afraid of him?

"Who is Yuansou?" Emily asked again. Aunt Elaine and her dad's eyes met for a brief second before they rested on Emily. "You've heard about him."

"Yes," said Aunt Elaine.

"When we were children," said her dad. "But he was just a story. He can't be real."

"He seemed pretty real tonight," said Emily. "Why are you all so scared of him? Even Meihua is."

It's not him, said Meihua in the mental equivalent of a whisper.

"What do you mean it's not him?" asked Emily.

"It's not him she's scared of," replied Aunt Elaine. "Your grandpa used to tell us stories. Yuansou was a sorcerer. He worked for The Demon."

"He's a demon that worked for another demon?" asked Emily.

"No," said her dad. "*The* Demon. He's a ghost story. Our family's boogeyman. It's the story *yeye* used to tell me and Elaine at night to scare us into doing what we were told. He can't be real."

He is, said Meihua.

"Okay, you need to tell us what's going on," said Emily aloud.

Everyone in the kitchen was staring at Emily.

"What?" asked her mom.

"Sorry, I was talking to Meihua," said Emily. "What's going on? Who is Yuansou? Who is The Demon?"

There was silence as everyone in the room continued to stare at Emily. Her dad settled into a seat at the island beside her and her mom moved in closer too.

It might be easier if you let me tell it through you, said Meihua.

"What do you mean?" asked Emily.

Let me have some control, use your voice to tell the story. I will tell the story to you and everyone else with your voice. I can even show you. They'll have to settle for hearing it though.

Emily exhaled. "Okay. This is going to be weird. She's going to tell us the story through me."

"You're going to give her control of your voice," said Aunt Elaine.

"What?" exclaimed Emily's mom.

"It's fine, Jessica," said Aunt Elaine. "She's just going to talk to us so we can hear the story. It's easier this way. Now, we hear it straight from her instead of secondhand. Emily will be fine."

Are you ready? asked Meihua.

Everyone's attention was on her when she let Meihua take control. Warmth tingled up her arms and down her legs until they reached the tips of her extremities. A breath rose and then it escaped quietly before she spoke.

"I'm not even sure where to begin," said Emily. Her voice was paired with Meihua's, creating an echo behind each other. *"It would be easiest to just tell you who he is. But I feel you deserve to know more. How our agreement came to pass. Where I come from. What I am. And why I hate and fear Yuansou and his master."*

An image exploded into Emily's mind. There was a rush of green and blue and white and brown. She soared over the sky and then came crashing down into a valley. In the valley was a settlement somewhere between the size of a village and a city. The buildings were an off-white and topped with glazed green roof tiles. Off to the side of the small city was a house with a small hill in its walled yard. And on that hill stood a single tree. It had spindly branches forking out from its trunk like lightning, and each branch was ablaze with white flowers. The wind blowing made them shift and every flower flickered like candlelight. Emily studied the tree and recognized it. She had walked up the hill to that tree. She had sat under it. And then she realized that it was Meihua.

"I wasn't always a sword. I was born a long time ago, before this country, before China, in a land far across the sea. I don't remember how I was born or if born was even the right word. I simply came to be, I suppose. Before I was a sword, I was a tree. A plum blossom tree."

The scenery spun round and round and everything in the background shifted from winter to spring to summer to fall then back to winter over and over again.

It stopped suddenly and they were in the middle of spring. Something rustled beneath her. Emily's body moved on its own bringing the base of the tree into view. A man and a woman were lying beneath the boughs of the tree. They both slept silently in the sunlight. Their fingers were intertwined with one another, each clinging to the other like vines on a trestle. Petals drifted around them like fresh snowfall leaving the hill with an air of winter instead of the spring that Emily could practically smell.

"What I do know is that a family built their home around me. They cared for me, lived their lives next to me, spoke to me, and soon I came to life. I have been called a lot of things. A spirit, a genius loci, a god, the title doesn't matter. To me, all that mattered was that I cared for that family as much as they cared for me."

The scene shifted again, and Emily's stomach pitched as she was launched into the air. The tiny village disappeared, and she flew over valleys, forests, and mountains until she was lingering over an enormous city.

"That peace was not meant to last," said Meihua.

Emily lurched forward again this time flying over mountains and steppes until she was floating over a vast dark shape. It was moving and pulsed as if it was alive.

"War came upon the land like a swarm of locusts. It swallowed everything up. Land, animals, resources, people. It wasn't long before it came to the tiny little corner that your family and I called home."

Again, the scene shifted. It showed a man dressed in fancy robes reading off a scroll to a crowd of people. The scene focused on one young man standing off to the side in the shade. A woman stood next to him with her arm wrapped through his. Their eyes met and fear was evident on both their faces.

"The only son of the family, the only living heir, was being forced into war. He was terrified, had just fallen in love, and had everything to lose. That night he sat at my roots and prayed. Prayed for protection for his family and his love. I decided to help him. I used up all of my power that I had accumulated and transformed myself into a sword."

A flash of light burst out from the tree. Emily and the man both shied away from the brightness of it, and when they had regained their vision, the tree was gone. A sword ornamented with plum blossoms was now laying sheathed where the tree had once stood.

"I told him to pick me up, called out to him, and when he did, I bonded with him as I have with everyone in your family line. He took me to war. He told me his fears, his love; he shared with me. In turn I protected him. I brought him back from the war in one piece. Physically, mentally, spiritually. I kept him

whole. And when he came back, he married the girl and tried to give me back to the earth.

"I had given up too much power though and was forced to remain a sword. He promised me then that he would pass me down to his children so that I would never be alone or forgotten."

Faces flashed before Emily's eyes. Men, women, young, old, each one different until suddenly all the faces disappeared, and Emily was surrounded by a sea of black. It was thick like fog and Emily held her breath trying not to take in any of the miasma.

"But then the cycle was broken. I was taken by The Demon. Heise." There was a hard edge to Emily and Meihua's voice when they said the name. *"That monster used me to do terrible things. He used me to attack things, people. I killed people.*

"Don't get me wrong. I had been used to kill people before, but there was a difference. Before I was used to help someone survive. With The Demon, he used me to kill for sport. For fun. Because he could." Meihua's voice along with Emily's cracked and Emily choked down a sob. *"To everyone else I was a partner. We were extensions of each other's wills. To The Demon I was just a tool, a weapon. Do you know what it's like to be used? To have no control? The things he made me do. The things I saw.*

"I am blessed because I can use my memory, my knowledge to help my wielders. I am cursed because of The Demon. I can never forget what he made me do."

"What happened?" Emily heard her mom ask. "How did you get away?"

"The family," said Meihua. *"They heard about what was happening and they came for me. They brought a wizard and a whole host of warriors. All of them combined managed to pry me*

from The Demon's hands. They couldn't kill him though, so they locked him away. And then I was given to a new family member so the cycle could start over again."

"What does Yuansou have to do with that?" asked Mom. "You said The Demon's name was Heise."

"We don't know The Demon's name. The family decided to call him Heise. Yuansou was his underling," replied their two voices. *"He's a summoner, a demon. He corrupts creatures with his magic. The process transforms them, and they become his thralls. He was defeated along with Heise, but he escaped while they were capturing The Demon. We never heard from him again. We thought him too cowardly to show his face after he was defeated, but he's back. And if he's back, Heise is close behind."*

"I don't understand," said Emily, taking control again. "Everyone's told me that you only work for who you want to work for. Why couldn't you just stop working for Heise?"

And then she remembered the rules that made everything make sense. The black flower on the tree. The charred sword locked in chains. Every flower, every weapon, was a past guardian.

"Oh my God," whispered Emily.

"What?" asked her dad.

"Heise isn't a demon," said Emily. "He's human. He's one of us."

"One of us?" asked her mom.

Emily couldn't say the words, so Meihua did.

"He is your ancestor."

CHAPTER 23

A GOOD FRIEND

EMILY FOUND HERSELF exiled to her room after Meihua finished telling the story. Aunt Elaine and Emily's dad had apparently decided that Emily's role that evening was finished, and Emily's mom was all too eager to agree with them. Now Emily was grounded for real. She wasn't allowed to leave the house at all. Not until they had figured out what to do about Yuansou.

She was just making her way to her room when there was a knock at the front door and Stephen and Bryan were admitted into the house. Bryan looked up and gave Emily a weak wave. She returned it and leaned on the bannister to watch.

"How is she?" asked Stephen. He sounded like he was actually worried about Emily.

"Fine," said Aunt Elaine. "Just a small cut on her shoulder. Used up a little qi. Nothing some rest won't fix."

"I knew this was too much of a responsibility for her," said Stephen. "If you had only listened, we—"

"Stephen!" cut off Aunt Elaine. "Now is not the time. Nor will it ever be the time. I have bad news."

"What?" asked Stephen.

"We identified who's after Emily and Meihua," said Aunt Elaine.

"Who?" repeated Bryan. "Not what?"

Aunt Elaine nodded. "Emily snuck out tonight and was attacked by a man. He called himself Yuansou."

Both Stephen and Bryan's bodies went rigid.

"You can't be serious," scoffed Stephen.

"I am," said Aunt Elaine. "I saw him myself tonight. He summoned monsters. Just like in the stories."

There was silence between the three of them now and then Bryan motioned up to Emily. "What do we do now then? About her?"

Aunt Elaine eyed Emily. "She's under house arrest. She snuck out and nearly died for it. I'm going to have to make some calls to see if I can find out any more about Yuansou. I was hoping you two could stay and protect the house."

"Yes," said Bryan immediately.

Stephen glowered at his son and then up at Emily, but when he turned to Aunt Elaine his face had changed.

"Worthy or not, she is the sword's guardian," he said. "I'll double check the barrier. Then we can keep watch of the area outside. Best to stop a threat before it gets too close."

"Agreed," said Aunt Elaine. She shook his hand. "Thank you."

"Don't thank me," said Stephen. "I haven't done anything."

He and Bryan turned to leave, and Bryan waved at Emily. She waved back and watched the two of them slip outside into the dead of night. Aunt Elaine shut the door behind them and let out a resigned breath. She turned and started to walk away when she noticed Emily still standing at the bannister.

"You should be in your bed resting," said Aunt Elaine. "You can't do anything to help if you're tired."

Emily turned without saying anything and disappeared into her room. She fell on her bed and pulled her phone out of her pocket. She was inundated with messages. Her phone had been on silent since the start of the show, and she hadn't had a chance to check it since being attacked by Yuansou.

She had multiple missed text messages, calls, and a voice mail. One of the texts was from Marina saying she ran into Allison after the show and Allison told her that Emily didn't need a ride home.

Then there were the messages from Allison. Emily opened them and thumbed through them all. "Where are you?" "Are you still here?" "Did you leave?"

Then there were missed calls and finally a voicemail. Emily put the phone up to her ear to listen.

"Hey, so I guess you just decided to leave? Did you even stay for the whole show? We were supposed to go out afterward. Okay, whatever. Bye."

Her phone dinged. A new text message from Allison.

"I guess this is just how things are between us now. I mean I should have seen it coming. You never want to hang out anymore. We never talk about things, and it feels like you're hiding something from me. We used to tell each other everything! Now I'm lucky if I can get more than a few words out of you! I'm done."

Emily tapped at her phone furiously until she was calling

Allison. The tone went off twice before Allison's voicemail kicked in.

"No," said Emily. She redialed. This time there was no ring, it just went straight to voicemail. "SHIT!"

She threw her phone at her bed, grabbed her pillow, and screamed into it. She screamed and she screamed until her throat was raw and then ripped the pillow from her face and threw it across the room. Emily wanted to scream at Allison and tell her everything.

Ding.

Emily scrambled for her phone and saw another new text message from Allison. "Don't call me again."

She stared at her phone for a long while then. The words ripped a part of her soul from her and tore a hole into her chest. She hit the home button and the text message disappeared. Her background showed off a photo of her and Allison together over the summer. After a few moments the picture dimmed, and then it turned to black.

The whole process might have taken a minute, it might have taken ten. She wasn't sure. Something tickled her cheek, and she brushed her face. Her hand came away wet and she held it out in front of herself. Emily couldn't remember starting to cry, but now there were tears staining her face leaving trails like streams drying up. The phone fell and she buried her face in her hands. Heavy sobs bore through her like she had been underwater for too long.

The door to her room opened suddenly and her mother came rushing in. "Emily, what's wrong?"

Her mom moved instantly to her side and Emily half

stood up before she was enveloped in her mom's arms. "It's okay honey. Tell me what's going on."

"It's… Allison," Emily managed to blurt out through sobs. "She hates me."

Her mother rubbed Emily's head and pulled her in tighter. "Oh, she doesn't hate you. Why would you think that?"

Emily told her mom about all the text messages and the angry voicemail.

"But what did she say?"

"She basically said she doesn't want to be friends with me anymore," said Emily.

"Basically," repeated her mom. "Did she actually say that?"

Emily shied away from her mother. "No."

"So, what did she actually say?"

Emily spun back toward her mother and wiped away some tears. "She told me that we never talk anymore. That she can tell I'm keeping something from her. That I never want to hang out with her."

"Is that true?" asked her mother.

"No!" screamed Emily. She breathed heavily and waited for her mom to yell at her in return, but she didn't. She just gave Emily a small smile that said continue. "I mean you know it's not."

"Did you tell her that?"

"She wouldn't let me."

"Well, she's probably mad right now," said her mom.

Emily snorted.

"It makes sense," replied Mom. "Just give her some time. You two have been friends all your life. She'll get over it and she'll call you back."

Emily sniffed loudly and wiped at her face with a tissue her mom handed her. "She was so mad. I'm such a bad friend."

"That's not true," said her mom.

"How do you know?" snapped Emily.

Her mother knelt in front of Emily. She took her daughter firmly by the shoulders and held her in place. She didn't say anything until Emily finally met her mom's eyes.

"I know because I know you. I have seen you these last few weeks. I have seen all the hard work you've put in, all the things you've gone through. You have been hated by someone who never gave you a chance. You were forced to fight someone you would rather get to know. You are risking your life so your aunt can finally live hers. You have fought monsters and men from ghost stories just to protect your best friend. Sure, there were other people there, but I imagine they just got lucky that Allison was there. You went through and did all those things, and here we are less than an hour after finding out that the family boogeyman is real… and you're worried that you are a bad friend. That is how I know you're not."

Her mom kissed Emily on her forehead, let go of her shoulders, and stood up to leave the room. She didn't even wait to see if her daughter was okay. She just left Emily alone with the aftermath of her words.

"Mom!" called Emily before her mother managed to leave the room.

Her mom stopped at the door and turned. "Hmm?"

"Thank you," she said with new tears in her eyes. "And I love you."

"I love you too, honey."

Emily lay on her bed in the quiet of her room trying to take in everything Meihua had told them that night. The black flower on the tree and the sword that was just wrong. How Heise got a hold of Meihua all made sense now. But there was more. There had to be.

"That doesn't answer everything," said Emily. "If he was so bad, if he made you do such terrible things, why didn't you stop working for him? Like how you did with Aunt Elaine?"

Emily shut her eyes and a vision of Meihua appeared in her head. It was just the two of them. Emily was standing in an expanse of endless black. It was the color of water in the dead of night, and it was deathly still like a fjord. Emily watched her feet. Each step rippled across the black water. Standing across from her was Meihua. She was dressed in a pure white *hanfu* that was a stark contrast to the darkness all around them.

"What is this?" asked Emily.

"I told you before that we all have our secrets," said Meihua. *"Now it's time I share mine with you. I haven't told this story in a long time. I don't know if I can tell everyone. Not yet. But I can tell you."*

Emily looked at Meihua now, really looked at her.

She was unsure, scared, nothing like the regal vision she had been in Emily's dreams so many weeks ago. Now she was like Emily on her first day of school, or maybe how Emily looked on the day of the duel. Worse, she had an ashamed expression on her face.

"Heise wasn't his name. That was what the family called him. His real name was Kuo," said Meihua. She gestured to her left with her hand and the water rippled until it showed a man.

He was handsome and confident in a black and gray *hanfu*. He had long black hair bound so it was above his head like a topknot. He held a sword in his hand and Emily instantly recognized Meihua. *"Kuo was the most skilled guardian I ever had. He was strong, courageous, kind, and loyal. He didn't need me to win fights. He carried me just so I could live with him."*

The image shifted to show the man with a beautiful woman and a small boy who couldn't have been older than ten. *"Kuo had a wife and son. His wife's name was Liling and his son's name was Sheng. They were happy together, and I was happy for them. Then one day Sheng went out to play with some friends. Those friends returned later covered in dirt and tears, and without Sheng. Kuo and Liling asked them what happened, and they told Kuo that they had gone into the woods and found an old cave that they were always told to stay out of. They dared each other to get close to it, but Sheng had gone inside. That was when they heard him scream, and then they ran home.*

"Kuo set out immediately with me in hand, determined to find out what happened to his son and to save him," said Meihua. The image shifted and it showed Kuo practically flying through the woods, jumping effortlessly from tree to tree like he was gliding through the forest. *"We found the cave and Kuo stepped inside. Sheng was seated in the center of the cave, waiting. He smiled at his father when we walked inside, but it was wrong."*

There was horror on her face, even after all these years. *"It wasn't Sheng's smile. They weren't Sheng's eyes,"* said Meihua. *"And when he spoke, it wasn't a child's voice."*

Emily turned back to the reflection, to the little boy who was just grinning evilly at the man who had come to save him.

"Yuansou?" asked Emily, fear in her own voice.

"No," said Meihua. *"Heise. You see, demons in China are rarely physical things. They are spirits, and Heise was no different. He was a very strong spirit, and he took over Sheng's body."*

Horror and revulsion rolled over Emily like a wave, and she fought the urge to vomit.

"Heise offered Kuo a trade," said Meihua. *"He would release Sheng and let him go free, in exchange for Kuo's body.*

"Kuo agreed immediately," continued Meihua. *"He tried to give me to his son to take back. He wanted to save me as well, but I refused to leave. I told him that I wouldn't leave him. I was as much his guardian as he was mine. I would help him, protect him from Heise. I would defend his mind, body, and soul. I thought I could save him."*

Meihua brushed at the corner of her eyes.

"I couldn't."

The scene shifted again and there was a new Kuo. He was still the handsome man he was before, but the smile was gone. Everything about him was sharper. He was more serious, and his kind face was replaced by something that was evil, threatening.

The scene dissipated back into black water and the two of them were alone. Meihua was in open tears now. She sobbed.

"Sheng made it home, and the family was told what happened. They dispatched warriors immediately to try and save Kuo, but Heise was stronger than any of us had realized. He had threatened Kuo that if he didn't uphold his end of the deal, he would go after his family again. So Kuo fought me. Heise used Kuo's body however he liked, and the whole time I was locked in combat against the very person I was trying to save."

Meihua focused on the water again. *It was no longer about me saving him. Now I was the one held captive. I couldn't save him, and I couldn't save myself. It was a long time before the family was able to stop Heise. Kuo's own son led the charge against his father. I think that was the only reason Heise was captured. Kuo stopped fighting me and fought against Heise. It lasted only a moment, but he let me go, and the family was able to subdue him. By then Heise had too strong a hold over Kuo's body, and the only thing they could do was lock him away.*

Meihua raised her head, tears streaming down her face, and Emily was reminded of the anguish on her family's faces when Aunt Elaine had told them she was dying.

They locked me away too, whispered Meihua.

"What?" said Emily, disbelief in her voice.

I had been with Heise a long time, replied Meihua. *They weren't sure that I hadn't been corrupted.* She gestured all around her. *This emptiness, this nothing, this was all I experienced for five years.*

Five years. How could you even measure time in a place like this? Did you count the days? What did you do in all that time?

"How do you know it was five years?" asked Emily in a whisper.

Sheng visited me once a year, said Meihua. *He wanted to free me. He wanted to use me, to help prove to the rest of the family that I wasn't corrupted. Five times in five years and each time I told him no. After the fifth time I was given to someone new.*

"Why didn't you go with Sheng?" asked Emily. "You could have been out of... this." She gestured around them.

Emily couldn't imagine being stuck in a place like this for longer than five minutes. Five years sounded awful.

"I was ashamed," said Meihua. She wiped tears from her eyes. Her cheeks and eyes were still red. *"I told you before, Emily. I love every one of my guardians. I remember them all. I couldn't save him, and I couldn't face his son after that."*

CHAPTER 24

A HERO

EMILY'S HANDS STARTED to shake, and she opened her eyes suddenly. She wasn't sure if she had fallen asleep or if she had gone into some deep, meditative trance with Meihua, but something had woken her up.

Bzzzt. Bzzzt.

Emily's phone buzzed in her hands. She turned the phone over in her hand and saw two things. The first was the time. It was just before midnight meaning Emily had been asleep for a couple hours. The second, more important thing, was that Allison was calling her. Her heart lit up like a fire and suddenly her whole world wasn't crumbling around her. She hit the answer button on her phone.

"Allison," Emily said groggily. "I'm so happy you called."

"Hello again," said many voices at once, none of which were Allison's. Emily's breath froze and she felt a mental recognition from Meihua. Emily imagined if Meihua could breathe, she would have stopped just then too. "Now don't go telling anyone who's talking to you. We would hate for something to happen to your dear friend here. What was her name again?"

"Allison," whispered Emily and her voice cracked while saying it.

"What was that? We couldn't hear you," replied Yuansou.

"Allison," Emily repeated. Her voice was clearer this time, but it was still layered in fear.

"Right. Beautiful name. Here's the deal. You come to us and we'll let your friend go free. You come alone. If you don't, then we'll know. Do you know what we will do to Allison if you don't listen to us?"

"You'll kill her," whispered Emily.

"No, I won't," was his reply, and this time it was one voice. "I will take her. I imagine Meihua has told you who I am by now? What I do? What I can do?" He paused as if waiting for a response, but Emily couldn't say anything. "I'll take that silence as a yes. I will take her, change her, she will serve me forever. It's harder to do with more intelligent life. They fight so hard to hold out. It will take time, but I will break her. Then she will be mine. Do you understand?"

"Yes," whispered Emily again.

"Now, meet us at your school," said the multiple voices again. "Can you do that?"

Emily jumped up from her bed and opened her door just a little bit. She peeked out into the darkness of the night-filled house. "I don't know," said Emily. "There are two people watching the house. I don't know where they are."

"We have already taken care of them," said Yuansou. "And their barrier."

Rage and fear burned inside her for Bryan, and yes, for Stephen too. "You better not have hurt them—"

"We do not think you are in any position to tell us what to do," broke in Yuansou. "Now, can you meet us at your school?"

"Yes," said Emily.

"Good." There was shuffling on the phone and then Yuansou spoke. His voice was a little farther away like he was talking to someone else. "You. What's this place called?"

"It's the stage in the quad," Emily heard a quiet voice say. Allison.

"Right. Come to the stage in the quad at your school. Understand?"

"Yes," replied Emily.

"Good. You live close. You've got fifteen minutes."

Click. Yuansou ended the call. Thoughts and panic flooded Emily all at once. She paced around her room and clutched her head in her hands. There wasn't time to do anything. She couldn't tell her family; they wouldn't let her go alone. If she didn't show up alone then Allison was worse than dead. She didn't have time to explain or to even sit around and think about it. She had to sneak out and go.

You can't go alone, chimed in Meihua. *He will kill you. He will take me from you.*

"If I don't go alone, then he's going to take Allison," spat Emily.

You don't even know that he has her.

"You heard her!" Emily replied.

It could be a trick.

"I can't take that chance," whispered Emily.

So what happens if you go? What do you do? What's your plan?

"I don't know!" cried Emily. She stopped and listened. She couldn't hear any footsteps outside her room, and no one had come to check on her. She grabbed the jacket from her bed and started pulling it on. "I have to do something though. I have to protect her."

I'm not saying you shouldn't do anything. But... I can't be taken again.

Emily had felt how scared Meihua was when she showed her the memory from so long ago. She had no idea how long ago it had happened or how many guardians had come and gone in the time since then, but the thought of Heise still shook Meihua to her core. She still remembered. Emily couldn't recall being so afraid of something that it still haunted her. She had had recurring nightmares but nothing that affected her daily life. Nothing that had scarred her so much.

But she knew something that might.

If she didn't do anything, if she didn't try to save Allison, and Yuansou took her. If he corrupted her, warped her into something of his own making, Emily would never be able to live with herself. She knew deep in her heart of hearts that doing nothing would break her in a way that could never be fixed.

Meihua had said that destiny was just small choices that led up to one big one. All the choices she had made brought her here to this exact moment. She was going to have to choose, but there was really no choice. She had to save Allison. She had to try.

"Meihua, I understand you're scared," replied Emily. She raised her hand up to her face, so the ring was at eye level. "But my best friend is in danger. A monster from your past, not mine, is holding her hostage. If you're too scared to help me, then I'll leave you here and go by myself. Do I have to do that?"

No, said Meihua quickly. Emily tried to hide her relief, but she realized it was probably silly since Meihua could basically read her mind.

"Will you help me?"

Of course, I will, replied Meihua.

Are you sure you know what you're doing? Meihua asked when the school came into sight.

"No," replied Emily. "I didn't really have time to come up with a plan, remember?"

I do, said Meihua.

"Do you regret choosing me yet?" Emily asked.

There was silence and Emily imagined Meihua was thinking it over. She wasn't sure if she should have been hurt at how long it was taking Meihua to answer, or if she should be okay with it considering what they were walking into. She'd always read scenes in books where people said that they appreciated candor, but she wondered if a white lie to comfort someone was better in potentially final moments.

Has Elaine ever told you about the first time I saw you? Meihua asked suddenly. *The first time I really saw you.*

"No."

It was the first time you met Allison, I believe.

"Really?"

Yes, came Meihua's reply. *It was years ago when you were little. Aunt Elaine had come by for a surprise visit and asked your parents if she could pick you up from school. They said yes and we waited outside for you. Now I'd seen you before, but I never gave you much thought. You were just a kid. Elaine was young. We both hadn't thought of who would inherit me. We wouldn't have to think about it for years.*

"I remember that now," said Emily. "I think I was in third grade."

Second, corrected Meihua.

"You sure?"

I have a very good memory. Plus, moments like that one are some of my most cherished memories.

"Moments like what?" asked Emily. Cold air bit into her skin despite her jacket, and Emily needed the conversation to distract her from the temperature.

When I know who my next guardian will be.

Emily and her breath stopped at the same time. She thought back to that day, to what had happened to Allison, and how they became friends.

"You've known since then?" Emily asked.

Yes, replied Meihua. *Do you remember what happened?*

"Yeah, Allison was new to school. She was in my class, but we didn't talk very much. She was shy and didn't talk to anyone actually. Then class got out and we all started leaving."

Right, and what happened next?

"I was walking out, and a boy started bullying Allison," said Emily, the memory flooded back uncontrollably now. Like when you're not sure how to tell a story, then you start stringing word after word and then it all just comes naturally. "Wait, are you talking about when I punched Jeff? He didn't like how she was dressed or the way she looked at him or something stupid."

And what did you do?

Emily snorted a small sound of derision. "I saw him picking on her and something just snapped. I shoved him. He shoved me back. He said something to me that made me really mad. I don't remember what it was. So, I punched him. He bled a lot."

You might have broken his nose, replied Meihua. *And that was when I knew you were going to be my next guardian. I think that's when Elaine knew, too.*

"When I broke a second grader's nose?"

No, said Meihua and Emily could tell she was trying not to laugh. *When you defended someone you didn't know who needed defending. You didn't have to help Allison. You didn't know her. Then you saw Elaine and your face lit up. You got in so much trouble though.*

"Well, I was happy to see Aunt Elaine," remarked Emily.

Right, and she kept you from getting in more trouble. And then the three of you sat there until Allison's parents came and picked her up.

"We've been best friends since then," said Emily.

Do you remember what you told your aunt after Allison left?

"No."

You told her you were scared, replied Meihua. *But you did it anyway. And that is why I picked you. You ran headlong into danger, afraid, and did something because you believed you should. That it was the right thing to do. And look. Here you are again. Running into danger. You didn't think about it. You did it because the only thing that mattered to you is that if you did, you could save Allison. You're a hero.*

"Or just stupid," remarked Emily, her cheeks starting to flush. "I'm only a hero if I succeed."

You're not a hero just because you succeed. You become a hero because of the choices you make. You're a hero because you tried.

"Yeah well, let's try to survive this one."

Emily started walking across the parking lot. The streetlights bathed it in a white glow. The parking lot was empty and Emily stifled a shiver while walking through it. The wind made the trees by the entrance sway gently but there were no sounds in their movement. There were no sounds at all. It was unnerving, but Emily told herself it was because of what she was there to do. The gates of the school were closed and locked.

Emily clutched Meihua by the sheathed blade and ran toward the wall. She kicked off the wall and vaulted over the gate. She landed lightly on the ground and internally praised herself for how good she had gotten at that.

She continued her lonely walk inside the school toward whatever fate had decreed for her. She passed the classrooms she had grown used to every day. Emily imagined the echoes of her classmates walking around her. She could hear their voices, see their faces, and she smiled despite her situation. She had always thought Allison was her only friend, but she had more. She had called them acquaintances in her head, but they were friends like everyone who went to the same school and saw each other every day. It was this unspoken bond. They were in this together. They were like family, and like all families they had disagreements, but for the most part they managed to coexist. Emily passed her locker and rested a hand against it. A chill ran down her body and she shivered.

She squeezed the sword in her hand for comfort and to focus on anything else.

Emily? said Meihua.

"I'm scared," whispered Emily.

I'm scared too. You'd be crazy not to be scared. Are you ready?

She didn't answer, not yet at least. She took the moment to understand her fear. What was she afraid of? Losing Allison, in more ways than one, and losing Meihua. These were things a fourteen-year-old girl shouldn't have to feel, but here she was. Fear itself wasn't a new thing, but the stakes were so much higher than she expected. She closed her eyes, tilted her head back a little, and took a deep breath of night air. She listened to the silence of the night. There was no chirping from crickets, or shuffling of trees and bushes, or anything that would have made her feel normal. Just nothing.

"Yeah," she said. "Let's go."

Emily stopped at the corner and poked her head around it. The planter that she usually sat at to eat lunch with Allison was right in front of her and over that was the quad. The quad had the outdoor stage that Yuansou had said to meet at. He was standing on the stage. A chair was next to him, and in that chair was a girl with flowing raven hair. Emily walked across the quad as quickly as she could. Yuansou raised his hand when she made it halfway through the quad. The signal for her to stop.

She did.

"Leave the sword on the table please," said Yuansou.

Emily laid Meihua down on the concrete table. Then he beckoned Emily closer. The arrogance in his smile made her insides roil in anger. The way the corners of his mouth curled up like he had already won. She was really starting to hate smiles like that.

He held up a hand for her to stop again when she was about ten feet away. Yuansou kept smiling at her while he lifted the hood revealing his face.

"Hello Emily," said Stephen with a sneer. "How would you like to make a deal?"

CHAPTER 25

A VILLAIN

MILY'S EYES WIDENED. Her jaw dropped. Shock, revulsion, betrayal, she felt it all. Stephen stood on the edge of the stage with that gloating smile plastered on his face. Here was the uncle who had hated her, and who was apparently behind all of her tragedies the past few weeks. And he was proud of it.

"Stephen? You?"

"Yes. Me." His face shifted until it bore malice. There was a wild gleam to his eyes, and they shifted from their dark color to a vibrant green. "And us."

When he spoke the second time, his voice had taken on the quality that Yuansou's had earlier that night. There was arrogance and evil in it. It sounded like a snake slithering on dry dirt, and claws raking on concrete.

"Emily?" Allison said. Her eyes were wide, and her breath was wild. It came out in plumes of steam from her lips every time she spoke. She was pale, and Emily was sure it wasn't just because of the moonlight.

Stephen rested a hand on her shoulder, and she tried to shy away from his touch. A whimper escaped Allison's lips and Emily took a step forward in response.

He patted Allison's shoulder and she started to cry. "Let's not get ahead of ourselves."

"Don't worry," Emily said to her best friend. "I'll protect you."

She tried to give her friend a reassuring look, but Allison just gaped at Emily, dumbfounded. Her eyes were still wide, and she was shaking. "What's going on? Do you know him?"

She screamed suddenly and it pierced Emily's heart. Stephen or Yuansou must have squeezed her shoulder because her body tensed up suddenly like someone had dropped an ice cube down her back.

"Enough of that," he said. "Stay quiet and let us talk or you won't be allowed to stay."

"Let her go!" screamed Emily. "She's got nothing to do with this!"

"She has something to do with you though," replied Stephen. "And that makes her fair game as far as we are concerned."

"We?" said Emily. She searched for the monkey or the coyote but there were only the three of them. Four if she counted Meihua resting on the table. "What do you mean *we*?"

"We see you have a limited understanding of us," said Stephen.

He spread his arms out wide and raised them in the air. His shadow swirled around him until he was surrounded in a pool of black. It was like ink in the water. It sent smoke like tendrils up into the air, and slowly figures started rising from the shadows. The forms of the coyote and monkey rose on either side of Stephen. Wings spread out from behind him and Emily remembered the bird that had whisked Yuansou away earlier that night. Something large loomed deeper in the shadows and circled Stephen just below the surface.

"We are Yuansou," said all the creatures together.

"Stephen isn't Yuansou?" she asked.

She knew the answer already from Meihua's story. Yuansou had been around for hundreds of years, there was no way it could have been Stephen. But here he was.

"Your uncle is the host," said Yuansou. "Yuansou is a collective. We live on through our hosts. We have been around for hundreds of years. Watching. Waiting."

"Waiting for what?" asked Emily.

"The right opportunity," replied Yuansou.

"Well, I'm here now so you can let Allison go," said Emily.

"She has only served half her purpose."

"Half?" repeated Emily. "What else do you need her for?"

Yuansou's face morphed into a frown like he had just eaten something particularly bitter. He took his hand off Allison's shoulder. She relaxed almost instantly but she was still deathly pale and shaking.

"My girl, from the moment we have laid eyes on you, we have found you utterly unworthy," said Yuansou. No, it was Stephen this time. "Your aunt spoke so highly of you and I expected so much more. Can't you think for yourself?"

"Now, now," said Yuansou this time. "Don't be too hard on her." His eyes darted to the sword then back to Emily. "Like we said at the beginning: Let's make a deal. You give us the sword of your own free will, and you and Allison get to walk away."

"What?"

"You heard us," said Yuansou. "We will let the two of you walk away. No strings attached. You get to live."

Emily thought about it. Meihua wasn't with her and since their mental connection required physical contact, she wasn't here to chime in. She could imagine what Meihua would have said. *Don't trust him.* It wasn't as simple as that though. He had Allison, and at the end of the day that was why Emily came. That was why Emily considered it. Allison was human, her best friend, someone who had been in Emily's life for so many years.

Allison had a wild desperate plea in her eyes. She had no idea what was going on, but she had heard Yuansou say the words. Give him the sword and they get to walk away. That was probably perfect to Allison. A sword for her life. There was fear in Allison's eyes, and Emily realized that Meihua was probably experiencing that fear too. A fear of being taken. Emily couldn't just give in to him. She couldn't trade one person's life for another. If she did, what made her any different from the monsters in the stories she read?

"Say I give her to you, then what?"

"Then what?" Yuansou repeated. "Then you and your little friend walk away."

"But what happens to Meihua?" Emily asked.

Yuansou grimaced at her with Stephen's face. "I'm not sure how that would be any concern of yours."

"You just take her back to Heise?"

Yuansou froze, and it was the first time that Emily recalled catching him or Stephen off guard. It was only for a moment, but it was there. A second later he was back to his arrogant, sneering self. He snorted and it actually made him sound human. "Heise? Hardly. I am here of my own accord."

"What?" said Emily. "I thought you worked together."

"We did not work together. We worked for him. He never recognized us for the asset that we were. We were his servants. A fact he always made apparent. When your family attacked us and locked him away, we ran. We waited. We planned. Heise's time has passed. It is our turn now. We will take the sword. We will be stronger. Better than he was."

"So, why didn't you take her earlier?" asked Emily.

Yuansou growled. "As we said, we are patient. We waited. We watched. We saw your teacher. We learned she was sick. We thought we must attack her before she gave it to someone strong. But then she said she was giving the sword to a child."

Something shifted in Stephen's face and the arrogance slipped into confidence, and Emily was worried. She had learned by now the subtle difference between the two, and she didn't like the idea of a confident Stephen. Yuansou. Whatever.

"I approached Stephen," started Yuansou, but the voice was different now. It was softer, older, and patient. "Slowly at first, cautiously. I learned of how angry he was, of who you were, and I was so happy. I had options now. A dying woman, still strong despite her disease, or a child with no knowledge of the world we live in.

"I offered Stephen the deal," said the new singular voice. "Become our host. Take what should be ours."

"So, you're a coward," said Emily. "You waited until you found someone you could beat, and you came after me. You can't use her. She chooses."

"So we have learned," said Yuansou. "We made a few

attempts to take her from you. The easiest was suggested by Stephen."

"I pressured my son to challenge you for the sword," said Stephen, and it really was his voice this time.

"He wasn't part of this?" asked Emily.

Stephen scoffed. "No, he could never. He never understood how great he could be. I figured once he took the sword from you, I could manipulate him or just take it for myself. And when that didn't work…"

"They sent me," said the coyote. "I attacked you, thinking I could just pry it from your corpse. But you proved resourceful, and your family got in the way."

"It was easy to find a creature willing to work with us," said the voices of Yuansou minus the coyote. "Everyone wants the same thing. Power. But when we had you in our grasp, we couldn't take the sword," said the collective. "So, if we can't take the sword, you must give it to us. We will work out the details on our own."

"Meihua isn't an *it*," retorted Emily.

Yuansou shrugged. "It doesn't matter to us what she is. Only what she will become. Ours. Now give her to me."

Emily remained still. She tilted her head down. She wiggled her toes and her sneakers flexed up. Finally, she raised her head.

"No."

Yuansou was taken aback, perplexed, and then disappointed. He raised his hand, palm down, and shadows swirled around it. Then something came out of the shadows. It was a brownish black spiraling shell like an ammonite, and it was the size of a cantaloupe.

Then a monster emerged from it. It was a snail, if snails were nightmares incarnate. It stretched out like an eel, peeking out of its shell with a pair of antennae that peered around. It loomed toward Allison and tentacles erupted from what must have been a mouth. The tentacles brushed against Allison's skin and ear and she started crying as soon as they touched. Allison squeezed her eyes shut and shied away from the snail while Emily fought down an urge to vomit.

"Are you sure?" asked the clear, resonant voice from before. It was coming from the snail. "I am the first of Yuansou. I am the one who created more. Her mind might not survive the ordeal, but one way or another she will be mine. And I will send her after you. Could you fight her? Kill her? You would have to because I would send her over and over and over again."

Emily tried not to imagine what it would be like to have Allison attack her. Which meant all she thought about was what it would be like to have Allison attack her. How long would it take, she wondered, to transform her from her best friend into something like the monsters that served him? She was a kind, caring, loving, and happy person. Had the other creatures been like her before Yuansou corrupted them?

Then it reminded Emily of what Meihua had told her. How Kuo had sacrificed himself to save his family. How Meihua had fought against him. Was that what was going to happen to Emily? Was she going to be forced to fight the monster version of Allison?

Surely Yuansou knew that Emily and her family would come after him if he took Allison. More than that, there would be others. Everyone would look for her. She couldn't just disappear.

But Yuansou could. He had already done it. Their family had no idea he was still around until he showed up as a very real threat. And Yuansou wasn't like the normal criminals that the police or anyone else could look for. He didn't even have a real body. He could take Allison and ditch Stephen. And then there was the risk that they would find him. Emily imagined a police officer stopping Stephen and then suddenly a monster appeared. What could they do against something like Yuansou? Against the monsters and nightmares at his disposal? But then again, what could Emily do?

She squirmed in her shoes and unease entered her heart. That unease turned to doubt, and Emily forced her gaze anywhere but at Allison. She couldn't imagine what Allison was thinking right now. How terrible a person she must seem to Allison, unwilling to trade a sword for her best friend's life. She couldn't do it though. She couldn't just trade one life for another. All she could do now was fight.

"Emily!" cried a voice from behind her. Both she and Yuansou turned. Her parents, Aunt Elaine, and Bryan were running toward them. Yuansou glared at the newcomers then at Emily.

"I told you to come alone!" seethed the snail.

"I did," whispered Emily in disbelief.

The snail hissed and it sounded like a thousand cats hissing at once. "You! You went easy on the boy! See him! He is already awake!"

"I didn't—" started Stephen and there was panic in his voice. Emily turned just in time for his face to shift again until he was glowering. It was like he had multiple personalities.

"It matters not," said Stephen with the voice of many. "They are here, but so are we."

"Dad," said Bryan when they had all lined up with Emily. "Dad please, tell me this isn't real."

The snail shifted into shadows and disappeared. "It is real, boy," said the collective of Yuansou.

"What the hell is going on?" asked her dad when he stepped in front of Emily.

"Not sure," said Aunt Elaine. "Attack now, ask questions later."

CHAPTER 26

SHOWDOWN

HER AUNT AND father sprung toward Yuansou. Bryan hesitated for a second before he charged and screamed to give him his dad back. The four of them met in a tempest of fists and kicks. Her dad, Aunt Elaine, and Bryan moved awkwardly with one another and Yuansou used that to his advantage.

Bryan came in with a front kick and Yuansou deftly spun out of the way. He shoved Bryan toward Emily's dad and turned to run but Aunt Elaine jumped in the way. Yuansou parried a punch and hopped back toward the center of the circle they had formed around him. Aunt Elaine pulled the dao she had taken from the monster earlier that night and brandished it at Yuansou.

"Enough!" yelled Yuansou with the voice of the nightmare snail. Stephen's shadow contracted toward him, pooling into a deep black covering the ground. It exploded out in a smoky ring and the ground was covered in a dark fog. Snarls and hisses emanated from the black smoke.

The first monster that appeared was the coyote that had attacked Emily and Allison the week before. It rose from the darkness, its head appearing like a shark's dorsal fin, and circled Yuansou snarling as it got closer to the trio of fighters.

A shape emerged next, like something swimming just beneath the water. A head rose up, followed by a long body, and Emily was reminded of the stories of sea serpents. The head came up from behind Yuansou and the snake circled around him protectively, creating a barrier between him and Emily's family. It was striped with scales as dark as obsidian and as light as milky quartz crystal. It hissed loudly and Emily stuttered back a step. She was mildly relieved that she wasn't the only one to do so.

Another shadow rose up behind the sorcerer and spread dark feathery wings that resembled scales in the night. They shimmered and a head appeared behind Yuansou. It had a long, hooked, jagged, gleaming black beak and it let out a piercing cry before it flapped its mighty wings once and rocketed into the sky.

The last to appear was a monkey, roughly the size of a short man, with sandy fur and a leathery dark face. It had one dao sheathed on its back and strapped to its armor. He scanned the warriors surrounding him and smiled contentedly. The monkey's eyes rested on Aunt Elaine and the dao she was carrying. He held up his hands with his left covering his right fist and bowed. Emily wondered how Yuansou had managed to get something like that to work for him.

Aunt Elaine's face said she was surprised but she returned the gesture.

"The sword you carry is one of a pair," said the monkey. "I have the other. A rematch? To determine who shall hold both."

Aunt Elaine nodded to him.

"I will wait for you on the side. Say your goodbyes."

Her aunt spun toward Emily as soon as he started walking away. "What were you thinking?"

"I was thinking I had to save Allison," said Emily.

"You're lucky Bryan woke up and found us," said her aunt.

"What happened to the barrier around the house?" asked Emily.

"Stephen was the one who put it up," said Aunt Elaine. "He probably tore it down. It would have been easy. Now, stay low, don't die. Let us handle this." And with that she walked off to where the monkey waited for her.

The coyote let out a bone shaking howl and advanced on Emily's dad. He had a bo staff in his hand and spun it around before pointing it at the beast. The bird circled above the group.

"Dad!" yelled Bryan. He advanced toward his father and the snake moved its head to track his movements. Bryan pulled out his hook swords and tapped the tips of them together. "Dad, don't make me do this."

The snake moved its head until it was in Bryan's way. And then it spoke with a voice that sounded like a rake against dry leaves. "Your father is one of us now."

"Not for long," said Bryan. He charged and the snake launched itself forward, its mouth spread wide enough it could have fit the entirety of Bryan's head inside it. Bryan dodged to the side toward a planter that was full of trees and darted up. The snake slithered after him and they began an acrobatic fight inside the branches.

All of this somehow left Emily alone with Yuansou.

He sneered at her and held his right hand out to the side. Shadows pooled on the ground again and a haft rose from the darkness until it reached Stephen's hand. He pulled and a spear erupted out. It was a dark storm, gray with no adornments whatsoever. He spun it and let the blunt end hit the ground, so the spear's tip was pointing up. "No one left to protect you now."

Emily's eyes darted to Allison for a split second, but Allison was backing away from Yuansou. A shadow shifted farther in the back and her mom came into view circling the quad, making her way toward Allison. Emily knew the potential danger if Yuansou noticed either of them. Neither of them could defend themselves like Emily could.

She remembered all the things that had gone wrong and how they could all be traced to this one man. This uncle of hers who had thrown his lot in with monsters all because he didn't get his way. Her blood boiled and a rage burned up inside her.

Emily ripped off her jacket and threw it to the side. She held her right hand out with her fingers flared. Meihua flew from where she rested on the table and spun in the air until she was in Emily's hand.

"No one left to protect *you* now."

Emily charged and Yuansou rushed forward to meet her with a flurry of thrusts. He was faster than Emily and his weapon was longer than hers, so she parried one to the side and dodged to her left. She lunged forward with her sword and came down with a slash but Yuansou stepped up and parried the blade with the haft of the spear.

He snorted at her and shoved his hands forward knocking Emily off balance and kicked her in the stomach. She saw it coming and kicked back just before his kick hit her, so she rolled with the momentum. She jumped up just as Yuansou swung the spear downward. Emily continued the roll and Yuansou landed hard on the ground where she had been moments ago. The spear crashed into the concrete, breaking it, and sending chunks rocketing out. He pulled it out with ease and then waved the spear again to get the dust off.

"You didn't tell me he could fight," Emily said.

It must be Stephen.

Yuansou rushed at her again and she met him head-on. They met in a storm of sword and spear. The air was full of ringing from when their blows were parried or blocked. Emily was just barely keeping up with him.

She slashed high at him again from her left, but he blocked it. Meihua's blade and the haft of his spear grated against one another. Yuansou spun the weapon and shoved Emily back before sweeping the spear at her head. She swerved and dipped to her right. The spear whipped past her head and she swore the edge brushed against her hair.

He swung the spear back faster than Emily expected, exchanging power for speed. The side of Emily's head exploded in pain as the metal haft smacked against her. She stumbled back, clutching the side of her head, desperate for a reprieve of some kind. Yuansou came at her again. Emily brought the sword up but Yuansou swiped it aside and landed a round-house kick on Emily's ribs. She cried out in pain and shut her eyes trying to run away. As soon as she closed her eyes, she remembered a sound like a thunderclap or two gloves being slammed together. She forced her eyes open just in time to meet his onslaught.

He came at her hard and fast with a front kick to where her head should have been. She jumped back and then lunged forward at him. Yuansou sidestepped her thrust and swung the spear at her. Emily raised her sword up to deflect the blow, but he pulled it back and kneed her in the stomach.

Emily clutched her abdomen and tried to breathe.

Yuansou grabbed her arm and threw her. She landed hard, skidded back, and felt her skin scrape against the concrete. She curled up into a ball after she stopped moving and heard a whimper escape through her lips. Tears were streaming down her face and she didn't know what was happening anymore except that her body was screaming with agony.

Her stomach and ribs felt like they had been beaten with a baseball bat. Her skin burned and when she glanced down, she could see dots of blood across her arms like tiny crimson constellations. She turned over and her world spun. She tried to empty her stomach, but nothing came out. All the while Yuansou was stalking toward her. His gloating smile was replaced by a line of grim determination.

Emily, you have to get up!

She tried to stand but staggered to the ground again.

"I can't," she managed to cough out. Something red and liquid flew out of her mouth and suddenly all she could taste was metal.

You have to, repeated Meihua.

She tried again but her body refused to listen to her. "Help me, Meihua."

You have to give me control, Meihua said. *Full control.*

Emily wheezed. Yuansou's spear gleamed in the moonlight and she saw her death in it. Everything was clearer to her now. The shimmer of light off the tip of the spear. The razor-sharp edges flowing up into a point. He had punctured concrete with it like it was nothing. Emily was made of softer things than that.

"Do it," she said.

Emily closed her eyes and a warmth spread through her, and then she felt nothing at all. Pain slipped away, fatigue was gone, and there was only the sword. Emily knew that it was a lie. Meihua could hide it all, but the damage was still there. She could hide Emily's skill level too, and right now that was what mattered.

Yuansou came in fast, but to Emily's Meihua-powered senses he was moving much slower than before. She stood, sidestepped to the right of his thrust, and jabbed the hilt of her sword into his stomach with a backhand. Yuansou grunted but didn't stop. She shifted the sword so the point was down in her grip and brought it up as hard as she could hilt first into his face. There wasn't much leverage there so the blow was soft but there was a satisfying crunch.

Emily put her weight onto her right foot and came in hard with a kick toward Yuansou's ankle. He stepped back in time to avoid it and tried to jump away, but Emily's hand shot out fast and grabbed his arm. She pulled him back down toward her and punched him in the face as he fell. He staggered back and Emily rushed forward.

She was pushing her body to the limits. Emily attacked with a flurry of thrusts and slashes that Yuansou was forced to block and dodge. He tried to counter, but Meihua pressed forward, pushing him back until he hit the stage and fell backward.

Emily saw it; he was open everywhere. She saw every vital point. The sword came up for a stab and Emily jumped forward aiming for the neck.

NO! screamed Emily.

Her body stopped. No—time slowed. Aunt Elaine was engaged in full-fledged combat with the monkey. Her father had just dodged another lunge from the coyote. Bryan was swinging from one tree branch to another to avoid the snake's bite. They were all moving, but the movements were miniscule.

Why? asked Meihua.

You can't kill him. The voice was coming from inside her own head. She spoke but her lips didn't move.

If we do not kill him, then he will escape, Meihua said. *He will escape and he could find Heise. Stephen knows enough of the family secrets. He will release Heise. I will not go back to that monster.*

You won't have to, said Emily. *Just because we don't kill him doesn't mean we let him go.*

No, he'll escape, repeated Meihua. *The bird is there, above. If we don't end it now, he will escape and we will lose him. I can't let that happen.*

If you kill him, what makes you different from any other monster? asked Emily. *You're killing him out of fear.*

I am sorry, Emily, said Meihua. *You gave me control. I will not be used for murder. Not again.*

Like you're about to use me? asked Emily.

Meihua faltered. Emily felt it in her mind even as time started again. Her arm was moving forward but the control, the certainty behind it, was gone. Yuansou might be a bad guy, her uncle might have allied with monsters, but she was not going to kill him. This was Emily's choice. She was more than a sword, more than a sharp edge. She used every ounce of her will, every part of her inner strength, and wrested control of her own body away from Meihua.

"No!" she screamed.

She managed to move her arm at the last second. The sword came screeching down and thrust itself into the concrete next to Yuansou's head. Shock lit up his face when he realized he wasn't dead. He shoved Emily off him with his feet and jumped into the air. A dark shape flew down and whisked him away into the night.

The bird soared away with Yuansou crouched on its back. She spun around. The coyote was turning back into shadow and shot up into the sky after him. The snake turned to darkness as well just as Bryan was about to strike at it. Her aunt was walking toward her, a dao in each hand, and a dark form lying motionless on the ground behind her. Someone yelled her name and she turned. Her mom and Allison were running over to her.

Emily fell to her knees.

"We won."

CHAPTER 27

THE GIRL THAT CHOSE HER DESTINY

THE FIRST CALL Aunt Elaine made in the aftermath was to Henry Black. Moments later, a portal opened in the middle of the quad and he came striding out in pajamas, a robe, and bed slippers again. If it weren't for the fact that the only two times she had met the man had been at night, she would have thought that he only wore pajamas.

Allison sat on the concrete table that Emily had put Meihua down on earlier that night. She was wearing Emily's dad's jacket and was leaning into Emily's mom who held her close like she was her own child. Emily wanted to be there for Allison more than anything, but her aunt and dad had insisted that Emily stay with them for the time being.

The body of the monkey monster started dissolving and turning to ash. Emily frowned while she watched. It was sad to her, considering how the monkey had seemed less a monster than the others, but he was an enemy still.

Her dad stood next to Emily, leaning on his bo staff. He was breathing almost as heavily as Emily was.

"I haven't done anything like that in almost twenty years," he said. He had an actual smile on his face like he was enjoying himself. He clapped Emily on the back and gave her shoulder a little shake. "Good job tonight, Emily. I mean, sneaking out of the house twice in one day was terrible. You're definitely grounded after that. But good job."

"Thanks?" said Emily, unsure how to react to her praise and her grounding. Her dad pointed at the monkey's body with his bo staff.

"What was up with him?" he asked. "Those other monsters were like… monsters. But this guy was honorable somehow."

"I mean this is the one that attacked me at Allison's show. He was going to cut my hand off."

"Oh," said her dad. He frowned and prodded the remains with the staff. It crumbled into dust and disappeared as if it was never there. "Good riddance."

"Emily!" yelled Aunt Elaine. "We need you for a second!"

"Okay!" Emily yelled back. Her dad waved at her to go. Emily walked over to her aunt who was standing with Henry. "What's up?"

Her aunt motioned to Allison. "I'm going to ask Henry to alter Allison's memory again."

"No," pleaded Emily. "You can't."

"We have to," replied her aunt. "It's safer for her this way. Safer for everyone."

"Actually," broke in Mr. Black. "I don't think this would be safe for her. This is a big trauma to try and block from her memory. I'm not sure I can do it."

"Are you serious?" Aunt Elaine asked.

"Quite," replied Henry. "I told you it would be no problem, but now that I'm here I can see everything I'm dealing with. There was only one creature left and by everyone's estimation, he was the nicest of the bunch. You say there were three others and a summoner of some strength. And he had her for who knows how long? She won't forget this. I could try to change her memory and it might even work. But it won't go away. Not completely. Maybe if she were younger, but not now. Then there's the risk that I wipe her memory completely. There would be nothing left."

"Aunt Elaine, no, you can't," said Emily.

Her aunt sighed. "I suppose we can't."

Emily squealed and hugged Henry. He stumbled back, sputtered, and rested his hands on Emily's shoulders.

"Oh my, I didn't do anything," he said.

"Exactly," Emily said. She backed away and beamed at him. "Thank you."

"You're welcome," he said. "Right now, I think the best thing we can do is have the kids go home while we clean up this mess."

"I'd rather not have Emily out of my sight," said Aunt Elaine.

"Elaine," said Henry. "Does this look like a place they should be right now?"

Both Emily and her aunt surveyed the scene and the carnage. The ground was torn up from the coyote's claws and the tree was sanded in parts where the snake had moved. Then her eyes rested on Allison, shivering in her mom's arms and not from the cold.

"All right," said Aunt Elaine finally. "I'll stay here and help you clean up, but we do it fast."

Emily turned away from the two of them and walked across the quad. Her mom raised her head when she got close. "Hey, they said we can go home."

A few minutes later Allison, Bryan, Emily, and her parents were seated in their house. Emily and Allison were in the kitchen while Emily's mom was doting on them with food. She had just called Allison's parents to say that Allison was staying the night and apologized for not telling them sooner. Then she put Allison on the phone and Emily was surprised at how easily Allison lied to them about what happened. Emily's mom left to put a bed together for Allison, leaving the two of them alone in the kitchen. They ate peanut butter and jelly sandwiches in silence.

Neither of them were eating very much. Now that Emily had time to think, she remembered what she had been so worried about before Yuansou had called from Allison's phone. She had thought she lost a friend. Now Allison knew the truth. She had seen the monsters and the magic, and she had seen Emily fight. She knew that Emily had lied to her. And now they were alone, and they weren't speaking. What if Allison hated her? What if she blamed her for everything that happened? What if she really didn't want to be friends anymore?

She sniffed her tears and feelings back in as quietly as she could. If that's what Allison wanted, if that's what she said, then Emily would respect her wishes. She took another bite of her sandwich, but it tasted like sand in her mouth.

"So, are you like a hero?" Allison finally said.

Emily stopped chewing and her eyes went wide like she was a deer caught in headlights. She forced herself to finish chewing and swallow.

"Not really," said Emily. She rested a hand on Meihua who was on the island counter. "It's mostly the sword."

"Yeah, when did you even get that?" asked Allison.

"Remember my ring?" Allison nodded. "That was Meihua."

"Meihua?"

"That's the name of the sword. Well, she's the sword. She's actually a spirit who used to be a plum blossom tree, but now she's a sword." Allison's face showed that she didn't understand anything Emily had just said. "It's complicated."

"So, all those times you couldn't hang out, you were training?"

"Yup," replied Emily. "I wanted to tell you. Really, Allison. But they told me I couldn't. Family secrets and keeping you safe and all."

"Keeping me safe?" she said incredulously. "I didn't know about any of it, and I ended up here anyway."

"I'm sorry," said Emily. "They said that knowing that monsters are real makes them real to you. I didn't get it. I'm still not sure I do."

"Am I in danger now?" asked Allison.

Emily couldn't answer. She didn't know. Stephen, Yuansou, was still out there, and Meihua was sure that Heise was going to come back. Yuansou had said that he wasn't working with Heise, but then she beat him. She could lie to Allison and say no, but she was tired of lying to her best friend.

"I don't know," said Emily. "But don't worry, I'll protect you."

Allison started to giggle. "You know, I actually believe you. I saw you tonight. You came to my rescue, and then you fought whoever that guy was. You know what my favorite part was?" Emily shook her head. "When you took your jacket off and threw it aside. Then you made that sword fly to your hand and said, 'No one left to protect you.' Totally badass. You really were a hero."

"Not really," said Emily. "I was just trying to do the right thing."

"Isn't that what a hero does?" asked Allison.

"I guess," said Emily. Loud yells broke out from the living room and both Emily and Allison turned toward the noise. "I'll be right back, are you okay by yourself?"

"Sure," said Allison. Emily slid off her stool, left Meihua by Allison, and walked into the living room.

Her dad and Bryan were facing off against one another. Bryan was trying to leave, and Emily's dad was trying to calm him down. Mom came down the stairs just as Bryan tried to get past him again.

"Hey!" yelled Emily. Bryan turned to face her. "What's going on?"

"I'm going after him," said Bryan. "My dad is my responsibility. I'm sorry about all this. If I had seen it sooner—if I had noticed—you and your friend wouldn't have been in danger."

"That's not true," said Emily. Bryan's face said he didn't believe her. "Trust me. Yuansou said he had been watching the whole time. Or they had. We've got it all wrong about him. He wasn't even working with Heise. He was going to come after me no matter what. This isn't your fault."

Bryan's uncomfortable expression screamed that there was

a war going on inside him. He began to cry, and Emily wasn't sure what to do. Luckily, Aunt Elaine walked into the house right then. She glanced at the scene in front of her and then she walked straight up to Bryan. She put an arm around him and pulled him into a hug. Emily's parents came up until they were all surrounding him.

"Shhh, this isn't your fault," said Aunt Elaine. "None of us had any clue. Don't worry though. We'll catch him."

"Yeah?" said Bryan. "And then what?"

"I don't know," said Aunt Elaine.

"We save him," said Emily immediately. "He was taken advantage of by Yuansou. I know it. We can save him."

"You really think so?" asked Bryan, hope in his voice.

"I do."

"We can't do anything about it right now," said Aunt Elaine. "I promise you though, we will find him."

They all separated, and Emily noticed who was missing. "Where's Mr. Black?"

"He said he had to run home real quick. He'll be here shortly," replied Aunt Elaine.

Emily turned to walk back to Allison but found her standing in the corner of the room. She was holding Meihua in her hands and was just watching them. She held Meihua out to Emily. "You forgot this."

Emily took the sword and Meihua turned into a ring in front of Allison's eyes. Emily slipped the ring on her right ring finger.

"Whoa, that was cool," said Allison.

"You've called your parents already?" Aunt Elaine asked Allison.

"Yeah," said Allison. "They were pretty pissed, and I wasn't sure what to say. Luckily Mrs. Lau talked to them first. I think they're still mad, but they were glad to hear from her."

"That's good," said Aunt Elaine. She let out a breath and when she did her whole body deflated a little. Emily was trying her hardest not to think about the toll the night's activities had taken on her aunt, but not thinking about something meant she was giving it attention anyway. Her aunt didn't look like she was in pain at least.

"Why don't the two of you go upstairs?" said Mom. "You both must be exhausted. And I'm sure you'd love a shower."

"That sounds amazing right now," said Emily.

Allison's face was unsure, but she relented. "Okay."

Emily's mom had set up a sleeping bag in Emily's room. Emily insisted on taking the sleeping bag and letting Allison sleep on the bed. Allison had tried to argue about it first, but Emily wouldn't budge. She climbed into the sleeping bag and refused to move until Allison crawled into bed. Someone knocked softly just as they were settling to sleep, and Henry stepped inside.

"Sorry to interrupt," said Henry. "I brought something for Allison."

He held his hand up and showed off a leather hoop hanging from a leather strap. There was string or something in the middle that was like a spider web. Trailing under the hoop were feathers and beads. It spun slowly in the air.

"This is an authentic dream catcher," said Henry. "I got it from a friend a long time ago. I thought you might like it."

"Oh, thanks," said Allison. "What does it do?"

"It catches dreams," said Henry with a smile. "Nightmares get caught in the web and good dreams trickle down through the feathers to you. After everything you've seen and experienced, I thought you might like to have it."

"Thank you," said Allison again, and there was genuine appreciation in her voice. Henry stepped around Emily and hung the dreamcatcher above Allison's head.

"Remember to take it home with you tomorrow," he said. Henry left the room afterward and shut the door softly behind him.

There was a little light plugged into a wall socket giving the room a soft glow to keep it from being completely dark. The two of them were quiet and Emily hoped the dream catcher was as authentic as Henry claimed it was. Allison was turning in her sleep.

"Hey," said Emily. "Are you awake?"

"Yeah," said Allison.

Allison had her back to Emily, and she didn't turn over. Emily locked her gaze on the ceiling. She had a question inside her that she had been too scared to ask all night. She had braved monsters and a mad man but the answer to this one question scared her more than almost anything else had that entire night.

"Do you hate me?" she asked.

Allison shifted in the bed until she was facing Emily, but Emily couldn't look at her. She just lay in the sleeping bag staring straight up with her hands folded on her belly. She refused to look over at Allison, just like she refused to wipe the tears that were coming down her face.

"How could you ask that?" she heard Allison say breathily.

"You were so mad at me earlier," said Emily. "For leaving the show. You said you didn't want to talk to me again."

"That was before I knew you were busy saving everyone from a monster," said Allison. "And even then, I never hated you. I was just so angry at the time. You're my best friend, Emily. I could never hate you."

"But I lied to you," said Emily.

"To protect me."

"I put you in danger," said Emily. "Something terrible could have happened to you."

Allison didn't say anything. She seemed content to let Emily stew in her own thoughts and overthink.

"Something bad could happen to me every day," said Allison finally. "You saved me from it this time. You'll do it next time, too."

The tears fell freely now but they had transitioned from sad to relieved. A heavy weight lifted from her chest and the dull ache in her throat dissipated.

"Thank you, Allison," said Emily. "And you're right, I'll keep you safe."

"I know," said Allison. "Thanks. Good night."

"Night," replied Emily.

She lay quietly on the floor of her bedroom and listened to Allison breathing. Over time it shifted from forced to rhythmic and Emily realized that Allison must have fallen asleep. She had no idea what Allison was thinking or how their friendship was going to change from this. She had won and saved her friend, but she was still scared that she was going to lose her despite everything Allison said. And then there was the other person she had managed to anger.

"You're awfully quiet," whispered Emily. "Aren't you happy, Meihua?"

You made a mistake.

All the good news they just received, everything that had happened, and all Meihua could say was that Emily had made a mistake.

You defeated Yuansou, but he got away. I won't lie to you, Emily. I am afraid. Yuansou is a spiteful being. He will come back for his revenge, and he will not come alone.

"You're scared?" Emily repeated in a whisper. "It's okay. If Heise comes we'll beat him too."

No, Emily, we won't.

Emily had been betrayed again. She had spent the majority of her weekend with Allison, filling her in on all the details she had missed out on over the last month. Then Monday morning came and she had expected that her parents and aunt would let her have the day off. Instead her mother woke her up at the butt crack of dawn.

"Emily, what are you doing?" asked her mother after she barged into the room and jolted Emily awake. "Did you sleep through your alarm?"

"Alarm?" asked Emily. "I turned it off."

"Why would you do that?" her mom asked.

"Um... so I could sleep in?" said Emily. She cracked an eye open. Her mom was standing at the foot of Emily's bed giving her daughter a heavy stare.

"Emily, it's a school day," said her mom.

"What?" said Emily. She sat up in her bed and was just as shocked by this betrayal as she was by Stephen being Yuansou.

"You can't be serious. Why am I going to school? I was just attacked by monsters *at school*. My own uncle attacked me!"

"Your uncle?" repeated Mom. "Since when is Stephen your uncle?"

"Since he decided to betray me and attack me at my own school," said Emily.

"Well, that doesn't get you out of school," said her mom.

Emily groaned. "Betrayed twice. First, he tries to steal Meihua, then he can't even get me out of a day of school."

"That's right," replied her mom. "You decided you wanted a magic sword. You said you would take responsibility for yourself. Now get up and get dressed. You're going to school."

"Mom!" groaned Emily. "I bet Allison isn't going to school!"

"I'm not Allison's mom," she said. "I'm your mom and I'm saying you're going to school."

Emily rushed through her morning routine and a few minutes later was out the door with her mom without eating breakfast. They drove through the junior parking lot past the trees that had been so ominous before. Then she passed the gate she had jumped. They were open now, and in the daylight, they were smaller than she remembered Friday night.

She moved quickly through the school, passing classmates and classrooms. She listened to the sounds of everyone around her. She remembered the sounds she had heard Friday night, and they sort of layered with the here and now creating a mishmash. Real life sounded better to her than the sounds she had made up. A feeling of contentment crept up on her and she started power walking.

Emily made a beeline toward her locker and pulled up

short just a few feet away. Allison was standing next to her locker pulling books out. Emily hadn't expected Allison to be at school today. If she was being honest, she hadn't expected to see Allison all week after everything that had happened.

Allison must have felt Emily's stare on her back because she looked over her shoulder. Allison's eyes widened in shock. Emily walked up to her best friend and the two of them just sort of gawked at one another. Allison closed her locker and pulled her backpack up.

"I'm surprised you're here," said Emily.

"Yeah, well, I couldn't really give my parents a good reason for me not to come to school," said Allison.

"Fair enough," said Emily. "How are you?"

"I'm fine," said Allison. "It's a little weird being here."

"Right?" whispered Emily louder than she meant to. "I told my mom I shouldn't have to go to school. I mean we were just attacked by monsters here!"

"Yeah, but I couldn't tell my parents about that," said Allison. She leaned against her locker while Emily grabbed her last set of books. "Who was Mr. Black anyway?"

"A wizard," said Emily. She closed her locker and zipped her backpack shut before she noticed that Allison was gaping at her. "What?"

"A wizard?" repeated Allison. "Like a real one?"

"Yeah," replied Emily. "He's a friend of my aunt's."

"So, magic is real?" she asked.

"Yup."

"You're serious?" asked Allison.

Emily hooked her arm through Allison's, pulled her in close, and shook her head.

"You saw monsters Friday night, but you don't think magic is real?" replied Emily.

"Good point," said Allison.

The two of them turned and started walking to their first class. They rounded the corner and walked by the planter where they normally ate lunch and then the quad came into view. And it was pristine, or it was as pristine as a high school quad *could* be. There were no claw marks in the ground. The tree was undamaged somehow. All signs of the battle were gone.

The only thing left over from last Friday night was the two of them. Allison's arm slipped out of hers. Emily turned. Allison was staring at the stage, frozen in place. Her lip quivered slightly, her skin had gone pale, and she was holding her breath. It had only been a few days, and a dream catcher might help at night, but Allison still had to face her demons during the day.

Emily walked back to her friend and nudged her with her shoulder. "Hey, it's going to be okay."

Allison took a breath and wiped something away from her eye. "Yeah. You're gonna keep me safe, right?"

"Right. I'm here for you. No looking back. We've just got to move forward. And how do we do that?" Allison didn't respond so Emily hooked Allison's arm in her own again and started walking, pulling Allison along with her. "One step at a time."

And so, she urged Allison forward, one step at a time, all the way to her first class.

The rest of her day was tedious and boring, but she enjoyed it. She missed the simple routine of her everyday life. She missed being normal. Later, she found herself in English class sitting with rapt attention. She was completely focused on Mr. Coulter who was leaning against his podium at the forefront of the room with a happy expression on his face. He watched everyone take their seats. The rest of her classmates were the exact opposite of Emily. They slouched in their seats and this aura of fatigue permeated out from them. Emily imagined a shield all around her keeping their energy away from her.

She didn't understand why they were so tired and so… grumpy. Sure, it was Monday, and it was the last class of the day. They probably just wanted to make it out of the first day of the week, but Emily had this new energy spring up inside her like a well.

You told me before that destiny isn't something set in stone, said Emily. *You said destiny is a bunch of small moments that lead up to one big one. All the things I've read and seen, I know it was all just made up. But books, games, movies, all those stories taught me to be me. That's why I couldn't let you kill Stephen.*

You're just like your aunt, said Meihua. *You do the right thing, even when it could kill you.*

There's a lot of uncertainty in the word 'could,' thought Emily. *Nothing's set in stone. And I remember that you made a similar decision to mine. You tried to save Kuo when he sacrificed himself. You didn't run away. You ran headfirst into trouble. Just like me.*

Meihua didn't respond and Emily wondered if she had pushed too far when her desk neighbor got a little too close to her. He turned to take his seat and his backpack swung out almost hitting Emily in the face. She shied away from it and almost fell out of her seat. She glowered at him and his obliviousness and then resituated herself.

I guess we're both pretty stupid, said Meihua.

Maybe, replied Emily. *Or maybe we're both just heroes.*

The bell chimed, cutting Meihua and Emily's conversation short, and Mr. Coulter stepped forward. "Wow, rough day guys?"

The room was deathly quiet, so everyone heard Emily snort with laughter. One by one they all turned and gave Emily different reactions. She covered her mouth with her hand and prayed the rush of heat to her face didn't show up as color while she tried to keep herself from dying of embarrassment. Thankfully, everyone turned away from her after a second or two.

"Well, I'm glad one of you is awake," said Mr. Coulter. "I thought we could go over one of my favorite poems. I know you guys still hate poetry, but I'm trying to change your minds. This one is called 'Invictus' and it was written by William Ernest Henley."

He held up his hand like he had during the time he read Robert Frost to them and the room went from quiet to quieter as everyone somehow slouched even farther into their seats. Emily, however, sat up straighter than she had before.

"'Out of the night that covers me, / Black as the pit from pole to pole, / I thank whatever gods may be / For my unconquerable soul,'" he started. And then, just as before, he had their attention. Or at least he had Emily's. The words stirred something inside her, or maybe Meihua was listening to Mr. Coulter too.

"'In the fell clutch of circumstance, / I have not winced

nor cried aloud. / Under the bludgeonings of chance / My head is bloody, but unbowed.'"

The emotions inside her turned to recognition. She listened to Mr. Coulter and actually heard him. The words were truth to her. She put to mind everything he had said and realized she had moments in her life that she could relate to his words.

"'Beyond this place of wrath and tears / Looms but the Horror of the shade, / And yet the menace of the years / Finds and shall find me unafraid.'"

She nodded with the words. Mr. Coulter looked up for a brief moment and their eyes met. He gave her a smile and lowered his gaze back to the book in his hand.

"'It matters not how strait the gate, / How charged with punishments the scroll, / I am the master of my fate, / I am the captain of my soul.'"

He slammed the book shut dramatically and everyone in the room jumped when he did. Smatterings of chuckles bubbled up all around her as everyone woke from their respective reveries. Emily pulled her pen out and wrote down the title of the poem so she could read it again later.

See, Meihua, we choose our own destiny.

Acknowledgements

First of all, I'd like to thank my editors, Carrie Jones and Lucia Ferrara. Carrie kept me sane and I can't even begin to quantify how much she helped me. Lucia helped me look like I knew what grammar was. This book wouldn't be what it is now if not for them. Thank you to my mother who got me reading which eventually led to writing. To my father who helped me with everything along the way. To my sisters for being there. Thank you to my cousins Matt and Sean. They were my very first readers and really got me thinking I could be a writer. To Deion for giving me feedback on my ideas. The first sparks of this story started with him, and thankfully it got so much better along the way. To Amber and Loosah for so much. They listened to me and have believed in me from the start. Thank you.

About the Author

Timothy Stone was born in Southern California to an American father and a Chinese mother. He writes fantasy and *Emily Lau and the Plum Blossom Sword* is his first novel. It took him a while to put pen to paper, or keystrokes really, but he got there eventually. He attended university and graduated with a degree in history from Cal State Fullerton, but part of him has always wanted to tell stories.

Made in the USA
Las Vegas, NV
30 March 2022

46574214R00184